Approval Voting

Steven J. Brams
Peter C. Fishburn

Birkhäuser
Boston • Basel • Stuttgart

Steven J. Brams
Department of Politics
New York University
New York, NY 10003

Peter C. Fishburn
Bell Telephone Laboratories
Murray Hill, NJ 07974

Library of Congress Cataloging in Publication Data

Brams, Steven J.
  Approval voting.

Bibliography: p.
  Includes index.
  1. Voting. I. Fishburn, Peter C. II. Title.
JF1001.B72 1983   324.6'3   82-17849
ISBN 3-7643-3108-9

CIP-Kurztitelaufnahme der Deutschen Bibliothek

Brams, Steven J.:
Approval voting/Steven J. Brams; Peter C.
Fishburn.—Boston; Basel; Stuttgart:
Birkhäuser, 1982.
  ISBN 3-7643-3108-9
NE: Fishburn, Peter C.:

With 4 illustrations.

Printed in the United States of America.

ISBN 3-7643-3108-9 (Hardcover)
ISBN 3-7643-3124-0 (Softcover)

I am not an advocate for frequent changes in laws and constitutions, but laws and institutions must go hand in hand with the progress of the human mind. As that becomes more developed, more enlightened, as new discoveries are made, new truths discovered and manners and opinions change, with the change of circumstances, institutions must advance also to keep pace with the times.

> Thomas Jefferson, Letter to
> Samuel Kerchaval, July 12, 1816

The method of choice . . . should be as scientifically framed and as efficiently adapted to its purpose as experience and political wisdom can make it. . . . It is not sufficient for every citizen to have the vote; he should also be assured of the greatest possible freedom and effectiveness in its use.

> Enid Lakeman and James D. Lambert,
> *Voting in Democracies*, 1955

The way we pick our presidents should not be fraught with danger and uncertainty. It should be a clear, secure, sensible procedure in which we can have confidence. . . .

> Terry Sanford,
> *A Danger of Democracy*, 1981

During lunch, a show of hands was taken, and the '47 [wine] received more first-place votes than any other wine. Because of more numerous second- and third-place votes, the '49 [wine] was judged the group's favorite, although this method of scoring caused controversy.

> Terry Robards, "Wine Talk,"
> *New York Times*, April 28, 1982

Contents

Preface

This book is about an election procedure called approval voting that appeared *de novo* about five years ago. As far as we can determine, five sets of people hit upon the idea of approval voting independently and deserve credit for recognizing its potential.[1] It seems like such a reasonable idea that we suspect other people thought of it earlier, but, for reasons best left to historians of science, only recently has it received general recognition.[2] At the time of this writing (June 1982), there are no extant uses of approval voting in public elections, but bills to implement this reform have been introduced in two state legislatures (New York and Vermont; for the text of the New York bill, see the Appendix).[3]

The idea behind approval voting is straightforward. In an election among three or more candidates for a single office, voters are not restricted to voting for just one candidate. Instead, each voter can vote for, or "approve of," as many candidates as he or she wishes. (Henceforth, we shall use only the masculine pronoun for convenience, but voting—at least in recent times—is not a subject with sexist overtones, and we intend none.) Each candidate gets a full vote from each voter who votes for him. The candidate with the most votes, and presumably acceptable to the most voters, wins the election. Thus, the winner is simply the candidate approved of by the largest number of voters.

Our research on election procedures over the past several years has led us to believe that approval voting is superior in many ways to commonly used procedures for determining a winner in elections with more than two candidates, including plurality voting (vote for one) and plurality voting with a runoff between the top two vote-getters. The purpose of the book is to explain our reasons for this conclusion.

We shall do this with a blend of theoretical analysis and case studies based on actual elections. Although we shall consider a variety of alternative election procedures, our comparisons will focus on the simpler procedures that are easy for voters to understand and hence are good candidates for adoption if they are not already widely used.

The book's analysis is fairly rigorous and will not be easy going for many readers. Accordingly, the first chapter gives an overview of what we think, from a normative perspective, are the main advantages of approval voting. This will allow practitioners and others who prefer not to involve themselves in technical details to gain a quick grasp of its essential features. The technical details are, however, the backbone of our work, and we have tried to present them in a clear and systematic manner. With a few exceptions that serve to illustrate the deductive method, proofs of theorems are omitted since they can be found elsewhere and would impede the present exposition.

It seems fair to us to characterize approval voting as a reform in the best sense of that word. It will, we think, improve the conduct of elections generally—including the manner in which campaigns are run—and, more specifically, lead to the selection of candidates with the most widespread support among voters. We readily admit that it will not solve all problems of public choice; indeed, one of the lessons of this books is that every practicable voting system suffers certain deficiencies, and good public policy rests on scrupulous comparisons that identify that system that best satisfies criteria one thinks important. Without downplaying what we consider to be the advantages of approval voting, we have attempted to present a balanced analysis of this and other election procedures, based on a number of criteria for the democratic selection of candidates. We see no incompatibility between the role of analysis and that of advocacy where the former supports the latter.

We are reasonably confident that the theoretical foundations developed in this book for analyzing and comparing voting systems will stand up over time. On the other hand, it must be conceded that because approval voting has not been used on any substantial scale (see Chapter 1, note 7, for nonpublic elections where it has been used), we lack the kind of empirical data that are needed to make informed judgments of how it works in practice. We do, of course, hope that this will change in the near future. In the meantime, we try here to give an idea of the probable effects approval voting would have had in several recent elections conducted by other procedures. Since our reconstructions and analyses of these elections are mixed with the more theoretical arguments, readers are cautioned not to confuse the two strands. They complement each other, we believe, in giving answers to certain questions that common sense alone cannot provide.

As an election reform, approval voting could have major policy consequences, for it may well affect the kinds of political leaders who are elected and who, in turn, influence public policy in many different areas. Judging from the interest and not infrequent apprehension that the idea has aroused, this viewpoint is shared by a growing number of people who range from professionals in various political arenas to analytical theorists. Approval voting, however, will probably never be the burning issue of the day, though this study shows, we think, that its impact could be more significant than many burning issues and that it has much to recommend it. But perhaps what is most important, and could make approval voting in the final analysis acceptable to both citizens and policy makers, is that it really is a very simple and logical idea.

Footnotes to Preface

1. Guy Ottewell, "The Arithmetic of Voting," *In Defense of Variety* **4** (July-August 1977), 42–44; John Kellett and Kenneth Mott, "Presidential Primaries: Measuring Popular Choice," *Polity* **11**, 4 (Summer 1977), 528–537; Robert J. Weber, "Comparison of Voting Systems" (mimeographed, 1977); Steven J. Brams and Peter C. Fishburn, "Approval Voting," *American Political Science Review* **72**, 3 (September 1978), 831–847; and Richard A. Morin, *Structural Reform: Ballots* (New York: Vantage Press, 1980). Weber, who coined the term "approval voting," and Brams discovered their common interest in this subject at a workshop at Cornell University, under the direction of William F. Lucas, in the summer of 1976. Brams had earlier been attracted by the concept of "negative voting," proposed in a brief essay by George A. W. Boehm, "One Fervent Vote against Wintergreen" (mimeographed, 1976), passed on to him by the late Oskar Morgenstern. He first analyzed this kind of voting, as well as approval voting, in "One Man, n Votes," Module in Applied Mathematics, Mathematical Association of America (Ithaca, NY: Cornell University, 1976) and S. J. Brams, "When Is It Advantageous to Cast a Negative Vote?" in *Mathematical Economics and Game Theory: Essays in Honor of Oskar Morgenstern,* edited by R. Henn and O. Moeschlin, Lecture Notes in Economics and Mathematical Systems, Vol. 141 (Berlin: Springer-Verlag, 1977), pp. 564–572. Later Brams made more detailed comparisons of negative and approval voting in S. J. Brams, *Comparison Voting,* Innovational Instructional Unit (Washington, DC: American Political Science Association, 1978), which will appear in slightly revised form in *Modules in Applied Mathematics: Political and Related Models,* Vol. 2, edited by Steven J. Brams, William F. Lucas, and Philip D. Straffin, Jr. (New York: Springer-Verlag, 1982); and S. J. Brams, *The Presidential Election Game* (New Haven: Yale University Press, 1978), Ch. 6, which also reports on results developed in Brams and Fishburn, "Approval Voting." Ottewell (personal communication to Brams, November 17, 1980) first thought of the idea of approval voting in 1967–1968, and Morin (personal communication to Brams, September 21, 1980), who refers to the reform as "direct approval voting," first wrote about it in 1977. Morin's book, *Structural Reform: Ballots,* deserves special notice because, as a nonacademic with little contact with the professional literature, Morin offers a substantial

and lucid analysis of approval voting, some dubious claims (e.g., that the paradox of voting cannot exist under approval voting) notwithstanding.

2. Approval voting has recently been discussed in a number of texts and monographs, including Dennis C. Mueller, *Public Choice* (Cambridge: Cambridge University Press, 1979), pp. 60–64; K. H. Kim and Fred W. Roush, *Introduction to Mathematical Consensus Theory,* Lecture Notes in Pure and Applied Mathematics, Vol. 59 (New York: Marcel Dekker, 1980), pp. 94–102; Philip D. Straffin, Jr., *Topics in the Theory of Voting,* UMAP Expository Monograph (Boston: Birkhäuser, 1980), pp. 49–50; Thomas E. Cronin, *The State of the Presidency,* 2d Ed. (Boston: Little, Brown, 1980), pp. 65–66; Alan L. Clem, *American Electoral Politics: Strategies for Renewal* (New York: D. Van Nostrand, 1981), pp. 146–147; Peter H. Aranson, *American Government: Strategy and Choice* (Cambridge, MA: Winthrop, 1980), pp. 600–601; and William H. Riker, *Liberalism against Populism: A Confrontation between the Theory of Democracy and the Theory of Social Choice* (San Francisco: W. H. Freeman, 1982), pp. 88–90, 91–94, 101, 105–110, 113, and 293. Riker says (p. 113), "In primary elections, I would use approval voting," though he would eschew it in a general election because he thinks it would destroy the two-party system. In *A Danger of Democracy: The Presidential Nominating Process* (Boulder, CO: Westview, 1981), Terry Sanford says (p. 119), "It is not my recommendation at this time that this system [approval voting] be generally adopted, but it is promising enough for the parties to encourage several states to act as public laboratories by trying it." A similar position has been taken in a Position Statement on approval voting (September 1981) by the Council on International and Public Affairs in New York for their Project on Political Change. Ward Morehouse, president of the Council, is author of the Position Statement; the Statement has also been endorsed by Robin J. Arzt, Steven J. Brams, William Cowan, Curtis B. Gans, Donald Harrington, Betty G. Lall, and Henry Teune. Others who have been instrumental in developing legislative support for approval voting are Daniel Feldman in New York, Dick Bennett in New Hampshire, and Frank Bryan, Norris Hoyt, and Mary Barbara Maher in Vermont.

3. One exception, perhaps, is its use in elections in the United Nations, wherein members of the Security Council can vote for more than one candidate for the post of Secretary General. For reports on such voting in fall 1981, see Bernard D. Nossiter, "U.N. Security Council Fails to Agree on Waldheim," *New York Times,* October 28, 1981, p. A14; B. D. Nossiter, "China Continues to Bar Waldheim Nomination," *New York Times,* October 29, 1981, p. A9; B. D. Nossiter, "Someone Is Trying to Fire Waldheim," *New York Times,* November 1, 1981, p. E5; and B. D. Nossiter, "Security Council Elects a Peruvian Secretary General," *New York Times,* December 12, 1981, pp. 1, 6.

Acknowledgments

During the short time that approval voting has been a research topic, we have benefited greatly from the ideas of a number of scholars and practitioners, whose writings and other contributions are cited in the footnotes. Extra thanks go to Samuel Merrill, III, Nicholas R. Miller, Hannu Nurmi, Jeffrey T. Richelson, Duff Spafford, and anonymous reviewers who read the manuscript and gave us valuable criticism and advice.

Most of the book is based on our joint papers, several of which have appeared or are forthcoming in academic journals acknowledged in the footnotes. We are grateful for permission to use this material, which in some instances includes technical arguments, omitted here, that specialists may want to consult.

Brams's work was partially supported by grant DAR-8011823 from the National Science Foundation to New York University for applied research in approval voting, beginning July 1980. Fishburn's research on approval voting began when he was at The Pennsylvania State University and has continued part time since he joined Bell Laboratories in 1978. While we have enjoyed and deeply appreciate the support of our sponsoring institutions, the views expressed in this book are our own and in no way reflect the policies of these institutions.

Our wives, Eva Brams and Jan Fishburn, liked the idea of approval voting from the start. In contrast to some of the esoteric ideas that we often work with, we view their approval of approval voting as recognition of a sound practical idea that can benefit a society which elects its political leaders. Their support and encouragement have been splendid. Similar reactions from friends, who represent a variety of interests and professional fields, strengthen our feeling that approval voting has a promising future.

List of Tables

List of Figures

Chapter 1
Introduction: Overview of the Problem and Its Solution

This chapter is deliberately written to provide a stark contrast with the formality of much of the rest of the book. It could well be the last chapter, offering a wrap-up summary and some examples that illustrate the main points of the analysis. (Several of these examples are analyzed in greater detail later.) We might say these things in a lecture or conversation about approval voting, and some people will have no need or desire to hear more.[1] Those who do can go on, but those who do not will be able to get the gist of our general arguments in the next few pages.

We shall begin by commenting on the problem posed by multicandidate elections (those with more than two candidates), suggest how approval voting would ameliorate this and related problems of elections, mention and briefly comment on several criticisms of approval voting, show, as an illustration of its effects, how the results of New Hampshire's 1980 presidential primaries probably would have changed under approval voting, and finally indicate the reform's prospects for adoption. Although we shall devote a good deal of space to presidential elections, the problem of selecting a winner in multicandidate elections is a general one, which we shall illustrate with several examples from nonpresidential elections.

1.1. The Multicandidate Problem

Elections under plurality voting often seem rigged against majority candidates. For example, James Buckley was elected a United States Senator from New York in 1970 with only 39 percent of the vote. Buckley, a conservative, was probably no more representative of New York state voters than John Lindsay, a liberal, was representative of New York City voters when he was reelected to a second term as mayor of New York in 1969 with 42 percent of the vote. The 61-percent majority that voted for Buckley's two opponents, and the 58-percent majority that voted for Lindsay's two opponents, were effectively denied representation, at least in terms of their apparent ideological preferences, for six and four years, respectively. Moreover, as these examples indicate, the apparent bias of plurality voting toward the strongest minority candidate is not ideological: either liberals or conservatives may be aggrieved by the results.

One can think of many examples in which three or more candidates in a plurality contest divided the total vote such that no candidate received a majority. A dramatic recent example is the 1977 New York City mayoral election, in which six candidates got between 10 and 20 percent of the votes in the Democratic primary. This contest was followed by a runoff between the top two vote-getters, Edward Koch (19.8 percent in the plurality election) and Mario Cuomo (18.6 percent), which Koch won.

The runoff, however, offered no assurance that one of the four other candidates in the 10–20-percent range could not have beaten Koch. Koch may well have been the strongest candidate in the Democratic field, but the plurality election, even followed by a runoff, did not offer incontrovertible evidence that he was.

Neither did the three-way United States Senate election in New York in 1980 prove that Alphonse D'Amato was a stronger candidate than Elizabeth Holtzman and Jacob Javits, whom D'Amato defeated with a 45-percent plurality to 44 percent for Holtzman and 11 percent for Javits. In fact, an ABC News exit poll of voters (taken as they left the polling booths) revealed that if Javits had not been in the race, twice as many of his supporters would have opted for Holtzman as for D'Amato, easily making Holtzman the winner in a two-candidate contest. Ironically, the Liberal Party nominee (Javits) helped defeat the most liberal of the three Senate candidates (Holtzman).

The problem in all these cases is that a candidate, with support from a relatively small percentage of the electorate, can either win a plurality election outright or qualify for a runoff. When four-fifths of the electorate vote for other candidates, as happened in the 1977 New York mayoral race, the winner can hardly claim a great popular mandate. Worse, if there is another candidate whom a majority would actually prefer, the election system, in our opinion, is working perniciously in depriving the electorate of its rightful public choice.

This was probably the case in the elections that Buckley and Lindsay won in 1970 and 1969, respectively (as well as in the most recent Senate election in which Javits played the spoiler role). If either Buckley or Lindsay had been in a head-to-head contest with just one of his opponents, he almost surely would have lost to him.

It is indeed unfortunate for the voters when the winner in an election is in fact a weaker candidate than one or more of the losers! This paradoxical result most often occurs when two or more moderate candidates split the centrist vote, allowing a more extremist candidate to eke out a victory with only minority support. It is precisely this shortcoming of our system that seems in part responsible for the presidential nomination of Barry Goldwater by the Republican Party in 1964, and the nomination of George McGovern by the Democratic Party in 1972. Although each nominee had vociferous minority support within his party, each was a disaster to his party in the general election.

1.2. A Solution: Approval Voting

We believe there is a simple, practicable solution to this defect in our election system. It is a new voting system called approval voting, which allows a voter to vote for, or approve of, as many candidates as he wishes in a multicandidate race.

Thus, if there were five candidates, voters would not be restricted to voting for just one candidate. They could vote for two or more candidates if they had no clear favorite. However, only one vote could be cast for every approved candidate—that is, votes could not be cumulated and several cast for one candidate. The candidate with the most approval votes would win.

Approval voting has several striking advantages over plurality voting, or plurality voting with a runoff.

1. It gives voters more flexible options. They can do everything they can under the present system—vote for a single favorite—but if they have no strong preference for one candidate, they can express this fact by voting for all candidates they find acceptable. On the other hand, voters who do have a clear favorite, but one who does not appear to have a good chance of winning, would not have to despair about wasting their votes but could also vote for a more viable candidate whom they considered acceptable.

Consider what might have happened if voters had had this option in 1980. A *Time* poll in mid-October, approximately three weeks before the presidential election, showed that 49 percent found independent candidate John Anderson "acceptable"—and presumably would have voted for him under approval voting. This compares with acceptability figures of 57 percent for Jimmy Carter and 61 percent for Ronald Reagan. In other words, John Anderson would have been almost competitive with the major-party nominees under approval voting; had he been perceived as such, he surely would not have been as severely hurt by the wasted-vote phenomenon. (Anderson actually received 7 percent of the popular vote, to 41 and 51 percent for Carter and Reagan, respectively.)

Apart from the question of wasting one's vote, plurality voting is fundamentally unfair to a voter who may have a hard time deciding who is the best candidate in a crowded field but can choose the two or more candidates considered most acceptable. Approval voting thus provides the voter with more flexible options and thereby encourages a truer expression of preferences than does plurality voting.

2. It could increase voter turnout. By being better able to express their preferences, voters would probably be more likely to go to the polls in the first place. Voters who think they might be wasting their votes, or who cannot decide which of several candidates best reflects their views, would not be on the horns of a dilemma. By not being forced to make a single—perhaps arbitrary—choice, they would feel that the election system allows them to be more honest. We believe this would make voting more meaningful and encourage greater participation in elections.

3. It would help elect the strongest candidate. Today, as the previous examples illustrate, the candidate supported by the largest minority wins, or at least makes the runoff. Under approval voting, by contrast, it would be the candidate with the greatest overall support—the one most widely approved of—who would win. This does not imply, incidentally, that a candidate with bland appeal and no ideology will inevitably win, as the approval strength of Ronald Reagan in 1980 testifies.

That a runoff may not succeed in electing the strongest candidate is illustrated by a three-candidate plurality race in which A wins 25 percent of the vote, B 35 percent, and C 40 percent. It is entirely possible that the loser, A, is the strongest candidate in the sense that he would beat B in a separate two-way contest (because C supporters would vote for A), and would beat C in a separate two-way contest (because B supporters would vote for A). A runoff election between the top vote getters (B and C) would not show up this fact. On the other hand, approval voting in all likelihood would reveal A to be the strongest candidate because some B and C supporters—who liked A as much or almost as much—would cast second approval votes for A, who would thereby become the winner. In other words, a candidate's strength would derive not from being the favorite of the largest fraction of voters but rather from having broad-based appeal in the entire electorate.

A related benefit is that approval voting would induce candidates to try to mirror the views of a majority of voters, not just cater to minorities whose votes could give them a slight edge in a crowded plurality contest, wherein a candidate with only 20 to 30 percent of the vote can win. The fact that Jimmy Carter won the 1976 Democratic Party primary in New Hampshire with only 28 percent of the vote, and Henry Jackson won the primary in Massachusetts one week later with only 23 percent of the vote, says nothing about how acceptable either candidate was to the approximately three-quarters of the voters in each primary who did *not* vote for them.

4. It would give minority candidates their proper due. Minority candidates would not suffer under approval voting: their supporters would not be torn away simply because there was another candidate who, though less appealing to them, was generally considered a stronger contender. Because approval voting would allow these supporters to vote for both candidates, they would not be tempted to desert the one who is weak in the polls, as under plurality voting.

Such desertions occurred in the 1968 presidential election, when George Wallace dropped from 21 percent support in the polls in September to 14 percent in the actual vote on Election Day in November. It seems likely that the one-third of Wallace supporters who deserted him in favor of one of the major-party candidates did so because they thought he had no serious chance of winning—the wasted-vote phenomenon, again. But if there had been approval voting, Wallace would almost certainly have retained his original supporters, some of whom would also have voted for Richard Nixon or Hubert Humphrey. One of these candidates would have won, probably with more than 50 percent of the vote (Nixon received 43.4 percent in the election; Humphrey, 42.7 percent), but Wallace would have registered much more substantial support than he did. Hence, minority candidates would probably receive their true level of support under approval voting, though majority candidates would generally win.

5. It is relatively insensitive to the number of candidates running. Because ballots may be cast for as many candidates as the voter wishes under approval voting, if new candidates enter it is still possible to vote for one or more of them without being forced to withdraw support from old candidates. Plurality voting, on the other hand, is very sensitive to the number of candidates running. As the number of contenders increases, the plurality contest becomes more and more one of who can inch out whom in a crowded field rather than who is the strongest and most acceptable candidate.

Thus, when Jimmy Carter won less than 30 percent of the vote in the New Hampshire Democratic primary in 1976, the significance of his victory could be questioned. This gave the media an opportunity to pass judgment, which they readily did. Approval voting, by contrast, better reveals the overall acceptability of the candidates independent of the field in which they run—and thereby more accurately mirrors each candidate's genuine support in the electorate. A side benefit would be that the voters, not the media, would have greater impact in the selection process.

A hypothetical example perhaps best dramatizes the different effects of plurality voting and approval voting:

	Plurality Voting	Approval Voting
Candidate X	25%	30%
Candidate Y	24%	51%

In this example, which assumes X and Y are the two top candidates in the race and several other candidates split the remaining vote, X just wins under plurality voting. Yet X is approved of by less than one-third of the voters, whereas Y is acceptable to more than one-half of the voters.

Is it fair that X, unacceptable to 70 percent of the electorate, should be considered the "winner" simply because he is the first choice of more voters than any other candidate in a crowded field? He may be liked by the biggest minority of voters (25 percent), but in our opinion the voting system should also register the fact that he is disliked—that is, not approved of—by all but 30 percent of the voters.

Approval voting would show up the fact that Y is acceptable to many more voters than X. Of course, the plurality voting winner and the approval voting winner are often the same, and then there is no problem. However, the discrepancy between plurality and approval voting winners seems not so infrequent, even in races with as few as three candidates, to be dismissed as a rare event.

6. It is superior to preferential voting. An election system that is used in a few places in the United States (for example, Cambridge, Massachusetts) shares many of the advantages of approval voting. It is called majority preferential voting, or "single transferable vote," and it allows each voter to rank the candidates from best to worst. If no candidate receives a majority of first-place votes, the candidate with the fewest first-place votes is dropped and the second-place votes of his supporters are given to the remaining candidates. The elimination process continues, with lower-place votes of the voters whose preferred candidates are eliminated being transferred to the candidates that survive, until one candidate receives a majority.

There are several practical and theoretical problems with preferential voting. First, it is difficult and costly to implement, and many voters do not understand how it works. For example, in New York City school board elections, in which this system has recently been used, it takes a week to count the ballots, make the transfers, and determine the winners. This delay could be alleviated by computerizing the system, but the capital expenditure needed to do this would be substantial. Moreover, it seems to be a system that voters do not comprehend very well, at least as measured by extremely low turnouts of less than 5 percent in recent school board elections under preferential voting.'

Second, under preferential voting, the candidate with the most first-place votes may be displaced after the transfers have been made to determine the majority winner. This may greatly upset that candidate's supporters, particularly if they are a large minority, and lead to questions about the legitimacy of the system—and ultimately its rejection by voters, as occurred in 1976 in Ann Arbor, Michigan. This challenge cannot be mounted against approval voting since approval votes are indistinguishable: whether these votes are first-place, second-place, or whatever is not recorded, so no portion of the winner's total can be judged "inferior."

Third, and more serious, is the possibility that preferential voting may eliminate the candidate acceptable to the most voters. For example, Charles Goodell would have been eliminated as low man in the 1970 United States Senate race in New York with 24 percent of the plurality vote (Buckley got 39 percent and Richard Ottinger 37 percent), though there is evidence he, like candidate A in the hypothetical example given in Section 1.2.3, could have beaten each of his opponents in face-to-face contests and would have won under approval voting.

Fourth, and probably most serious, is preferential voting's violation of a fundamental democratic ethic: a candidate may do better under this system by getting fewer, rather than more, first-place votes. For example, a candidate can win an election when, say, 10,000 voters rank him first but lose it when an extra 5,000 voters move him from a lower rank into first place (without changing their ordering of other candidates). In other words, it may be in the interest of a candidate to tell some of his supporters not to rank him first to ensure his victory—a truly perverse result. Without going into details, this perversity arises not because additional votes are counted against a candidate but rather because of the successive eliminations of the ostensibly weakest candidates and the transfer of their votes to ostensibly stronger candidates, as we shall illustrate later.

Because of this perversity, preferential voting is said in the technical literature to violate a "monotonicity condition." It is a pathology that does not afflict approval voting, because the more approval votes a candidate receives relative to the other candidates, the better he does. Under no circumstances can a candidate be hurt under approval voting by receiving additional first-place votes, which seems to us an extremely damaging flaw of preferential voting.

7. *It will add legitimacy to the outcome.* Large fields of candidates, especially in party primaries, are now commonplace. For example, gubernatorial primaries in New Jersey in June 1981 attracted a combined total of 21 candidates in the Democratic and Republican Party races. Such elections demonstrate that the fields often burgeon as new candidates, sensing an opportunity to win with only a small fraction of the vote, enter the race and cause the vote to splinter even further, in turn inducing additional candidates to enter and thereby aggravating the problem of large numbers.

While approval voting would not generate such a "snowball effect," it may encourage new candidates to enter who sense that they will be approved by supporters of other candidates. Whether more candidates would run under approval voting than under plurality voting is hard to say, but because approval voting is insensitive to numbers (point 5 above), large numbers would not ineluctably lead to a hopelessly splintered vote that facilitates a "divide-and-conquer" strategy.

Indeed, both party nominees in the New Jersey gubernatorial primaries won with less than one-third of the plurality vote, but they would have won by much larger margins under approval voting. The Democratic winner would have been approved of by 46 percent in a field of 13, and the Republican winner by 54 percent in a field of eight, demonstrating that they both had substantial popular mandates despite their relatively small plurality totals.[2] Thus, while approval voting often will do no more than confirm the plurality winners, in doing so it will confer legitimacy on their victories to the extent that it shows their support to be widespread in the electorate.

A variation on approval voting would add legitimacy to the presidential nomination process, in which both major parties now require delegates pledged to a candidate from the state caucuses and primaries to vote for him on the first ballot in national party conventions. It has been argued, most recently by supporters of Edward Kennedy in the divisive 1980 Democratic party convention, that this rule does not give delegates any flexibility in making a choice, perhaps months after they were selected, though circumstances might have changed.

One possible solution to this problem would be to retain the rule but also, as under approval voting, allow delegates to vote on the first ballot for any *other* candidates they deem acceptable. Thus, while not relinquishing support of the candidate he is pledged to, a delegate could, by supporting other(s) if he thought it advisable to do so, have greater weight in the convention.

The greater leeway delegates would have would, in our opinion, enhance the legitimacy of the selection process—as well as reinvigorate the role delegates play. At the same time that it takes account of voter preferences in the earlier caucuses and primaries, it does not lock delegates into these exclusive choices later. Moreover, by fostering the emergence of "compromise" choices—acceptable to opposing factions—in a sharply divided convention, it could also diminish rancor within a party.

8. It is eminently practicable. Approval voting can readily be implemented on existing voting machines. With paper ballots, the counting of votes would be somewhat more tedious, but this should not, in our view, be a major barrier to its implementation.

To enact, approval voting will require a statutory, not a constitutional, change in most jurisdictions. Consider the statute in New Hampshire for voting in the presidential primaries. To enact approval voting in these elections would require only the substitution of the italicized words in parentheses for the preceding words:

Every qualified voter . . . shall have the opportunity . . . to vote his preference (*preferences*), on the ballot of his party, for his choice (*choices*) for one person (*any persons*) to be the candidate (*candidates*) of his political party for president of the United States and one person (*any persons*) to be the candidate (*candidates*) of his political party for vice president of the United States . . . .

It may be thought that, even given the virtues of approval voting, it would make little difference in a real election. This is so because the candidates would encourage voters to vote just for themselves (bullet voting) to keep down the vote totals of their opponents. Yet, even if the candidates made such an appeal, it would probably not be effective, particularly in a crowded race in which voters had difficulty distinguishing their single favorite.

As evidence to support this contention, data from a variety of sources indicate that the average voter would approve of two or more candidates in most multicandidate races. In the gubernatorial primaries in New Jersey alluded to earlier, for example, only 13 percent of the voters considered there to be no candidate, other than their first choice, who was acceptable and for whom they would have voted. The fact that voter support can be shared under approval voting would, we think, mitigate candidate infighting—particularly in primaries, which can adversely affect a party nominee's support in the general election—and instead focus attention on the issues.

The commonsensical reasons we have outlined for adopting approval voting are supported by a number of technical arguments, which are developed in detail in subsequent chapters and which we shall just mention here in passing. Among all nonranked voting systems, approval voting is more "sincere," "strategy-proof," and has a strong propensity to elect so-called Condorcet candidates—those who, if they exist, would defeat all others in a series of pairwise contests—and these results carry over to the election of committees; it maximizes the "efficacy" or power of voters and is, in a particular sense, more equitable than other nonranked systems; it has several advantages over runoff and preference systems, some of which were described earlier. In addition, computer simulations, experiments, reconstructed ballot data, and survey data lend empirical support to several of the postulated and derived theoretical effects.

1.3. What's Wrong with Approval Voting?

It seems only fair to acknowledge objections to approval voting that some people feel detract from its positive features. We note four objections here and offer brief comments:

1. Gradations of preference allowed by voting systems that use voters' rankings of candidates are lost under approval voting. Since most voting systems in widespread use, especially in the United States, in fact allow voters *less* opportunity to differentiate among candidates than does approval voting (see point 1 in last section), this objection has little force in the context of present practices. We question also the acceptability and practicality of "ranking methods" in large-scale elections (see Section 1.2.6), particularly in single-winner elections in which the question of proportional representation is not pertinent. Moreover, gradations offered by ranking methods will most likely be dampened by aggregation, and rankings, if reported truthfully (a potentially significant problem in itself, as we shall show in Chapter 2 and later), would be very likely to elect the same candidate as approval voting.

2. Approval voting could encourage the proliferation of candidates with fuzzy or ambivalent issue positions, thereby giving the electorate no real basis for choice. As explained in Chapter 10, with documentation given earlier, we think this is most unlikely to occur. Among other reasons, we do not believe that the electorate is sufficiently naive or undiscerning to support bland or nebulous candidates.

3. Approval voting could undermine and perhaps destroy the two-party system. This contention, of course, applies only to jurisdictions with strong two-party systems believed to be worth preserving and notably excludes party primaries, wherein approval voting would almost certainly abet the choice of the strongest party nominee (see Section 1.2.3). The evolution of party structures depends on many factors besides voting methods, so we think, especially without experience with approval voting, it is premature to predict the demise of the two major parties. Even if additional candidates should be drawn into

the fray in general elections under approval voting, we see no reason why strong party candidates should not continue to do well, particularly since other candidates need not drain support away from them under approval voting (see Section 1.2.5). To be sure, if the parties fail to nominate candidates with broad popular appeal, they may be hurt, but their poor performances will then not be attributable to approval voting.

4. Approval voting could create significant inequities among voters, depending on the number of candidates for whom they vote. This objection involves issues of efficacy and equity that we analyze in Chapter 5. It is in fact groundless because approval voting tends to be both more efficacious and equitable for voters than other simple voting systems, such as plurality voting.

1.4. An Illustration of the Effects of Different Rules: The 1980 New Hampshire Primaries under Approval Voting

The results from New Hampshire's presidential primaries on February 26, 1980 turned the tide for Ronald Reagan, after his loss to George Bush in the Iowa caucuses a month earlier, and gave an additional boost to Jimmy Carter over his principal rival, Edward Kennedy. On the Republican side, Reagan was the big winner with 50 percent of the vote, with George Bush and Howard Baker trailing far behind with 23 and 13 percent, respectively. No other Republican candidate received more than 10 percent of the vote.

Would these results have changed significantly under approval voting? To approximate approval voting, ABC News asked voters in exit polls in New Hampshire to indicate *all* the candidates they considered acceptable if they could have cast more than one vote. The responses indicate that Reagan would have increased his total by 8 percentage points to 58 percent, Bush by 16 percentage points to 39 percent, but by far the biggest gainer would have been Baker: he would have climbed a dramatic 28 percentage points to finish in second place, behind Reagan, with 41 percent of the vote.

In other words, under approval voting Howard Baker would have more than tripled his plurality vote total and wound up a very creditable second-place candidate instead of finishing a dismal third. Although not the first choice of most Republicans, he had greater residual support than his closest rival, George Bush, on Election Day in New Hampshire. Unfortunately for Baker, the returns never revealed this fact, and he dropped out after second poor showings in the Massachusetts and Vermont primaries one week after the New Hampshire primary.

On the Democratic side, the order of finish probably would not have changed under approval voting. Even if Edward Kennedy had been approved by all Jerry Brown's supporters (10 percent), this still would not have been sufficient to wipe out Jimmy Carter's 11-percent lead (49 to 38 percent). To be sure, some of Carter's supporters would also have approved of Kennedy, and vice versa, but it seems very unlikely that Kennedy would have defeated Carter under approval voting. In fact, the ABC News approval voting figures confirm this proposition: Carter would have received 60 percent approval, Kennedy, 48 percent, and Brown, 36 percent.

In sum, the results reveal a more tightly packed race in the Republican primary, with one candidate displacing another, but no displacement would have occurred in the Democratic primary. To us the most important finding is that the race in both parties would have been more competitive and, in the Republican Party, also looked significantly different for one candidate (Baker), generally considered a "moderate," coming out of New Hampshire at the beginning of the nomination race.

1.5. Prospects for Adoption

We believe that approval voting may well become the most significant election reform of the twentieth century, just as the Australian, or secret, ballot—printed by the government with the names of all authorized candidates—was the election reform of the nineteenth century. If effect, the principle of "one person, one vote" under plurality voting becomes the principle of "one candidate, one vote" under approval voting. That is, each voter makes judgments about every candidate under approval voting, so the tie-in of a vote is not to the voter but rather to the candidate.

One of us (Brams) has campaigned for the adoption of approval voting in the elections of several states as well as overseas, particularly Great Britain. This campaign has received coverage in the *New York Times*[3]—wherein an Op-Ed essay also appeared[4]—the *Los Angeles Times,*[5] the *Baltimore Sun,*[6] and many other newspapers, and also on network radio and television here and abroad, including ABC, PBS, and the BBC. Editorials have also appeared, and the reform has been discussed in such magazines as *Scientific American.*[7]

Over the past few years, Brams has had voluminous correspondence from presidential candidates, Secretaries of State, state legislators, state chairpersons of the Democratic and Republican parties, as well as officials of each party's national committee, major public interest organizations such as the League of Women Voters and Common Cause, and many others about the adoption of approval voting. In New Hampshire, he testified before both House and Senate committees on approval voting for use in that state's presidential primaries, and in New Jersey two forums were held at the Eagleton Institute at Rutgers University to debate its use in state elections there. Legislators from about a dozen other states have indicated a strong interest in introducing bills to implement approval voting in their state elections, especially party primaries, which usually attract large fields of candidates; in spring 1982, bills were formally introduced in the New York and Vermont legislatures. At the local level, a University of Pennsylvania group recommended, in a commissioned study, that approval voting be used in nonpartisan elections in Atlantic City, New Jersey, in a proposed charter revision for that city.[8]

Many voters are cynical today. Their choices are artificially limited. Approval voting could go a long way toward defusing their anger and frustration with a system that has nominated patently unrepresentative candidates like Barry Goldwater and George McGovern, who stymied their parties' presidential hopes in the years in which they ran and gave many voters no viable alternative to their opponents. In averting the nomination of such candidates, approval voting would strengthen the parties by electing their strongest nominees; this would increase competition in the general election. Moreover, by letting voters express themselves better at the polls, approval voting would greatly enhance democratic choice. This essentially costless reform thus seems well suited for voters, parties, and the heightening of competition among candidates that maximizes a voter's viable options.

Footnotes to Chapter 1

1. In fact, these things have been said in a few informal surveys. See "One Voter, Two Votes . . . or Three, or Four . . .," *Research for Managers at Penn State* (University Park, PA: College of Business Administration, Pennsylvania State University, 1978), pp. 22–23; Steven J. Brams, "Approval Voting: A Practical Reform for Multicandidate Elections," *National Civic Review* **68**, 10 (November 1979), 549–553, 560; S. J. Brams, "One Candidate, One Vote," *Archway: The Magazine of Arts and Science at New York University* **2** (Winter 1981), 10–14; S. J. Brams, "Approval Voting in Multicandidate Elections," *Policy Studies Journal* **9**, 1 (Autumn 1980), 102–108; S. J. Brams, "Approval Voting: One Candidate, One Vote," in *Representation and Redistricting Issues in the 1980s*, edited by Bernie Grofman, Arend Lijphart, Robert McKay, and Howard Scarrow (Lexington, MA: Lexington, 1982), pp. 137–142; S. J. Brams, "Is This Any Way to Elect a President?" in *Selection/Election: A Forum on the American Presidency,* edited by Robert S. Hirschfield (Hawthorne, NY: Aldine, 1982), pp. 173–177; Barbara J. Heil and S. J. Brams, "Approval Voting: How to Improve DC's Crazy Elections," *DC Gazette* **13**, 220 (May 1982), 2–4; and S. J. Brams, "Approval Voting: A Better Way to Elect a President?," *Annal of the Science and Public Policy Section*, New York Academy of Sciences (forthcoming). Some of these publications give citations to the technical literature, which we shall not give in this chapter but mention in later chapters, wherein the academic fine points are discussed. The *National Civic Review* article generated an exchange of letters between S. J.

Brams and George H. Hallett and Harold M. Olmstead, published in the following issues of the *Review*: **69**, 1 (January 1980), 10–13; **69**, 5 (May 1980), 247; and **69**, 8 (September 1980), 425–426, 434. Hallett and Olmstead defend single transferable vote, which we discuss in Section 1.2.6 and also in Section 7.5.

2. Based on an exit poll of 2,637 voters directed by Steven J. Brams, Arnold Urken, Douglas Muzzio, and George Sharrard and supported by The Fund for New Jersey. For more information on the results of this poll, see Arnold Urken, "Two from Column A . . . ," *New Jersey Reporter*, June 1981, pp. 9–12; and Gerald de Maio, Douglas Muzzio, and George Sharrard, "Approval Voting: The Empirical Evidence," *American Politics Quarterly* (forthcoming).

3. Warren Weaver Jr., "New System Urged in Presidential Primary Voting," *New York Times*, April 13, 1979, p. A15; and Malcolm W. Browne, "Can Voting Become Safer for Democracy?" *New York Times*, June 1, 1980, p. E7.

4. Samuel Merrill, "For Approval Voting," *New York Times*, July 20, 1979, p. A25. See also S. J. Brams's letters in *New York Times* (New Jersey section), January 11, 1981, p. 28; *New York Times Magazine*, March 22, 1981, p. 130; and *New York Times*, July 25, 1982, p. 18E.

5. Bud Lembke, "A Proposal for Legal Ballot-Box 'Stuffing,' " *Los Angeles Times* (Orange County section, Part 2), May 12, 1979, p. 13.

6. Stephen Hess, "Approval Voting," *Baltimore Sun*, May 8, 1981, p. A23.

7. Martin Gardner (written by Lynn Arthur Steen), "Mathematical Games (From Counting Votes to Making Votes Count: The Mathematics of Elections)," *Scientific American* (October 1980), pp. 16ff.

8. Henry Teune, Morton Lustig, Jack Nagel, and Oliver P. Williams, *A New Government for Atlantic City: A Strong Mayor-Strong Council Plan* (Philadelphia: Government Study Group, Department of Political Science, University of Pennsylvania, 1979), pp. 3, 28–31, and 75–78. Although we are not aware of its use in any public elections, approval voting has been used in several universities, including New York University, the University of Pennsylvania, University of New Hampshire, University of North Carolina at Charlotte, College of the Virgin Islands, and University of Saskatchewan, where it was used to help select a university president. It is also used in the election of a Secretary General in the United Nations Security Council, as reported by Bernard D. Nossiter, "U.N. Security Council Fails to Agree on Waldheim," *New York Times*, October 28, 1981, p. A14; in the selection of Fellows of the Econometric Society, as reported in Julie P. Gordon, "Report of the Secretary," *Econometrica* **48**, 1 (January 1981), 232; in the selection of members of the National Academy of Sciences at the stage of final balloting, as reported in *National Academy of Sciences: Constitution and Bylaws* (April 28, 1981), 33; and in the selection of members of the Council of the Consortium for Mathematics and Its Applications. In seventeenth century Massachusetts and Connecticut, a limited form of approval voting was used, with voting for each candidate in sequence. However, negative votes could be cast against a candidate, and only those candidates who had more approval than disapproval were elected. See Cortlandt F. Bishop, *History of Elections in the American Colonies* (New York: Burt Franklin, 1968; originally published in 1893), pp. 142–143, 150–151. We are grateful to Duff Spafford for this reference.

Chapter 2
Sincerity and Strategy-Proofness: Which System Is Most Honest?

2.1. Introduction

In this chapter we shall introduce some basic ideas about voting that will be helpful in distinguishing better from worse voting strategies. By "better" we mean roughly those strategies that a voter would seriously consider in deciding for whom to vote. Crucial to this determination will be eliminating those "worse" strategies that a voter would never consider because they are "dominated"—under no circumstances would they yield a better outcome than some other strategies, and sometimes they would give unequivocally worse outcomes. Those strategies which are not dominated will be called "admissible."

In general, a voter has more than one admissible strategy, so his problem is to choose from among them. Those admissible strategies which are "sincere," and more honestly reflect a voter's preferences in a sense to be made precise later, will be distinguished from those that are not under approval voting and other single-ballot voting systems that do not require voters to rank candidates. Different voting systems themselves will be characterized as sincere and, more stringently, "strategy-proof," for different configurations of voter preferences.

It will be shown that no system is absolutely invulnerable to strategic manipulation, but, among all nonranked voting systems (i.e., those in which a voter can vote for, but not order, the candidates according to his preferences), approval voting is less vulnerable than any other. Of course, the ability of a voter to exploit a system to his advantage depends not only on his preferences but also information that he has about the preferences of the other voters.

In this chapter, voters will be assumed not to be privy to information about other voters' preferences. However, this minimal-information assumption will be relaxed in later chapters, permitting voters to make more precise calculations about their optimal strategies on the basis of polls and other information they may have. Also, the possibility of there being more than one ballot, as in runoff systems, will be considered along with the effects that information from earlier ballots has on later ballots.

Surprisingly, having no information about the preferences, and hence probable voting behavior, of other voters still enables a typical voter to narrow his range of possible choices considerably in single-ballot elections. The extent of this narrowing depends on his preferences and the voting system, which are defined and discussed, along with the heretofore mentioned strategic concepts, in subsequent sections.

2.2. Voter Preferences and Dominance

Denote individual candidates by small letters a, b, c, . . . , and subsets of candidates by A, B, C, ... For any two subsets A and B, $A \cup B$, called the *union* of A and B, is the set of all candidates who are in A or in B. $A \backslash B$, called the *difference* of A and B, is the set of all candidates who are in A and not in B. In addition, $\{a\}$ is the subset of candidates that contains only candidate a, $\{a,b\}$ is the subset consisting of candidates a and b, and so on.

A voter's *strict preference relation* on the candidates will be denoted by P, so that aPb means that the voter definitely prefers a to b. Similarly, R will denote a voter's *nonstrict preference relation* on the candidates, so that aRb means that the voter likes a at least as much as b. Alternatively, aRb means that the voter either strictly prefers a to b or is indifferent between a and b.

It will be assumed that each voter's preferences are *connected*: he has a definite preference order on the candidates so that, for any two candidates, a voter prefers one to the other or is indifferent between them. Also, a voter's preference and indifference relations on all candidates are assumed to be *transitive*: if he strictly prefers a to b, and b to c, he will strictly prefer a to c, and similarly for nonstrict preference and indifference relations.

Given connectivity and transitivity, the set of all candidates can be partitioned into nonempty subsets (i.e., divided so that the subsets have no members in common), say A_1, A_2, . . . , A_n, for a given P so that the voter is indifferent among all candidates within each A_i and strictly prefers every candidate in A_i to every candidate in A_j if $i < j$— that is, he ranks all the "indifferent" candidates in A_i higher than the "indifferent" candidates in A_j.

According to this designation, A_1 is the voter's subset of most-preferred candidates, and A_n is the voter's subset of least-preferred candidates. If the voter is indifferent among all candidates, then A_1 and

A_n are the same, but otherwise A_1 and A_n are disjoint. The following comprehensive definition introduces a number of terms that will be used in this and later sections:

Definition 2.1. Suppose P partitions the set of all candidates into $n \geq$ 1 nonempty subsets $A_1, A_2, \ldots, A_n$, so that the voter is indifferent among all candidates within each A_i and has aPb when a is a member of A_i and b is a member of A_j if, and only if, $i < j$. Then P is *unconcerned* if and only if $n = 1$; P is *dichotomous* if and only if $n = 2$; P is *trichotomous* if and only if $n = 3$; and P is *multichotomous* if and only if $n \geq 4$. In addition, a subset of candidates B is *high for P* if and only if whenever it contains a candidate in A_j it contains all (more-preferred) candidates in A_i for every $i < j$; and B is *low for P* if and only if whenever it contains a candidate in A_i it contains all (less-preferred) candidates in A_j for every $j > i$.

A voter who has an unconcerned P will be referred to as an *unconcerned voter* since he is indifferent among all candidates. If P is unconcerned, then every subset of candidates is both high and low for P.

When P is concerned—that is, when P is either dichtomous, trichotomous, or multichotomous—exactly two subsets of candidates are *both* high and low for P, namely the empty set and the set of all candidates. If P is trichotomous on a set of five candidates $\{a,b,c,d,e\}$, say with $A_1 = \{a\}$, $A_2 = \{b,c\}$, and $A_3 = \{d,e\}$, then P has six high subsets in addition to the empty and whole sets, namely $\{a\}$, $\{a,b\}$, $\{a,c\}$, $\{a,b,c\}$, $\{a,b,c,d\}$ and $\{a,b,c,e\}$; and P has six low subsets in addition to the empty set and the whole set, namely $\{e\}$, $\{d\}$, $\{e,d\}$, $\{c,d,e\}$, $\{b,d,e\}$ and $\{b,c,d,e\}$. In all cases, the number of high subsets is equal to the number of low subsets since a subset is high if and only if its complement (i.e., all other candidates) is low.

The characterizations of dominance and admissible strategies to be developed in Sections 2.3 and 2.4 depend not only on the relations P and R as applied to individual candidates but also on extensions of these relations to subsets of candidates. The reason for this is that dominance and admissibility are viewed as based on individual preferences between potential outcomes of a vote, where the *outcome* of a given vote is the set of all candidates who have the greatest vote total on the ballot. In most real cases, there will be no ties and hence the outcome will consist of the one candidate with the largest vote total. However, if ties occur for the largest total, then the outcome will be a subset of two or more candidates.

Instead of specifying a method for determining an ultimate winner when the outcome of a vote contains two or more candidates, we shall proceed on the basis of assumptions that relate preferences between potential vote outcomes to preferences for the individual candidates. The symbols P and R that are used for a voter's preferences between individual candidates will also be used for the voter's preferences between subsets of candidates, viewed as potential outcomes. Thus, APB means that the voter prefers outcome A to outcome B, and ARB means that he finds A at least as good as B (i.e., he either prefers A to B or is indifferent between the two).

When A and B are one-candidate subsets, say $A = \{a\}$ and $B = \{b\}$, it is natural to assume that APB if and only if aPb, and that ARB if and only if aRb. Assume also that, for any nonempty A and B, APB and BRA cannot both hold. In addition, the following will be assumed for all candidates a and b and for all subsets of candidates A, B, and C.

Assumption P. If aPb, then $\{a\}P\{a,b\}$ and $\{a,b\}P\{b\}$.

Assumption R. If $A \cup B$ and $B \cup C$ are not empty and if aRb, bRc, and aRc for all a belonging to A, b belonging to B, and c belonging to C, then $(A \cup B)R(B \cup C)$.

Assumption P asserts that if candidate a is preferred to candidate b, then outcome $\{a\}$ is preferred to the tied outcome $\{a,b\}$, which in turn is preferred to $\{b\}$. This seems quite reasonable, regardless of how the tie between a and b might be broken when $\{a,b\}$ occurs, if the voter believes that a and b each has a positive probability of being elected when the two are tied after the initial ballot. This will surely be the case if ties are resolved probabilistically (e.g., by coin flips), but it seems also likely to hold for most other tie-breaking procedures.

Assumption R says that if everything in A is at least as good as everything in B and C, and if everything in B is at least as good as everything in C, then outcome $A \cup B$ will be at least as good as outcome $B \cup C$. If ties are broken randomly, then the conclusion of Assumption R says that the random choice of a winner from the union of A and B is as good as the random choice of a winner from the union of B and C.

Although Assumption R can be expected to hold in most cases, it is possible to imagine situations that challenge its credibility. For example, suppose $\{a,b,c,d\}$ is the set of candidates, and aPb, bPc, and cPd. Suppose further that there are two ballots, and the lowest candidate is eliminated on the first ballot. If there is a tie between a and d for the lowest vote total, then either $\{a,b,c\}$ or $\{b,c,d\}$ will be in the runoff.

Suppose that $A \cup B = \{a,b,c\}$ and $B \cup C = \{b,c,d\}$. If the voter with preference order P is convinced that c will be elected in a runoff among a, b, and c, and that b will be elected in a runoff among b, c, and d, then it is likely that this voter will prefer $B \cup C$ to $A \cup B$, in contradiction to Assumption R. Despite this possibility, Assumption R seems plausible in most situations and will be used in the subsequent analysis.

2.3. Dominance between Strategies

Define a *strategy* to be any subset of candidates. Then *choosing* a strategy means voting for all candidates in the subset. For identification purposes, let S and T rather than A, B, C, . . . identify strategies. A voter uses S if he votes for each candidate in S and no candidate not in S.

A strategy is *feasible* for a particular voting system if and only if it is permitted by that system. We assume that the abstention strategy— which is the empty subset of candidates—is always feasible. For every other strategy, a voter's ballot is counted if and only if he uses a feasible strategy. In addition to abstention, plurality voting has m feasible strategies when there are m candidates. By comparison, all strategies are feasible under approval voting.

The notion of admissible strategies to be developed in Section 2.4 depends on feasibility and on dominance. Roughly speaking, strategy S dominates strategy T for a particular voter if he likes the outcome of S as much as the outcome of T in every possible circumstance, and strictly prefers the outcome of S to the outcome of T in at least one circumstance.

To define dominance precisely, define a *contingency* as a function f that assigns a nonnegative integer to each candidate. A contingency is interpreted as specifying the numbers of votes each candidate receives from all voters *other than* the voter for whom dominance is being defined.

Call the latter voter the *focal voter*. Given a contingency f and a strategy S for this voter, let $F(S,f)$ denote the *outcome* of the vote. That is, $F(S,f)$ is the subset of candidates who have the greatest vote total under f and S. For any candidate a and strategy S, let $S(a) = 1$ if a belongs to S, with $S(a) = 0$ otherwise. Then, with $f(a)$ the integer assigned by contingency f to candidate a, a belongs to $F(S,f)$ if and only if $f(a) + S(a) \geq f(b) + S(b)$ for all candidates $b \neq a$. That is, a necessary and sufficient condition for candidate a to be contained in the outcome is that he receive at least as many votes from all voters (including the focal voter) as does every other candidate.

These concepts are illustrated by the data in Table 2.1 for the set of three candidates $\{a,b,c\}$. Voters other than the focal voter have created a contingency f in which a and b are tied with two votes each to one vote for c. If the focal voter's strategy S is to vote only for a, he breaks

Table 2.1

Illustration of a Contingency and a Focal
Voter's Strategy

Candidate i	Contingency $f(i)$	Strategy $S(i)$	Vote Total: $f(i) + S(i)$
a	2	1	3
b	2	0	2
c	1	0	1

the tie between a and b, making a the winner with three votes. Formally, because

$$f(a) + S(a) = 3 \geq f(b) + S(b) = 2$$

$$\geq f(c) + S(c) = 1,$$

the outcome $F(S,f)$ equals $\{a\}$.

One of the main tasks of the subsequent analysis is to determine strategies for a voter that lead to outcomes he most prefers. Although different strategies may be preferred under different contingencies, some strategies are uniformly as good as, or better than, other strategies, regardless of the contingency. That is, one strategy may dominate another strategy.

Definition 2.2. Given the strict and nonstrict preference relations P and R for a voter, strategy S *dominates* strategy T, or S *dom* T for this voter, if and only if $F(S,f)RF(T,f)$ for all possible contingencies f and $F(S,f)PF(T,f)$ for at least one contingency.

This definition does not require S and T to be feasible strategies and it is therefore applicable to all nonranked voting systems. Feasibility will enter the analysis explicitly through the definition of admissibility in Section 2.4.

Assumption R implies that an unconcerned voter (Definition 2.1) will be indifferent among all outcomes as well as among all individual candidates. Because Definition 2.2 requires that $F(S,f)PF(T,f)$ for some contingency f, it follows that no strategy is dominated for a voter with preference order P if P is unconcerned. The following theorem characterizes dominance between strategies for all concerned P. The definitions of high and low subsets are given in Definition 2.1, and $S\backslash T$ is the set of all candidates that are in S and not in T.

Theorem 2.1 (Dominance). *Suppose* P *is concerned and Assumptions* P *and* R *hold. Then* S dom T *for* P *if and only if* S $\neq$ T, S\T *is high* *for* P, T\S *is low for* P, *and neither* S\T *nor* T\S *is the set of all candidates.*

Proofs of Theorem 2.1 and other theorems and corollaries in this chapter are given elsewhere.[1] The intuitive reasoning underlying Theorem 2.1 is that because dominance is based on all contingencies, and the focal voter votes for all candidates in $S \cap T$ (i.e., the intersection of S and T, or the set of all candidates who are in both S and T) when he uses either S or T, S dominates T for P if and only if S\T dominates T\S for P. That is, dominance shows up in the nonoverlapping candidates, with those in S being high and those in T being low.

Although Theorem 2.1 is predicated on Assumptions P and R, the necessary and sufficient conditions for S dom T do not explicitly use the P and R relations on the outcomes. That is, *dominance between strategies can be determined completely on the basis of a voter's strict preference relation* P *over the individual candidates.* This greatly simplifies the identification of dominated strategies for a voter.

For example, if the set of candidates is $\{a,b,c\}$, and P is trichotomous with a preferred to b and b preferred to c, then Theorem 2.1 says that strategy $\{a\}$, under which the voter votes only for his most-preferred candidate, dominates strategies $\{c\}$, $\{a,c\}$, $\{b,c\}$, $\{a,b,c\}$, and the abstention strategy. Moreover, these are the only strategies that $\{a\}$ dominates.

Thus, for example, $S = \{a\}$ dominates $T = \{b,c\}$ because $S \neq T$; $\{a\}\backslash\{b,c\} = \{a\}$ is high for P—it contains only the candidate in A_1 (i.e., a); $\{b,c\}\backslash\{a\} = \{b,c\}$ is low for P—it contains all candidates in A_3 (i.e., c) whenever it contains a candidate in A_2 (i.e., b); neither $\{a\}$ nor $\{bc\}$ is the set of all candidates.

Theorem 2.1 also says that $\{a\}$ does not dominate $\{b\}$ since $\{b\}\backslash\{a\} = \{b\}$ is not low for P—it does not contain c. However, $\{b\}$ is dominated by $\{a,b\}$ according to Theorem 2.1 since $S \neq T$, $\{a,b\}\backslash\{b\} = \{a\}$ is high for P, $\{b\}\backslash\{a,b\} = \emptyset$ (the empty set, or abstention) is low for P, and neither $\{a\}$ nor $\emptyset$ is the set of all candidates.

Under approval voting, Theorem 2.1 says that if voters consider voting for their second choice b, then they should also vote for their first choice a since the latter strategy is as good as, and sometimes better than, the strategy of voting for b alone. However, under plurality voting, a vote for b alone could be a voter's best strategy since in this case $\{b\}$ is not dominated by any other feasible strategy. As we shall show in Section 2.4 (see Definition 2.4), strategy $\{b\}$ is "admissible" for plurality voting but "inadmissible" for approval voting.

Without giving the proof of Theorem 2.1 (and subsequent theorems in this chapter as well), it is hard to grasp why its particular conditions should distinguish those strategies which dominate others from those which do not. Why, for example, is $\{b\}$ dominated by $\{a,b\}$ under approval voting if a voter's preference order is *abc* (shorthand for *aPbPc*)?

To show why, intuitively, strategy $\{a,b\}$ in this instance is at least as good and sometimes better than $\{b\}$, consider the contingency $(2,1,0)$ [shorthand for $f(a) = 2, f(b) = 1, f(c) = 0$]. Clearly, if the focal voter chooses $S = \{a,b\}$, $F(S,f) = \{a\}$—that is, *a* wins with 3 votes to 2 and 0, respectively, for *b* and *c*. On the other hand, if $S = \{b\}$, $F(S,f) = \{a,b\}$—that is, the focal voter creates a tie between *a* and *b* with 2 votes each. By Assumption *P*, outcome $\{a\}$ is preferred to $\{a,b\}$ if *aPb*, so $S = \{a,b\}$ is better in this contingency.

But this is only half the story to prove dominance: while we have shown that there is at least one contingency in which strategy $\{a,b\}$ is better than $\{b\}$, we have not shown that in all other contingencies $\{a,b\}$ is at least as good as $\{b\}$. In fact, there are fifteen other distinct contingencies, and it can be demonstrated by exhaustive enumeration that in *none* does strategy $\{b\}$ induce a better outcome for a voter with preference scale *abc* than does $\{a,b\}$.[2]

Fortunately, Theorem 2.1 relieves one of the necessity of checking each and every contingency, which becomes virtually impossible if there are more than three candidates. Rather, it provides a general statement of conditions under which dominance obtains for any finite number of candidates, given a focal voter's preferences but assuming that, when he makes his strategy choice, he has no information about the preferences of any other voters.

2.4. Admissible Strategies

In this section we shall discuss a theorem that characterizes all admissible strategies for every concerned *P* and for all nonranked voting systems. Admissible strategies under approval voting and two other simple voting systems will then be compared.

To begin the analysis, two definitions are needed. The first makes the concept of a nonranked voting system precise by tying it to the numbers of candidates that voters are allowed to vote for (e.g., one, two, one or two, etc.) in order that their ballots be considered legal.

Definition 2.3. Suppose there are *m* candidates. Then a nonranked *voting system*[3] is a nonempty subset *s* of $\{1,2, \ldots , m - 1\}$.

As noted in Section 2.3, abstention—voting for no candidates—will be considered feasible for all voting systems. Since a vote for all candidates is tantamount to an abstention insofar as the determination of the outcome of a vote is concerned, we do not include *m* as a possible number in s in Definition 2.3. This will not present problems with the later analysis of admissibility since, when it is allowed, a vote for all m candidates (like an abstention) is dominated by some other feasible strategy whenever P is concerned.

According to Definition 2.3, plurality voting is system $\{1\}$. In other words, under plurality voting, a voter is allowed to vote for only one candidate. Under system $\{2\}$, each voter must vote for exactly two candidates for his ballot to be legal. System $\{1,2\}$ allows a voter to vote for either one or two candidates. System $\{1,2,\ldots,m-1\}$ is approval voting. Every system s that omits one or more integers in $\{1,2,\ldots,m-1\}$ is, of course, different from approval voting. As will be demonstrated in Section 2.5, approval voting is superior to all these other systems in eliciting "honest" choices.

For any subset A of candidates, let $|A|$ denote the *number* of candidates in A. Then strategy S is *feasible* for system s if and only if either S is the abstention strategy or $|S|$ belongs to s. This characterization of feasibility is consistent with Definition 2.3 and its use in Section 2.3, for it says that feasible voting strategies are exactly those that are permitted by the system—vote for none, or vote for only numbers of candidates contained in s.

Next, to provide a formal definition of admissibility, feasibility and dominance are combined.

Definition 2.4. Strategy S is *admissible* for system s and preference order P if and only if S is feasible for s and there is no strategy T that is also feasible for s and has T dom S for P.

Although a certain amount of formal development has been needed to give a precise definition of admissibility, its intuitive sense is easily understood. In effect, Definition 2.4 says that a voting strategy is admissible for a voter under a nonranked voting system if and only if (i) that strategy is permitted by the system, and (ii) there is no other permissible strategy—for all possible ways in which other voters may vote—that yields an outcome that is as good for a focal voter, and better in at least one contingency, as the admissible strategy. In other words, no other voting strategy dominates an admissible strategy, so admissible strategies are simply the set of undominated strategies.

Definition 2.4 suggests that, because of the feasibility requirement, a strategy feasible for each of two voting systems may be admissible for one system but inadmissible for the other. Indeed, in the example in Section 2.3 in which P was abc, it was noted that strategy $\{b\}$ is admissible for plurality voting but inadmissible for approval voting.

Before examining these specific systems in more detail, it is useful to have a theorem that characterizes all admissible strategies for every voting system and every concerned preference order P. This is so because the analysis that follows is based on the assumption that nonabstaining voters use only admissible strategies.

To facilitate the statement of the admissibility theorem, let

$M(P) = A_1$, the subset of most-preferred candidates under P,

$L(P) = A_n$, the subset of least-preferred candidates under P,

where A_1 and A_n are as given in Definition 2.1. The admissibility theorem below appears formidably complex, but as later corollaries will make clear, it is not difficult to apply to particular voting systems. Moreover, comparisons among several systems will show that they possess striking differences that bear on their strategic manipulability.

Theorem 2.2 (Admissibility). *Suppose* P *is concerned and Assumptions* P *and* R *hold. Then strategy* S *is admissible for system* s *and preference order* P *if and only if* S *is feasible for* s *and either C1 or C2 (or both) holds:*

C1: *Every candidate in* M(P) *is in* S, *and it is impossible to divide* S *into two nonempty subsets* S₁ *and* S₂ *such that* S₁ *is feasible for* s *and* S₂ *is low for* P;

C2: *No candidate in* L(P) *is in* S, *and there is no nonempty subset* A *of candidates disjoint from* S *such that* A ∪ S *is feasible for* s *and* A *is high for* P.

Since the abstention strategy satisfies neither C1 nor C2, it is never admissible for a concerned voter. Because abstention is inadmissible in the formal sense, a vote for all m candidates must likewise be inadmissible if it is permitted. Thus, though the abstention and "vote for all" strategies are assumed to be feasible, they can be omitted from the formal analysis since they are always inadmissible for a concerned voter.

The criteria of Theorem 2.2 can be applied to determine all admissible strategies for a given s and concerned P. To illustrate, suppose $m = 5$ and $s = \{1,3\}$, which is a rather unorthodox system that allows a voter to vote for either one or three candidates. Given P defined by $A_1 = M(P) = \{a\}$, $A_2 = \{b,c\}$, $A_3 = \{d\}$ and $A_4 = L(P) = \{e\}$, one can readily verify that

strategies $\{a\}$, $\{a,b,c\}$, $\{a,b,d\}$ and $\{a,c,d\}$ are admissible both by criterion C1 and by criterion C2;

strategies $\{a,b,e\}$ and $\{a,c,e\}$ are admissible by C1 only;

strategy $\{b,c,d\}$ is admissible by C2 only;

and no other feasible strategy is admissible. For example, strategy $\{b\}$ fails C1 since it excludes a; and it fails C2 since, if $A = \{a,c\}$, S is disjoint from A, $A \cup \{b\}$ is feasible for s, and A is high for P. In other words, feasible $\{a,b,c\}$ dominates feasible $\{b\}$.

Theorem 2.2 provides general criteria of admissibility for all non-ranked voting systems. Although these criteria do not have a simple interpretation in the general case, they can be rendered much more perspicuous in particular cases, as we shall next show.

When Theorem 2.2 is applied to approval voting, the following result is obtained.

Corollary 2.1. *Strategy* S *is admissible for approval voting and a concerned* P *if and only if* S *contains all candidates in* M(P) *and none in* L(P).

Hence concerned voters use one of their admissible strategies under approval voting if and only if they vote for every one of their most-preferred candidates and do not vote for any of their least-preferred candidates. Thus, if $m = 4$ and a voter has preference order $abcd$, then his admissible strategies are $\{a\}$, $\{a,b\}$, $\{a,c\}$ and $\{a,b,c\}$. To illustrate a case in which this voter would consider $\{a,c\}$—consisting of the voter's first and third choices—the best admissible strategy, consider a result simple to prove[4] that follows directly from Corollary 2.1.

Corollary 2.2. *A voter has a unique admissible strategy under approval voting if and only if his preference order* P *is dichotomous. This unique strategy is the voter's subset of most-preferred candidates.*

Now consider again a voter with preference order $abcd$, and suppose that all other voters have dichotomous preferences with a indifferent to b, and c indifferent to d. Some of the others prefer a and b to c and d, which we write as $(ab)(cd)$—with parentheses denoting indifference subsets—while the rest prefer c and d to a and b, or $(cd)(ab)$. Suppose further that these other voters use their unique admissible strategies, which are $\{a,b\}$ and $\{c,d\}$ for each of the two classes of other voters. It follows immediately that for the focal voter with preference order $abcd$, $f(a) = f(b)$ and $f(c) = f(d)$ for whatever contingency arises: a and b, and c and d, will each receive the same numbers of votes from all other voters.

Now assume that the voter with preference order $abcd$ estimates that the difference between $f(a)$ and $f(c)$ is likely to be more than one vote. Then, assuming that $f(a) > f(c) + 1$ and $f(c) > f(a) + 1$ are each thought to be fairly likely, $\{a,c\}$ will probably be the best strategy for the focal voter since $f(a) > f(c) + 1$ implies that

$$F(\{a,c\},f) = F(\{a\},f) = \{a\}$$

whereas

$$F(\{a,b\},f) = F(\{a,b,c\},f) = \{a,b\};$$

and $f(c) > f(a) + 1$ implies that

$$F(\{a,c\},f) = F(\{a,b,c\},f) = \{c\}$$

whereas

$$F(\{a\},f) = F(\{a,b\},f) = \{c,d\}.$$

Hence, strategy $\{a,c\}$ ensures (I) the election of the focal voter's most-preferred candidate when $f(a) > f(c) + 1$, and (II) the defeat of the focal voter's least-preferred candidate when $f(c) > f(a) + 1$, thereby affording him protection whether $\{a,b\}$ or $\{c,d\}$ is the social choice of the other voters.

Because approval voting offers more feasible strategies than plurality voting and the other nonranked systems identified in Definition 2.3, it might appear that it will (i) confuse voters by its large number of options, and (ii) be more liable to strategic manipulation than other systems. Not only is (ii) categorically false, as we shall show in Section 2.5, but (i) is not justified either, as we shall next show.

If concerned voters do not abstain, it is reasonable to assume that they will entertain only admissible strategies since all other strategies are dominated. Given this assumption, comparisons between different voting systems need only depend on *admissible* strategies for these systems. Thus, the question of the number of options that a voter faces under different systems really turns on the number of admissible strategies and not on the number of feasible strategies.

We shall compare approval voting with two other systems to illustrate the numbers of admissible strategies they offer different types of voters. The first system is plurality voting. The second system is $s = \{1, m - 1\}$, in which a voter can vote for either one, or all but one, candidate. Although the latter system may be unfamiliar, it is equivalent to the "negative voting" system proposed by Boehm that has been analyzed elsewhere.[5]

Under negative voting, each voter is allowed to cast one vote. This vote can be either for or against a candidate. A *for* vote adds one point to the candidate's score, and an *against* vote subtracts one point from the candidate's score. The outcome of a negative voting ballot is the subset of candidates with the largest *net vote* total (algebraic sum of for and against points), which may, of course, be negative.

Since a vote against a candidate has the same effect as a vote for every other candidate, the negative voting system is tantamount to system $\{1, m - 1\}$. When $m = 3$, this system is equivalent to approval voting, because a vote against one candidate has the same effect as approval votes for each of the other two. But for $m > 3$, negative voting has fewer feasible strategies than approval voting.

This argument can be made more precise. If there are $m \geq 3$ candidates, under approval voting a voter can cast either an approval vote or no vote for each candidate, giving each voter 2^m feasible voting strategies. However, since an abstention (vote for none) has the same net effect as a vote for all candidates, the number of effectively different choices is $2^m - 1$. By contrast, plurality voting allows $m + 1$ different choices (a vote for one of the m candidates or an abstention), and various other systems allow between $m + 1$ and $2^m - 1$ different strategies. Negative voting, for example, allows a voter $2m + 1$ strategies, because he can vote for or against each of the m candidates or abstain. If $m = 4$, there are nine feasible strategies, whereas under approval voting a voter would have 15 feasible strategies.

The following corollaries of Theorem 2.2 identify the admissible strategies of a concerned voter under plurality and negative voting. Recall that $L(P)$ is the voter's subset of least-preferred candidates. In Corollary 2.4, $\bar{a}$ denotes the strategy in which the voter votes for all candidates other than candidate a (or casts a vote against candidate a).

Corollary 2.3 *Strategy* {a} *is admissible for* plurality voting *and concerned* P *if and only if* a *is not in* L(P).

Corollary 2.4. *Suppose* m $\geq$ *3. Then (i) strategy* {a} *is admissible for* negative voting *and concerned* P *if and only if the voter strictly prefers* a *to at least two other candidates, and (ii) strategy* ā *is admissible for* negative voting *and concerned* P *if and only if the voter strictly prefers at least two other candidates to* a.

Corollaries 2.1, 2.3, and 2.4, which provide necessary and sufficient conditions for admissible strategies under three different simple voting systems, can be used to identify and compare sets of admissible strategies for various preference orders of voters for the candidates. For example, given the trichotomous preference order $(ab)cd$ for the set of four candidates $\{a,b,c,d\}$, the sets of admissible strategies for each of the systems is:

1. *Approval*: $\{a,b\}$, $\{a,b,c\}$. These are the only feasible strategies that contain all the voter's most-preferred, and none of his least-preferred, candidates.

Table 2.2

Numbers of Admissible Voting Strategies for
Three Voting Systems with Four Candidates*

Concerned Preference Order		Number of Admissible Strategies for		
		Approval Voting	Negative Voting	Plurality Voting
Dichotomous:	$a(bcd)$	1	1	1
	$(abc)d$	1	1	3
	$(ab)(cd)$	1	4	2
Trichotomous:	$(ab)cd$	2	4	3
	$ab(cd)$	2	4	2
	$a(bc)d$	4	2	3
Multichotomous:	$abcd$	4	4	3

*Source: Steven J. Brams and Peter C. Fishburn, "Approval Voting," *American Political Science Review* **72**, 3 (September 1978), 837, Table 1; reprinted with permission.

2. *Plurality*: {*a*}, {*b*}, {*c*}. These are the only feasible strategies that do not contain the voter's least-preferred candidates.
3. *Negative*: {*a*}, {*b*}, $\bar{c}$, $\bar{d}$. These are the only feasible strategies in which the voter strictly prefers the candidate to at least two others, or strictly prefers at least two other candidates to the barred candidate.

The numbers of admissible strategies for all concerned *P* orders for four candidates are shown in Table 2.2. It is clear that the relative numbers of admissible strategies for the three systems are very sensitive to the specific form of *P*. Although approval voting may offer more admissible strategies than other systems, as when *P* is $a(bc)d$, it may also offer fewer admissible strategies than the others, as when *P* is $(ab)cd$. Hence, it is not generally true that, in comparison with other voting systems, approval voting will overwhelm the voter with a wealth of *viable* options, even though it offers him more feasible, or theoretically possible, strategies than any other nonranked system.

2.5. Sincere Voting and Strategy-Proofness

To facilitate a general comparison of approval voting and all other simple voting systems in terms of their ability to elicit the honest or true preferences of voters, the following notions of sincere strategies and strategy-proofness are helpful.

Definition 2.5. Let P be a concerned preference order on the candidates. Then strategy S is *sincere* for P if and only if S is high for P; voting system s is *sincere* for P if and only if all admissible strategies for s and P are sincere; and voting system s is *strategy-proof* for P if and only if exactly one strategy is admissible for s and P (in which case this strategy must be sincere).

Sincere strategies are essentially strategies that directly reflect the true preferences of a voter, i.e., that do not report preferences "falsely." For example, if P is $abcd$, then $\{a,c\}$ is not sincere since a and c are not the voter's two most-preferred candidates. Because we believe that a democratic voting system should base the winner of an election on the true preferences of the voters, sincere strategies are of obvious importance to such systems.[6]

They are also important to individual voters, for if a system is sincere, voters will always vote for *all* candidates ranked above the lowest-ranked candidates included in their chosen admissible strategies. (To illustrate when this proposition is not true, if P is $abcd$, $\{a,c\}$ is admissible under approval voting but obviously not sincere since this strategy involves voting for candidate c without also voting for preferred candidate b.) Thus, if a candidate that a sincere voter approves of should win, the sincere voter can rest assured that he could not have brought about the election of a preferred candidate by choosing a different admissible strategy.

Consider, for example, a focal voter whose preference order is $abcd$, and let contingency f be $f(a) = 0, f(b) = f(c) = f(d) = 1$. Then, if the focal voter chooses his insincere admissible strategy $A = \{a,c\}$, the outcome is $F(S,f) = \{c\}$, the next-worst candidate for the focal voter. On the other hand, if the focal voter had chosen his sincere admissible strategy $\{a,b,c\}$, his next-best choice $\{b\}$ would have been the outcome. Thus, the voter has reason to regret his insincerity.

This cannot happen, however, if the voting system is sincere and voters choose admissible strategies. Although a voter may not obtain his best choice under such a system, after the election he cannot regret having failed to vote for a candidate (b in the previous example) preferred to the lowest-ranked candidate he voted for (c in the previous example).

Using Corollaries 2.1, 2.3, and 2.4, one can easily verify that, for the seven prototype preference orders for four candidates given in Table 2.2, approval voting is sincere in six cases (only $abcd$ is excluded), negative voting is sincere in four cases, and plurality voting is sincere in only the first three cases. In fact, it is no accident that approval voting is "more sincere" than both of the other systems given in Table

2.2; as the following theorem demonstrates, approval voting is the uniquely most sincere system of all the nonranked voting systems described by Definition 2.3.

Theorem 2.3. *If* P *is dichotomous, then every voting system* s *is sincere for* P. *If* P *is trichotomous, then approval voting is sincere for* P, *and this is the only system that is sincere for every trichotomous* P. *If* P *is multichotomous, then no voting system* s *is sincere for* P.

No system is sincere when P is multichotomous because, for every s and every P with four or more indifference subsets A_i, there is an admissible strategy that is not sincere. When there are relatively few candidates in a race, however, it is reasonable to expect many voters will have dichotomous or trichotomous preference orders. Indeed, Theorem 2.3 says that when voters do not (or cannot) make finer distinctions, approval voting is the most sincere of all nonranked voting systems, and this result can be extended to voters with multichotomous preferences.[7] Its pertinence to elections today is evident, especially in races in which insincere voting is rampant (examples will be given later).

Even if a voting system is sincere for P, however, it is not strategy-proof for P if it allows more than one admissible strategy. Although manipulation of election outcomes by strategic voting in multicandidate elections is an old subject, only recently has it been shown, beginning with the pioneering work of Gibbard and Satterthwaite,[8] that virtually every type of reasonable election method is vulnerable to strategic voting.

Like sincerity, strategy-proofness seems a desirable property for a voting system to possess. If voters have only one admissible strategy, they will never have an incentive to deviate from it even if they know the result of voting by all the other voters. For this is a dominant, or unconditionally best, strategy, so whatever contingency arises, a voter cannot be hurt, and may be helped, by choosing it.

Sincerity, on the other hand, does not imply such stability but instead asserts that whatever admissible strategy a voter chooses, whenever it includes voting for some candidate, it also includes voting for all candidates preferred to him. A voting system that does not force voters to "sacrifice," for strategic reasons, more-preferred for less-preferred candidates would seem to have several salutary consequences, both for individual voters and the election system.

Approval voting would, for example, probably produce higher voter turnout. By allowing voters to tune their preferences more finely, and by encouraging them more often to make sincere choices, it could well stimulate more voters to express themselves at the polls and thereby enhance the legitimacy of the outcome.

Since the demands of strategy-proofness are more stringent than those for sincere voting, the circumstances that imply strategy-proofness are less likely to obtain than the circumstances that imply sincerity. Nevertheless, as with sincerity, the approval voting system is the uniquely most strategy-proof of all systems covered by Definition 2.3.

Theorem 2.4. *If* P *is dichotomous, then approval voting is strategy-proof for* P, *and this is the only system* s *that is strategy-proof for every dichotomous* P. *If* P *is trichotomous or multichotomous, then no voting system* s *is strategy-proof for* P.

The second part of Theorem 2.4 simply says that if P has at least three indifference subsets A_i, then any system s has at least two strategies—say, one from A_1, and one from $A_1 \cup A_2$—that are admissible for s and P. Hence, s can be manipulated by a choice of one and not another admissible strategy. For example, if P is the trichotomous abc, and s is approval voting, then the only admissible strategies are the sincere strategies $\{a\}$ and $\{a,b\}$. The former is optimal for a focal voter if, say, $f(a) = f(b) = f(c)$, because its choice would ensure outcome $\{a\}$. But the latter sincere strategy, $\{a,b\}$, would be optimal if, say, $f(b) = f(c) > f(a) + 1$, because it would ensure outcome $\{b\}$, whereas strategy $\{a\}$ would not.

The first part of Theorem 2.4 depends on Corollary 2.2: if P is dichotomous, then $M(P)$ is the unique admissible strategy for approval voting—vote for all candidates in the preferred subset A_1. By contrast, if s is not the approval voting system, then there is a dichotomous P such that there are at least two admissible strategies for s and P. For example, if P is the dichotomous $(ab)c$, then $\{a\}$ and $\{b\}$ are both admissible under plurality voting, rendering it not strategy-proof because strategy $\{a\}$ is optimal in some contingencies [e.g., $f(a) = f(c) > f(b) + 1$], and strategy $\{b\}$ in other contingencies [e.g., $f(b) = f(c) > f(a) + 1$].

Theorems 2.3 and 2.4 provide very strong support for approval voting when evaluated against the important criteria of sincerity and strategy-proofness, which have been investigated in more general settings by Fishburn.[9] Taken together, these two theorems establish that approval voting is the most sincere and strategy-proof of all systems in which a voter can vote for, but not rank, candidates.

Yet, the limitations of these results should not be forgotten: strategy-proofness depends entirely on the preferences of all voters' being dichotomous; sincerity extends to trichotomous preferences, but it is a weaker criterion of nonmanipulativeness than strategy-proofness. For multichotomous preferences, the election of Condorcet (majority) candidates is at least possible using sincere strategies under approval voting but may not be under other systems—including those that allow for runoffs—as we shall show in Chapter 3.

Despite the restriction of the foregoing positive results to dichotomous and trichotomous preferences, multicandidate races in which voters make only two-way or three-way preference divisions of the candidates seem quite common. Particularly in races in which the voters do not have much information about the candidates (e.g., the early presidential primaries), voters may still be able to distinguish "best" and "worst," and sometimes "medium," candidates. In these circumstances, voters can be more honest in expressing their preferences under approval voting than under other nonranked voting systems.

2.6. Conclusions

In this chapter, the basic theoretical structure for much of the subsequent analysis has been laid. The numerous definitions and assumptions may be difficult to assimilate, even when accompanied by examples intended to highlight their significance, but this foundation is essential if terms like "dominance" and "admissibility" are to have a precise meaning and serve as building blocks to achieve more substantive results.

The substantive results of this chapter all concern honesty in voting. By "honesty," we do not mean to imply that a voting system, which is nothing more than an impersonal set of rules and procedures, deceives voters. Rather, voting systems may not succeed in eliciting honest or truthful responses because they are vulnerable to strategic manipulation. If some voters can do better by strategically voting for candidates other than those they most prefer, then, instead of accusing them of dishonesty in making rational strategy choices, it seems better to try to design systems that make dishonesty unnecessary or costly in order for voters to achieve their aim of electing desired candidates.

Among all simple nonranked voting systems, approval voting does this job better than any other single-ballot system. (Multiple-ballot systems, including runoffs, will be analyzed later.) First, it discourages insincere voting; up to trichotomous preferences, it is *never* advantageous for a voter to vote for one candidate without also voting for all those he ranks higher. Put another way, a sincere strategy does not require a voter to "lie" about his preferences, as would be true of an insincere strategy wherein he votes for a candidate whom he prefers less to some candidate for whom he does not vote.[10]

Second, approval voting is more strategy-proof than other non-ranked voting systems. In particular, if a voter divides candidates into only two classes—preferred and nonpreferred—there is *never* an incentive to vote for those not preferred. Moreover, if preferences are indeed dichotomous, a voter can completely express his preferences by voting for all his preferred candidates, which he cannot in general do under other voting systems.

In fact, approval voting offers voters the maximum number of choices possible in an election in which the ranking of candidates is not permitted. Yet, it does not present voters with too many viable options, because the number of admissible strategies it offers voters— and which they would presumably seriously consider—approximates the number that less flexible nonranked systems offer.

Approval voting, nevertheless, is not foolproof. Polls, as we shall show in Chapter 7, may give voters reason to switch from sincere to insincere strategies, and they may also confound "popular" choices. But to examine the second question more carefully, one needs a precise notion of popular choice, which will be defined in Chapter 3 and whose implications under different voting systems—including runoff systems—will be investigated.

Footnotes to Chapter 2

1. Steven J. Brams and Peter C. Fishburn, "Approval Voting," *American Political Science Review* **72**, 3 (September 1978), 831–847.

2. Steven J. Brams, *The Presidential Election Game* (New Haven: Yale University Press, 1978), pp. 199–202.

3. We assume that if a voter votes for k candidates (k in s), then each candidate he votes for receives one full vote in the aggregation process (see Section 3.3). Cases in which votes receive different weights, depending on the number of candidates a voter votes for, are analyzed in Peter C. Fishburn, "Symmetric and Consistent Aggregation with Dichotomous Voting," in *Aggregation and Revelation of Preference*, edited by Jean-Jacques Laffont (Amsterdam: North-Holland, 1979), pp. 201–208. This has been extended to ranked voting in P. C. Fishburn, "Dominant Strategies and Restricted Ballots with Variable Electorate," *Mathematical Social Sciences* **2**, 4 (June 1982), 383–395. Among all systems examined in these articles, approval voting does very well on the basis of the criteria used for comparing systems.

4. Steven J. Brams, "One Man, N Votes," Module in Applied Mathematics, Mathematical Association of America (Ithaca, NY: Cornell University, 1976); S. J. Brams, *Comparison Voting*, Innovative Instructional Unit (Washington, DC: American Political Science Association, 1978), which will appear

in slightly revised form in *Modules in Applied Mathematics: Political and Related Models*, Vol. 2, edited by Steven J. Brams, William F. Lucas, and Philip D. Straffin, Jr. (New York: Springer-Verlag, 1982); and S. J. Brams, *Presidential Election Game*, Ch. 6.

5. George A. W. Boehm, "One Fervent Vote against Wintergreen" (mimeographed, 1976); and Steven J. Brams, "When Is It Advantageous to Cast a Negative Vote?" in *Mathematical Economics and Game Theory: Essays in Honor of Oskar Morgenstern*, edited by R. Henn and O. Moeschlin, Lecture Notes in Economics and Mathematical Systems, Vol. 141 (Berlin: Springer-Verlag, 1977), pp. 564–572.

6. It can happen that more complex voting systems than those discussed here are able to induce the same outcome from "strategic voting" as would obtain if all voters voted sincerely. See Bezalel Peleg, "Consistent Voting Systems," *Econometrica* **46**, 1 (January 1978), 153–162; and Bhaskar Dutta and Prasanta K. Pattanaik, "On Nicely Consistent Voting Systems," *Econometrica* **46**, 1 (January 1978), 163–170.

7. Peter C. Fishburn, "A Strategic Analysis of Nonranked Voting Systems," *SIAM Journal on Applied Mathematics* **35**, 3 (November 1978), 488–495.

8. Allan Gibbard, "Manipulation of Voting Schemes: A General Result," *Econometrica* **41**, 3 (May 1973), 587–601; and Mark Allen Satterthwaite, "Strategy-Proofness and Arrow's Conditions: Existence and Correspondence Theorems for Voting Procedures and Social Welfare Functions," *Journal of Economic Theory* **10**, 2 (April 1975), 187–217. Recent results on manipulability relevant to approval voting are given in P. C. Fishburn, "Dominant Strategies and Restricted Ballots with Variable Electorate."

9. P. C. Fishburn, "A Strategic Analysis of Nonranked Voting Systems." Other properties that approval voting satisfies are delineated in different axiomatizations of approval voting in P. C. Fishburn, "Axioms for Approval Voting: Direct Proof," *Journal of Economic Theory* **19**, 1 (October 1978), 180–185; and P. C. Fishburn, "Symmetric and Consistent Aggregation with Dichotomous Voting."

10. Lying may also refer to the false announcement of preferences by a deceiver in a game of incomplete information that induces the deceived player(s) to change strategies that lead to better outcomes for the deceiver. This concept connotes more than "mere" insincerity and is formally analyzed in Steven J. Brams, "Deception in 2 × 2 Games," *Journal of Peace Science* **2**, 2 (Spring 1977), 171–203; Steven J. Brams and Frank C. Zagare, "Deception in Simple Voting Games," *Social Science Research* **6**, 3 (September 1977), 257–272; and S. J. Brams and F. C. Zagare, "Double Deception: Two against One in Three-Person Games," *Theory and Decision* **13**, 1 (March 1981), 81–90. For a more informal development of deception in voting games, see S. J. Brams, *Paradoxes in Politics: An Introduction to the Nonobvious in Political Science* (New York: Free Press, 1976), pp. 172–176.

Chapter 3
The Condorcet Criterion:
Which System Best Finds the
Majority Candidate?

3.1. Introduction

We showed in Chapter 2 that approval voting promotes sincere voting and discourages strategic or manipulative voting more than other nonranked voting systems. This is in part due to the fact that, unlike other nonranked systems, approval voting imposes no restrictions on the number of candidates for whom an individual can vote. Thus, voters can express their approval for all candidates they consider acceptable, without worrying about abandoning their favorite candidates when such candidates have only a slim chance of winning.

Approval voting would seem, therefore, to enhance the likelihood that a candidate who is acceptable to a large proportion of the electorate will be elected. Yet, it is certainly possible, especially in crowded races, that no candidate may be approved of by a majority of voters, let alone be a majority winner under plurality voting.

When there are three or more candidates, and only one is to be elected to a specified office, there are widespread differences of opinion as to how the winner should be determined. These differences are perhaps best epitomized by Condorcet's criticism of Borda's method,[1] which is recounted by Duncan Black, who also provides an historical treatment and analysis of other proposed voting methods.[2] Borda recommended that in an election among three candidates, the winner be the candidate with the greatest point total when awards, say, of two points, one point, and zero points are made, respectively, to each voter's most-preferred, next most-preferred, and least-preferred candidates. Condorcet argued to the contrary that the winner ought to be the candidate who is preferred by a simple majority of voters to *each* of the other candidates in pairwise contests—provided that such a majority candidate exists—and showed that Borda's method can elect a candidate other than the majority candidate.

Although many analysts accept Condorcet's criterion, it leaves open the question of which candidate should win when there is no majority candidate—that is, when the so-called paradox of voting occurs (see Section 3.2 for an example of the paradox).[3] Fishburn, Richelson, Straffin, Riker, Nurmi, and others have reviewed a number of methods for determining a winner from voters' preferences when there is no majority candidate and conclude that, although some methods are better than others—in the sense of satisfying properties considered desirable—there is no obviously best method.[4]

If there is a paradox of voting, approval voting does not eliminate it but instead finds the candidate acceptable to the most voters, which is, we think, a most sensible way to choose a winner even when there is no candidate who is invincible in a match against every other. But the focus of this chapter will not be on such paradoxical situations but instead on how well different simple voting systems satisfy the Condorcet criterion of electing the majority candidate. This criterion seems to us compelling, and we shall show that if the preferences of voters are dichotomous, approval voting is the *only* nonranked voting system that ensures the election of the Condorcet (majority) candidate, given one exists.

We shall then introduce runoff voting systems into the analysis and compare them with single-ballot systems. These systems consist of voting procedures whose first ballots are similar to the ballots of the single-ballot nonranked systems studied in Chapter 2; the second or runoff ballot is a simple majority ballot between the two candidates who receive the most first-ballot votes.

The concepts defined in Chapter 2 for single-ballot systems will be extended to runoff systems, and new results will be given for these systems. For example, it can be shown that, for most preference orders, the set of admissible voting strategies for any ordinary (single-ballot) system is a proper subset of (i.e., included in and smaller than) the set of first-ballot admissible strategies for the corresponding runoff system.

Next, we shall use the admissibility results to determine the abilities of various systems to elect a strict (single) Condorcet candidate when one exists. After investigating the existence of admissible and sincere admissible strategies that elect the Condorcet candidate, we shall then consider cases in which the Condorcet candidate is invariably elected, whatever admissible strategies voters use.

To give some flavor of what constitute proofs of the theoretical results, we shall depart from the practice of Chapter 2 and give a simple proof of one theorem in Section 3.2. It illustrates the way in which a sound deductive argument, using a minimum of mathematical symbolism, can be developed. (Other elementary proofs to propositions in

Chapter 8 will illustrate how different intuitive ideas can be demonstrated to be correct.) It will be helpful, nevertheless, to introduce some symbolism to avoid long verbal circumlocutions and state as precisely as possible assumptions, definitions, and theorems. We have, however, endeavored to avoid encumbering the main arguments with formalism that does not render them more cogent.

3.2. Dichotomous Preferences

In this section, as in the previous chapter, we shall restrict the analysis to single-ballot nonranked voting systems. This restriction will be dropped in subsequent sections. The main result shown here is that when voters' preferences are dichotomous, approval voting is the uniquely best system with respect to the Condorcet criterion. But before proving this result, some definitions, which we shall illustrate, are needed.

Let V denote a finite list of preference orders for the candidates, with each order in the list representing the preferences of a particular voter. Clearly, each allowable preference order may appear more than once in V, or not at all. The *Condorcet candidates* with respect to any given V are the candidates in the set Con(V), where

Con(V) = {all candidates a such that, for each candidate $b \neq a$, at least as many orders in V have a preferred to b as have b preferred to a}.

Thus, candidate a is in Con(V) if and only if at least as many voters prefer a to b as prefer b to a for each b other than a.

When there is a paradox of voting that includes all candidates, Con (V) will be empty, which occurs, for example, if $V = (abc,bca,cab)$. Here a majority of two voters prefers a to b, a different majority b to c, and a still different majority c to a. Thus, while a defeats b, and b defeats c, c defeats a, making the majorities cyclical. Because each candidate can be defeated by one other, there is no candidate who does at least as well against all other candidates as they do against him.

Condorcet's basic criterion asserts that candidate a wins the election when Con(V) contains only a and no other candidate. But because it is possible for more than one candidate to be in Con(V), as when the same number of voters prefer a to b as prefer b to a, it is useful to extend Condorcet's rule to assert that if Con(V) is not empty, then *some* candidate in Con(V) wins the election. In particular, if every candidate who is in the outcome from the ballot is in Con(V), provided it is not empty, the extended rule will apply.

It has been shown by Inada that if all preference orders in V are dichotomous, then Con(V) is not empty.[5] Using the results of Chapter

2, which presume Assumptions P and R (Section 2.2), we shall establish much more than this, namely that the use of admissible strategies under approval voting when preferences are dichotomous always yields Con(V) as the outcome. Moreover, we shall indicate without proof that, for any *other* nonranked voting system s, the use of admissible strategies, given dichotomous preferences for all voters, may give an outcome that contains no candidate in Con(V).

The following formulation will be used to express these results more rigorously:

Definition 3.1. For any finite list V of preference orders for the candidates, and for any voting system s as identified in Definition 2.3 (Section 2.4), let $V(s)$ be the set of all functions that assign an admissible strategy to each of the terms in V. For each function α in $V(s)$, let $F(\alpha)$ be the outcome (the set of candidates with the greatest vote total) when every voter uses the admissible strategy that is assigned to his preference order by α.

As an illustration, assume $V = (abc, abc, c(ab))$, consisting of two voters who prefer a to b to c and one voter who is indifferent between a and b but prefers c to both a and b. If s is plurality voting, then $V(s)$ contains $(2)(2) = 4$ functions since each of the first two voters has two admissible strategies and the third voter has one admissible strategy according to Corollary 2.3 (Section 2.4). The outcomes for the four α functions are $\{a\}$, $\{a,b,c\}$, $\{a,b,c\}$, and $\{b\}$. $F(\alpha) = \{a,b,c\}$, for example, if α assigns strategy $\{a\}$ to the first voter and strategy $\{b\}$ to the second voter; the third voter would necessarily choose strategy $\{c\}$ because it is his only admissible strategy.

Theorem 3.1. *Suppose all preference orders in* V *are dichotomous and* s *is the approval voting system. Then* F(α) = Con(V) *for every* α *belonging to* V(s).

In other words, if all voters have dichotomous preferences, their use of admissible strategies under approval voting invariably yields Con(V) as the outcome.

Proof. Corollary 2.2 (Section 2.4) implies that $V(s)$ consists of the unique function α that assigns the subset of most-preferred candidates to each preference order in V. [For example, if an order were $(ab)c$, α would assign the subset $\{a,b\}$ to this order.] The outcome of this function, $F(\alpha)$, must be Con(V) since as many orders in V have a preferred to b as b preferred to a if and only if a receives as many votes as b. This completes the proof.

More informally, the reasoning underlying the last statement in the proof is that if a gets more votes than b, then more voters prefer a to b than prefer b to a, and conversely. Consequently, all candidates not in Con(V) will lose and not be in $F(\alpha)$. Those in $F(\alpha)$ will all tie one another in votes, and likewise be tied in preference counts by pairwise comparisons [i.e., each member of a candidate pair in $F(\alpha)$ will be preferred to the other by the same number of voters].

To show how the dichotomous-preference situation differs under plurality voting, suppose that the candidate set is $\{a,b,c\}$ and there are $2n + 1$ voters in V: One is $a(bc)$, with the other $2n$ orders divided evenly between $b(ac)$ and $(ac)b$. Then Con(V) = $\{a\}$. However, if as few as two of the n voters who have the order $(ac)b$ vote for c rather than a under plurality voting, then $F(\alpha) = \{b\}$, and $F(\alpha)$ and Con(V) are therefore disjoint. The following theorem shows that a similar result holds for every system other than approval voting.

Theorem 3.2. *Suppose* s *is a voting system as described in Definition 2.3 (Section 2.4) but not approval voting. Then there exists a* V *consisting entirely of dichotomous preference orders and an* α *belonging to* V(s) *such that no candidate in* F(α) *is in* Con(V).

Hence, among all nonranked voting systems, there is a uniquely best system by Condorcet's criterion when preferences are dichotomous. Since approval voting is both strategy-proof and selects Con(V) when voters use admissible strategies and have dichotomous preferences, it is the best possible voting system in two important respects when preferences are dichotomous.

In contrast to the definitive picture obtained for dichotomous preferences, comparisons among approval voting and other single-ballot systems are less clear-cut when some voters divide the candidates into more than two indifference subsets. The main work to date on the propensities of different voting systems to elect a Condorcet candidate when Con(V) is not empty has been reported by Fishburn, Fishburn and Gehrlein, and Gillett.[6]

The conclusions in these studies are based primarily on computer simulations to estimate the probabilities that various voting systems will elect the Condorcet candidate when there is a unique such candidate. Without going into details, the general conclusion that emerges from these studies when all voters have strict preference orders (no indifference) and vote sincerely is that approval voting's propensity to elect Condorcet candidates is comparable to if not better than the propensities of other nonranked systems. Additional support for approval voting is provided by Weber, who develops a measure of the "effectiveness" of voting systems in electing the "socially optimal" candidate in a "random society" based on a probabilistic model, and by Bordley and by Merrill using computer-simulation models.[7]

3.3. Runoff Systems

All the theoretical results discussed so far in this and the previous chapter pertain only to nonranked voting systems in which the election outcome is decided by a single ballot. But there are more complicated nonranked voting systems, the most prominent being runoff systems, and in the remainder of this chapter we shall compare these with what will be called ordinary (single-ballot) systems. In making this comparison, we shall begin by reviewing some aspects of ordinary systems discussed in Chapter 2 to clarify relations between the two types of systems.

A specific system of either type is identified by a nonempty subset s of $\{1,2, \ldots, m - 1\}$ (Definition 2.3 in Section 2.4), where $m \geq 3$ is the number of candidates. Since there are $2^{m-1} - 1$ such subsets, there are $2^{m-1} - 1$ different systems of each type.

This definition of a voting system precludes those systems in which voters can vote for all m candidates—an inadmissible strategy for the concerned voter (see Section 2.4)—as well as those in which they can vote for no candidates or abstain. Thus, if $m = 3$, the three possible systems allow one to vote for exactly one candidate, vote for exactly two, or vote for either one or two; abstention is also feasible.

Each *ordinary system* is a single-ballot system. Each voter either abstains or votes for exactly k candidates for some k belonging to s. Voters do not rank their chosen candidates, and a candidate receives a full vote from each person who votes for that candidate. The candidate with the most votes is elected. Thus, $s = \{1\}$ is the usual plurality system, and $s = \{1,2, \ldots, m - 1\}$ is the approval voting system.

Each *runoff system* s is a two-ballot system. On the first ballot each voter either abstains or votes for exactly k candidates for some k belonging to s. The two candidates with the most first-ballot votes go onto the second, or runoff, ballot.[8] The runoff ballot is a simple-majority ballot; the candidate who receives the greater number of votes on this ballot is elected.

What about ties? For ordinary systems we assume that all candidates who tie with the largest vote total have some chance of winning, and that all others have no chance of being elected. But no procedure for breaking ties is assumed. Given the possibility of ties, an *ordinary outcome* is the *set* of candidates who have the greatest vote total in an ordinary election.

Ties can occur in runoff systems at two points. First, a tie can affect who goes onto the runoff ballot. If more than two candidates have the largest first-ballot total, then we assume that each of these candidates, and no others, has a chance of being in the runoff, which always involves exactly two candidates. On the other hand, if exactly one candidate has the largest first-ballot total, and two or more candidates have the next-largest first-ballot total, then we assume that the former candidate is assured of being in the runoff whereas each of the latter tied candidates (but no others) has a chance of being in the runoff.

The second point at which a tie can occur is on the runoff ballot. When this occurs, we assume that each candidate *not* in the runoff has no chance of being elected. As with ordinary systems, specific tie-breaking procedures will not be prescribed for runoff systems.

For later purposes, define a *runoff outcome* as a triple $(A,B,>)$ where:

A   is the set of candidates who must be on the runoff ballot on the basis of the first-ballot vote;
B   is the set of candidates who have some chance, but are not assured, of being in the runoff on the basis of the first-ballot vote;
>   specifies what would happen in the runoff for every pair of distinct candidates from $A \cup B$ who might be on that ballot; $x > y$ means that x would beat y.

Let $|A|$ denote the number of candidates in A, and $\emptyset$ be the empty set, so that $|A| = 0$ if and only if $A = \emptyset$. Preceding assumptions require that $|A|$ belong to $\{0,1,2\}$, with $B = \emptyset$ if $|A| = 2$ and with $|A| + |B| \geq 3$ if $|A| < 2$. Within a runoff outcome, (A,B) may take the following forms: $(A,B) = (\{x,y\}, \emptyset)$ says that x and y have more first-ballot votes than all other candidates; $(A,B) = (\{x\}, \{y,z\})$ says that x has the most first-ballot votes, followed by y and z, who are tied; and $(A,B) = (\emptyset, \{x,y,z\})$ says that x, y, and z have the same largest first-ballot total.

Several important differences between ordinary and runoff systems are worth mentioning here. First, runoff systems are more costly than ordinary systems since they require two elections.[9] Second, runoff systems provide voters with more opportunities for strategic manipulation. In particular, runoff systems may encourage some voters to vote for candidates on the first ballot only because they could be beaten by the voter's favorite (whom he may think does not need his help to get on the second ballot) in a runoff. Since the degree of manipulability in this sense is most likely to be positively correlated with the number of candidates a person can vote for on the first ballot, the plurality *runoff* system would appear to be the least manipulable, the approval *runoff* system the most manipulable.

We shall only briefly analyze the comparative sincerity and strategy-proofness of different runoff systems. One reason for giving less attention to these concepts here than we gave to them in Chapter 2 is that the strategic calculations for runoff systems are a good deal more complex than for ordinary systems. More important, though, is the fact that runoff systems, because they are so manipulable, simply do not hold out much promise for encouraging honest or sincere voting.

Coupling approval voting to a runoff system, for example, produces a combination that is *never* strategy-proof. We shall not only demonstrate the deep flaw in runoff *approval* voting but also illustrate, in the context of an actual election described in Chapter 4, that when the notion of runoff is extended to elimination contests that may require more than two ballots, additional problems arise.

It is (two-ballot) runoff systems, however, that are by far the most common multiballot election systems in use today and what we shall focus on in this chapter. They are used extensively in state and local elections, particularly in party primaries; their main rationale is to provide a device to ensure the election of the strongest candidate should he not triumph in the first plurality contest. As we shall show later in this chapter, however, if "strongest" is defined to be the Condorcet candidate (if one exists), this claim on behalf of the runoff is dubious, particularly when compared with ordinary approval voting.

3.4. Dominance, Admissibility, Sincerity, and Strategy-Proofness of Runoff Systems

We assume that the definitions and assumptions introduced in Sections 2.2 through 2.4 for ordinary systems obtain. In this section, we shall introduce their counterparts for runoff systems. These will serve as a prelude to theorems of dominance and admissibility for runoff systems.

For runoff outcome $\gamma = (A,B,>)$, defined in Section 3.3, let Γ denote the set of all pairs of candidates that might constitute the runoff ballot, and let $\Gamma(>)$ be the set of all candidates who have some chance of winning the election when γ obtains. For example, if $\gamma = (\{x\},\{y,z\},\{x > y,z > x\})$, $\{x\}$ must be on the runoff ballot, one of $\{y,z\}$ will be the other candidate on this ballot, and though $\{x\}$ will beat $\{y\}$, $\{z\}$ will beat $\{x\}$. Hence, $\Gamma = \{\{x,y\},\{x,z\}\}$ and $\Gamma(>) = \{x,z\}$—that is, two runoff pairs are possible, but only $\{x,z\}$ could win the election because if $\{y\}$ should make the runoff, he would be defeated by $\{x\}$.

For preferences between runoff outcomes, let Γ_i correspond to γ_i, and let $\Gamma_i \backslash \Gamma_j$ denote the set of all pairs in Γ_i that are not in Γ_j. The following will be presumed to hold for runoff elections for all runoff outcomes $\gamma_1 = (A_1,B_1,>)$ and $\gamma_2 = (A_2,B_2,>)$:

Assumption P'. If $\Gamma_1(>) = \{x\}$ and $\Gamma_2(>) = \{x,y\}$, then $\gamma_1 P \gamma_2$ if xPy, and $\gamma_2 P \gamma_1$ if yPx;

Assumption R'. $\gamma_1 R \gamma_2$ if either $\cup \{\{x,y\}:\{x,y\}$ belongs to $\Gamma_1\} \subseteq M(P)$ or $\cup \{\{x,y\}:\{x,y\}$ belongs to $\Gamma_2\} \subseteq L(P)$ or $[\cup \{\{x,y\}:\{x,y\}$ belongs to $\Gamma_1\backslash\Gamma_2\} \subseteq M(P)$ and $\cup \{\{x,y\}:\{x,y\}$ belongs to $\Gamma_2\backslash\Gamma_1\} \subseteq L(P)]$.[10]

These assumptions are analogous to Assumptions P and R in Section 2.2.

Assumption P' is straightforward and is similar to Assumption P. Although $>$ does not appear explicitly in Assumption R', the same $>$ is presumed to apply to both γ_1 and γ_2 so that if $\{x,y\}$ belongs to $L_1 \cap L_2$ (i.e., intersection of L_1 and L_2, or set of candidates included in both L_1 and L_2) and $x > y$, then x will win in either case if x and y are on the runoff ballot. The first alternative in Assumption R' implies that $\Gamma_1(>) \subseteq M(P)$ regardless of $>$; the second alternative implies that $\Gamma_2(>) \subseteq L(P)$ regardless of $>$; and the third alternative guarantees the election of a most-preferred candidate if the runoff pair is in Γ_1 but not Γ_2, or the election of a least-preferred candidate if the runoff pair is in Γ_2 but not Γ_1. Hence, R' seems quite reasonable from the viewpoint of an individual's preferences.

Given Assumptions P' and R', dominance can now be defined for runoff systems, which in turn can be used to characterize admissible strategies under such systems. As under ordinary systems, we assume that voters either abstain or use admissible strategies on the first ballot in a runoff election. On the second or runoff ballot, we assume voters vote for their preferred candidate on that ballot. Hence, a voter's only strategic choice in a runoff election is what to do on the first ballot since he will always vote sincerely on the runoff if he is not indifferent between the two candidates.

To explicate the notions of dominance for runoff systems, consider a focal voter with preference order P, allow any finite number of other voters, and consider all ways that the others might vote. Assume that the focal voter votes on the runoff if he votes on the first ballot and is not indifferent between the runoff candidates.

Others' votes on the first ballot, as well as what might happen on a runoff ballot, are accounted for by contingencies. An *ordinary contingency* (see Section 2.3) lists the number of votes for each candidate by all voters, other than the focal voter, in an ordinary election. A *runoff contingency* specifies the vote totals for all other voters on the first ballot *and* specifies by $>$ what would happen on every runoff ballot that might arise from the first ballot. Ordinary outcomes and runoff outcomes as defined in Section 3.3 are unambiguously specified by a corresponding contingency and the strategy used by the focal voter on the only (or first) ballot. For example, a runoff contingency plus a strategy S for the focal voter uniquely determines a runoff outcome $(A,B,>)$.

Recall (Definition 2.2 in Section 2.3) that strategy S dominates strategy T in an ordinary election with respect to the focal voter with preference order P, or S *dom* T for P, if and only if the focal voter likes the ordinary outcome when he uses S as much as (R) the ordinary outcome when he uses T, for every possible ordinary contingency, and strictly prefers (P) the ordinary S-outcome to the ordinary T-outcome for at least one ordinary contingency. By comparison, for a runoff election, let S *dom'* T for P if and only if the focal voter with preference order P likes the runoff outcome when he uses S as much as (R) the runoff outcome when he uses T, for every possible runoff contingency, and strictly prefers (P) the runoff S-outcome to the runoff T-outcome for at least one runoff contingency.

In Section 2.3 we showed that dominance for ordinary systems (Theorem 2.1) depends on whether the candidates in S but not T ($S \backslash T$) dominated those in T but not S ($T \backslash S$). Runoff dominance can be similarly characterized but requires, in addition, that P be dichotomous as well as some other conditions.

Theorem 3.1 (Runoff dominance). *Suppose* P *is concerned and Assumptions* P' *and* R' *hold. Then, for all strategies* S *and* T, S *dom'* T *for* P *if and only if* P *is dichotomous,* S $\neq$ T, S\T *is either* $\emptyset$ *or* M(P), *and* T\S *is either* $\emptyset$ *or* L(P).

Proofs of Theorem 3.1 and other theorems in this chapter are given elsewhere.[11]

Clearly, runoff dominance demands much more of S, T, and P than does ordinary dominance, with S dom T for P whenever S dom' T for P. In general, more strategies will be admissible for runoff system s and preference order P than for ordinary system s and preference order P.

We showed in Section 2.4 (Theorem 2.2) that admissibility for ordinary systems requires that either one or both of two conditions, C1 and C2, be satisfied. Similarly, admissibility for runoff systems requires that either one or both of two new conditions, C1' and C2', are satisfied.

Theorem 3.2 (Runoff admissibility). *Suppose* P *is concerned and Assumptions* P' *and* R' *hold. Then strategy* S *is admissible for runoff system* s *and preference order* P *if and only if* S *is feasible for* s *and either C1' or C2' (or both) holds:*

C1': P is not dichotomous;
C2': P is dichotomous, and it is false that:

    i. every candidate in L(P) *is in* S, *and* S\L(P) *is feasible for* s; *and*

    ii. every candidate in S *is in* L(P), *and* M(P) $\cup$ S *is feasible for* s.

Now Theorem 2.2 in Section 2.4 implies that the abstention strategy $\emptyset$ under *ordinary* systems, though feasible, is never admissible for a concerned voter—it is always better to vote for one or more candidates. By contrast, under *runoff* systems, every feasible strategy, including $\emptyset$ and voting for least-preferred candidates, is admissible if P is concerned and not dichotomous. This is so because there in general will exist a contingency in which it is optimal for a focal voter to vote, say, for one or more candidates in $L(P)$—his subset of least-preferred candidates—because these candidate(s) will not fare well in this contingency against a more-preferred candidate in the runoff.

But what if P is dichotomous? Corollary 2.3 (Section 2.4) says that, under *ordinary* plurality voting, every strategy is admissible except $S = \emptyset$ and voting for any candidate(s) in $L(P)$. Under *runoff* plurality voting, according to Theorem 3.2, there are still restrictions: if $| M(P) | = 1$, then when $S = \emptyset$, (ii) in Theorem 3.2 is true so $\emptyset$ is not admissible—it is better to vote for the unique most-preferred candidate than to abstain; if $| L(P) | = 1$, then when $S = L(P)$, (i) in Theorem 3.2 is true so $L(P)$ is not admissible—it is better to abstain, or vote for candidates in $M(P)$, than to vote for the unique least-preferred candidate. However, while there are situations like the above in which abstention and voting for candidate(s) in $L(P)$ are dominated, and hence inadmissible strategies under runoff plurality voting, in general a runoff provision makes these apparently "inferior" strategies admissible when P is dichotomous.

When P is dichotomous, Corollary 2.2 (Section 2.4) says that, under *ordinary* approval voting, a voter's unique admissible strategy is to vote for all candidates in $M(P)$. Under *runoff* approval voting, according to Theorem 3.2, a voter has more leeway: S is admissible if and only if at least one candidate in $M(P)$ is in S [this renders the first part of (ii) always false], and at least one candidate in $L(P)$ is not in S [this renders the first part of (i) always false]. Since the last parts of (i) and (ii) are always true under approval voting, this admissibility condition in the runoff case is both necessary and sufficient. Among other things, it implies that $\emptyset$ is never admissible under runoff approval voting when P is dichotomous because it does not include at least one candidate in $M(P)$.

Although we have tried to highlight the implications of Theorem 3.2 for runoff systems under plurality and approval voting, and contrast them with the results of Chapter 2 for ordinary systems, we realize that it is not easy quickly to grasp the full significance of admissibility differences under the two types of systems. Perhaps the most salient finding is that runoff systems give the voter freer rein in choosing strategically viable strategies, including the strategy of not voting. Although abstention is never a viable option under ordinary systems for concerned voters, it sometimes is under runoff systems, which suggests why voters may be less disposed to vote in elections in which there is a runoff.

In runoff systems, historically, it is almost always true that fewer voters go to the polls to vote in the second election than the first.[12] But Theorem 3.2, when compared with Theorem 2.2 and its corollaries, indicates why even the first election may not entice voters: abstention, at least in a plurality runoff system—by far the most common kind of runoff system—is in general an admissible strategy (exception: abstention is not admissible when a voter ranks just one candidate best).

The concept of sincerity does not require much elaboration for runoff systems. As with ordinary systems (Definition 2.5 in Section 2.5), strategy S is *sincere* for P if and only if S is high for P (Definition 2.1 in Section 2.2).

In Section 2.5, we showed that ordinary approval voting is the only ordinary system that is sincere for every trichotomous P. Theorems 3.1 and 3.2 demonstrate that a runoff system is sincere for concerned P only if P is dichotomous. This follows from the fact that a voter always has an incentive to vote for *any* candidate(s) if his preferences are trichotomous or multichotomous (C1' of Theorem 3.2); only if P is dichotomous *may* there be an incentive to vote only for candidates in $M(P)$ (C2' of Theorem 3.2) because of dominance considerations (Theorem 3.1).

More specifically, given that P is dichotomous, runoff *plurality* voting is sincere for P if and only if $| L(P) | = 1$; in this case, S is admissible if the candidate in $L(P)$ is not in S by C2' of Theorem 3.2— by voting for him, one can only help to put him in the runoff—and obviously sincere since P is dichotomous. Runoff *approval* voting is sincere for P if and only if either $| M(P) | = 1$ or $| L(P) | = 1$; the former condition is allowed by the fact that S is admissible as long as it includes the candidate in $M(P)$—if it did not, one might prevent his making the runoff—and sincere since $| M(P) | = 1$, and the latter condition for reasons just given for runoff plurality voting. Thus, when there are exactly three candidates, runoff approval voting is sincere for every dichotomous P since either $| M(P) | = 1$ or $| L(P) | = 1$.

Like the results on admissibility, the results on sincerity vary under different runoff systems and can become quite difficult to sort out and keep straight. The general conclusion that emerges is that *runoff systems are less sincere than ordinary systems,* with runoff plurality less sincere than runoff approval because it requires a more restrictive condition when preferences are dichotomous. Thus, under both ordinary and runoff systems, approval voting is more sincere than plurality voting.

Neither runoff system is strategy-proof, however, even when preferences are dichotomous, except when $| M(P) | = 1$ and $| L(P) | = 1$. But then the contest has only two candidates, violating the assumption in Section 3.3 that $m \geq 3$, and the first election is exactly the same as the second election.

The reason why strategy-proofness breaks down under runoff approval voting in the dichotomous case is worth considering, especially in light of the supposition offered in Section 3.3 that the manipulability of runoff systems is directly related to the number of candidates a voter can vote for on the first ballot. If $|M(P)| > 1$ and $|L(P)| = 1$, voting for all candidates in $M(P)$ under runoff approval voting is not a unique admissible, or dominant, strategy (as under ordinary approval voting) because one may send to the runoff a candidate weaker against the $L(P)$ candidate than had one voted, say, just the one candidate in $M(P)$ who could defeat the $L(P)$ candidate in the runoff. Similarly, if $|L(P)| > 1$ and $|M(P)| = 1$, though one would always vote for the $M(P)$ candidate, voting also for one or more of the $L(P)$ candidates is an admissible strategy, too, since these additional approval vote(s) may be crucial in putting one candidate in the runoff whom the $M(P)$ candidate can defeat.

Thus, runoff approval voting, as noted earlier, is subject to severe manipulation effects. It is even more manipulable when the preferences of voters are not dichotomous. For example, if a plurality of voters has preference order abc and is fairly sure that a would beat c but lose to b in a runoff, these voters may well vote for a and c on the first ballot in an attempt to engineer a runoff between a and c. In Chapter 4 we shall discuss a concrete example of this type of thinking involving the election of the Majority Leader of the United States House of Representatives in 1976.

3.5. Condorcet Possibility Theorems

In this section and the next we shall consider whether a candidate x either can, or must, be elected under different voting systems. In both sections we assume that all voters use admissible strategies on the only ballot in ordinary systems, or on the first ballot in runoff systems.

In this section, we shall investigate the existence of admissible, and sincere admissible, strategies that *can* elect a Condorcet candidate. Cases in which the Condorcet candidate *must* be elected are examined mainly in Section 3.6.

Two simple examples with candidate set $X = \{x,a,b\}$, and Condorcet candidate x, illustrate the results given below. Suppose first that there are seven voters such that:

2 voters have preference order xab;
2 voters have preference order xba;
3 voters have preference order $(ab)x$.

Candidate x is the Condorcet candidate since he is preferred to both a and b by four voters (the first two sets) to three (the last set).

Both plurality and approval voting, with or without a runoff, can elect x when all voters use sincere admissible strategies by voting for their single most-preferred, or one or two most-preferred (last set), candidates. To be sure, if the first set of voters vote for $\{x,a\}$, the second set for $\{x,b\}$, and the third set for $\{a,b\}$, x will not win under either ordinary or runoff approval voting. But the voters have other sincere admissible strategies that can elect candidate x.

But now consider what happens when $s = \{2\}$, in which case each voter must vote for exactly two candidates on the only (or first) ballot if he does not abstain. For either the ordinary or runoff system $\{2\}$, the only admissible strategy for the third set of voters is $\{a,b\}$. This is easily verified from Theorem 2.2 (Section 2.4) for ordinary systems and Theorem 3.2 (Section 3.4) for runoff systems. It follows that ordinary system $\{2\}$ *must* elect either a or b when all voters use admissible strategies since x will get exactly four votes whereas a and b will get five votes each.

In addition, if voters use sincere admissible strategies in runoff system $\{2\}$, then x will not go onto the runoff ballot for, regardless of which (if any) of the first four voters abstain(s) rather than vote(s) for his first two choices on the first ballot, both a and b will get more votes than x. [Because $\{a,b\}$ is the unique admissible strategy of $(ab)x$ voters, they will never abstain.]

On the other hand, insincere admissible voting on the first ballot can get x elected with runoff system $\{2\}$. For example, if the first four voters vote for x and b on the first ballot—with the first two voting insincerely in this case—then x and b will be in the runoff, wherein x will beat b by a simple majority. Thus, system $\{2\}$ can elect the Condorcet candidate x only if some voters vote insincerely—and then only when there is a runoff—whereas sincere admissible strategies suffice under approval and plurality voting systems, with or without a runoff.

The second example with five voters illustrates another situation in which it may be necessary to vote insincerely to elect the Condorcet candidate x:

1 voter has preference order xab;
2 voters have preference order axb;
2 voters have preference order bxa.

In this case, ordinary approval voting but not ordinary plurality voting can elect x when all voters use *sincere* admissible strategies, although x can be elected by ordinary plurality voting when some voters use insincere admissible strategies. For example, if the first two sets of voters vote sincerely for x and a, respectively, at least one of the third set of voters must vote insincerely for x to ensure his election. Furthermore, if no voter abstains on the first ballot under the plurality runoff system, then some voter must vote insincerely to ensure that x gets on the runoff ballot. Now even ordinary plurality voting fails to elect the Condorcet candidate x if voters vote sincerely, whereas ordinary approval voting succeeds.

To generalize these observations, let V be a finite list of preference orders over the candidates, as in Section 3.2. We assume that V assigns a preference order P to every voter. Among all possible voter preference profiles V, let $V(x)$ denote the set of V in which candidate x is a strict Condorcet candidate in the sense that more voters have xPy than yPx for each y, other than x, in candidate set X.

We shall next state two theorems, one for ordinary systems and one for runoff systems, and offer interpretations of each. Although these theorems do not cover all conceivable cases, they bring out the main Condorcet features of each type of system.

Theorem 3.3 (Ordinary systems). *The following hold for ordinary systems* s *in which* m $\geq$ *3:*

1. Nonadmissibility. *There is a* V *belonging to* V(x) *and an* s *such that no combination of admissible strategies for the voters in* V *will elect* x;
2. Admissibility. *If 1 belongs to* s, *then, for every* V *belonging to* V(x), *there are admissible strategies for* V *that will elect* x;
3. Sincerity. *If* s *is the approval voting system, then for every* V *belonging to* V(x), *there are sincere admissible strategies for* V *that will elect* x;
4. Nonsincerity. *If* s *is any system other than the approval voting system, then there is a* V *belonging to* V(x) *such that no combination of sincere admissible strategies will elect* x.

Taken together, parts 3 and 4 of Theorem 3.3 say that approval voting is the only ordinary system that is invariably able to elect a strict Condorcet candidate x when voters use sincere admissible strategies. This does *not* say that approval voting *must* elect x for some V belonging to $V(x)$ when voters use sincere admissible strategies—only that it is possible to assign sincere admissible strategies to the voters such that x will be elected. (However, as shown in Section 3.2, if every P is dichotomous, then x must indeed be elected when all voters use admissible strategies under approval voting.)

Part 2 of Theorem 3.3 says that some systems besides approval voting have the capability of electing x whenever V belongs to $V(x)$ and voters use (not necessarily sincere) admissible strategies, whereas part

1 says that there are other ordinary systems that cannot make this claim. The first example of this section shows a case in which $s = \{2\}$ can never elect x when $m = 3$, V is as specifiied in the example, and voters use admissible strategies. On the other hand, as long as s allows one to vote for just one candidate, as under plurality or approval voting, there are admissible strategies—sometimes sincere—that can elect s.

Theorem 3.4 (Runoff systems). *The following hold for runoff systems when each voter in V votes on the runoff ballot if and only if he is not indifferent between the candidates on that ballot:*

1. Admissibility. *For every s and every V belonging to V(x), there are admissible strategies for V that give x at least as many first-ballot votes as every other candidate;*
2. Admissible election. *If s ∩ {1, 2} ≠ ∅, then for every V belonging to V(x), there are admissible strategies for V that will elect x;*
3. Sincerity. *If s contains every strategy in {1,2, . . . , m − 2}, then for every V belonging to V(x), there are sincere admissible strategies for V that will elect x;*
4. Nonsincerity. *If s = {k} for some k belonging to {1,2, . . . , m − 1}, then there is a V belonging to V(x) such that no combination of sincere admissible strategies will elect x, except when k = 1 (plurality voting) and m = 3. In the latter case, there is a V belonging to V(x) such that no combination of nonempty sincere admissible strategies will elect x.*

Parts 2, 3, and 4 of Theorem 3.4, in conjunction with part 3 of Theorem 3.3, imply the following for runoff systems {1}, {2}, and {1,2} when $m = 3$:

{1,2} (approval voting) can always elect Condorcet candidate x through nonempty sincere admissible strategies for V belonging to $V(x)$ (the proof of part 3 of Theorem 3.3 shows that nonempty sincere admissible strategies can be constructed that will elect x on the first ballot; as the Condorcet candidate, he will necessarily win the runoff);

{1} (plurality voting) can always elect x through sincere admissible strategies for V belonging to $V(x)$, but it may be unable to elect x using nonempty sincere admissible strategies (parts 3 and 4 of Theorem 3.4);

{2} (vote for exactly two) can always elect x through admissible strategies for V belonging to $V(x)$, but some of these strategies may have to be insincere (parts 2 and 4 of Theorem 3.4).

Although part 1 of Theorem 3.4 says that Condorcet candidate x can always get as many first-ballot votes as every other candidate when V belongs to $V(x)$ and runoff system s is used, it does not say that admissible strategies can always ensure the election of x. For example, if V has exactly one voter with preference order $xabc$ for four candidates, and if there is no other voter and $s = \{3\}$, then either the voter abstains or he votes for three of the four candidates. In either case, more than two candidates are tied after the first ballot and, according to an assumption made in Section 3.3, each of these has a chance of being in the runoff. Hence, x might not make the runoff ballot.

All four parts of Theorem 3.4, in comparison with their counterparts in Theorem 3.3, reflect the greater diversity of admissible strategies for runoff system s than for ordinary system s. For example, the "1 belongs to s" condition of part 2 of Theorem 3.3 is replaced in part 2 of Theorem 3.4 by "1 belongs to s or 2 belongs to s." And part 3 of Theorem 3.4 says that runoff system $\{1, 2, \ldots, m - 2\}$ can always elect the strict Condorcet candidate x, whereas parts 3 and 4 of Theorem 3.3 say that only approval voting can assuredly elect x with the use of sincere admissible strategies.

Because the plurality runoff system is so widely used, it is appropriate to note from part 4 of Theorem 3.4 that, when $m \geq 4$, there may fail to exist sincere admissible plurality voting strategies for V belonging to $V(x)$ that will elect x. On the other hand, part 3 of Theorem 3.3 says that ordinary approval voting always has nonempty sincere admissible strategies for V belonging to $V(x)$ that will elect x.

It is also worth pointing out that if the general condition of Theorem 3.4, which says that a voter votes on the runoff ballot if and only if he is not indifferent between the candidates on that ballot, is not assumed to hold, then the conclusions of the theorem remain true when "elect x" is replaced by "give x some chance of being in the runoff" in part 4. Indeed, the proof of Theorem 3.4 (not given here) only considers whether x can, must, or cannot be in the runoff. Effects of abstentions on the chances of the Condorcet candidate on a runoff ballot being elected are examined by Fishburn and Gehrlein.[13]

As a counterpoint to the Condorcet results of Theorems 3.3 and 3.4, one might consider the propensities of voting systems to elect, or prevent the election of, "inferior" candidates. Because runoff systems permit a great diversity of admissible strategies, the runoff choices may be candidates who almost surely would not have been elected by an ordinary system like approval voting. On the other hand, runoff systems guard against the election of a "worst" candidate since such a candidate would be beaten in the runoff should he make the runoff ballot.

3.6. Condorcet Election Guarantees

So far we have shown that under both ordinary and runoff systems, sincere admissible strategies can elect Condorcet candidate x under approval voting, whereas sincerity and sometimes admissibility may have to be sacrificed if approval voting is not used. But this is not to say that all sincere admissible strategies will guarantee x's election, even under approval voting. Occasionally, however, it is possible to make this guarantee, as the following example for three candidates $\{x,a,b\}$ illustrates:

1 voter has preference order xab;
1 voter has preference order $(ax)b$;
1 voter has preference order $(bx)a$.

Candidate x is the Condorcet candidate because he is preferred by two voters to a and two voters to b. Under ordinary approval voting, the only admissible strategies of the second two voters is to vote for their two preferred candidates. The first voter has two sincere admissible strategies: vote for his most-preferred, or two most-preferred, candidate(s). Whichever strategy the first voter uses, x wins the election. Hence, ordinary approval voting *must* elect x when voters use sincere admissible strategies.

Now consider ordinry plurality voting, and runoff plurality and runoff approval voting as well. Under these three other systems, the following strategies of each voter are both admissible and sincere: the first voter votes for x, the second voter for a, and the third voter for b. These strategies do not guarantee the election of x under plurality voting, nor do they guarantee the election of x under either runoff system since the runoff pair could be $\{a,b\}$. Therefore, ordinary approval voting is the only one of the four systems to guarantee the election of Condorcet candidate x when voters use sincere admissible strategies.

A second example demonstrates the proposition that when all voters use admissible (though not necessarily sincere) strategies, a Condorcet candidate's election may again be ensured only under ordinary approval voting:

2 voters have preference order $(xa)b$;
1 voter has preference order xba;
1 voter has preference order bxa.

Once again, x is the Condorcet candidate, and ordinary approval voting ensures his election no matter what admissible strategies voters choose. (In this example, as in the previous one with only three candidates, all admissible strategies are necessarily sincere under ordinary approval voting since no voter's preference order can be multichotomous.) On the other hand, if the second two voters voted for *b* under ordinary plurality voting (one would have to vote insincerely), *x* would not be ensured election.

Should this occur, and should the first two voters also vote for *a*, neither runoff system would elect *x* either. Thus, not only may approval voting be the only system to guarantee the election of a Condorcet candidate when voters are restricted to sincere admissible strategies, but it also may be the only system to provide this guarantee when voters are less constrained and can use any admissible strategies.

In generalizing these results, we shall assume that voters use admissible, but not necessarily sincere admissible, strategies. Moreover, to simplify matters, only the four systems previously discussed will be analyzed, namely ordinary and runoff plurality voting and ordinary and runoff approval voting.

In the preceding examples, *x* was a *strict* Condorcet candidate—he did not share his status with any other candidate. This is not a coincidence since, as shown by the following theorem, *x* must be a strict Condorcet candidate if some system—ordinary or runoff—guarantees his election when voters use admissible strategies.

Theorem 3.5. *Suppose that regardless of which system is used, all voters use admissible strategies on the only (or first) ballot and, in the case of a runoff system, each voter votes on the runoff ballot if and only if he is not indifferent between the candidates on that ballot. Then the four systems can be ordered in terms of the strength of their guarantees as follows:*

1. No guarantee. *There is no* V *for which* x *must be elected under runoff plurality voting;*
2. m = 3 guarantee. *There are* V *for which* x *must be elected under runoff approval voting if and only if* m = 3; *for any such* V, x *must also be elected under ordinary plurality voting;*
3. m ≥ 3 guarantee. *For every* m ≥ 3, *there are* V *for which* x *must be elected under plurality voting; for any such* V, x *must also be elected under ordinary approval voting;*
4. Strict Condorcet guarantee. *If* x *must be elected under ordinary approval voting, then* x *is a strict Condorcet candidate, i.e.,* V *belongs to* V(x).

Theorem 3.5 yields the following chain of implications for any $m \geq 3$, where $\Rightarrow$ is the logical relation "implies."

[*x* must be elected under runoff plurality voting]
$\Rightarrow$ [*x* must be elected under runoff approval voting]

$\Rightarrow$ [x must be elected under ordinary plurality voting]
$\Rightarrow$ [x must be elected under ordinary approval voting]
$\Rightarrow$ [x must be a strict Condorcet candidate].

Since examples can be constructed to show that the converse implications are false for some m, the ability of a system to guarantee the election of a strict Condorcet candidate under the conditions of Theorem 3.5 is highest for ordinary approval voting, next highest for ordinary plurality voting, third highest for runoff approval voting, and lowest—in fact, nonexistent—for runoff plurality voting.

3.7. Conclusions

Perhaps the best way to draw the findings of this chapter together is to summarize what each of the four nonranked voting systems we have concentrated on can and must do if there exist several Condorcet candidates—or a strict Condorcet candidate x—and all voters are concerned and use admissible strategies:

1. *Ordinary approval*: if voter preferences are dichotomous, *all* Condorcet candidates must be elected; if voter preferences are not dichotomous, x can be elected by *sincere* strategies and must be elected if *any other system* guarantees his election.
2. *Ordinary plurality*: if voter preferences are dichotomous, *no* guarantees; if voter preferences are not dichotomous, x can be elected by *possibly insincere* strategies and must be elected if *runoff approval voting* guarantees his election.
3. *Runoff approval*: if voter preferences are dichotomous, *no* guarantees; if voter preferences are not dichotomous, x can be elected by *sincere* strategies and must be elected for some sets of voter preferences if and only if there are exactly three candidates.
4. *Runoff plurality*: if voter preferences are dichotomous, *no* guarantees; if voter preferences are not dichotomous, x can be elected by *possibly empty sincere* strategies, but his election cannot be guaranteed whatever voter preferences are.

Clearly, the ability of the different systems to elect, or guarantee the election of, Condorcet candidates decreases in going from ordinary to runoff systems, and from approval voting to plurality voting. However, runoff systems, because they do not require insincerity to elect x under approval voting, would appear more sincere, but here one has to distinguish between a voter's ability to use sincere strategies and the likelihood of his doing so.

On balance, it seems, one is more likely to vote insincerely when there is a runoff because of the incentive under approval voting to vote not only for preferred candidates but also for nonpreferred candidates if it seems probable that a preferred candidate will beat a "weak" nonpreferred candidate in the runoff. On the other hand, if there is no runoff, one might vote for more of one's preferred candidates to help ensure that some acceptable candidate gets elected, even if not one's favorite. Insincere voting would probably be more prevalent in the first case (voting for preferred and "weak" nonpreferred) than in the second (voting for more of one's preferred), which is a supposition reinforced by the finding that ordinary approval voting is the only system that is sincere if preferences are trichotomous.

In runoff systems, approval voting is more sincere than plurality voting. If voter preferences are dichotomous, for example, a voter will always vote for a *single* best choice under runoff approval voting but not under runoff plurality voting, for under the latter it may be better in some circumstances to vote for a "weak" loser to help ensure that he goes into the runoff against one's favorite. Yet, this is not necessary under runoff approval voting, because one can also vote for one or more preferred candidates, thereby helping the (assumed) single preferred candidate, too, to make the runoff by voting for him.

To return to the main theme of this chapter, in general approval voting helps elect the Condorcet candidate(s), and with more sincere voting, than does plurality voting. Runoffs muddy the picture somewhat, but they do not in general give additional help to Condorcet candidates or encourage sincere voting—quite the opposite. As noted before, they make elections more costly and may also decrease voter turnout, even in the first election, by rendering abstention an admissible strategy for a concerned voter.

Runoffs do assuredly prevent the election of the weakest candidate—the one who would lose to all others in pairwise contests, the reverse of the Condorcet candidate. They may also discourage the entry of fringe candidates, who would lose in a runoff unless matched against another fringe candidate.

But the possibility of such a runoff between fringe candidates increases as the number of candidates increases; correspondingly, the probability of a Condorcet candidate's winning drops. Whether plurality voting encourages a greater proliferation of candidates—with or without a runoff—than would approval voting is difficult to say, but certainly new candidates are encouraged to run under plurality voting as the percentage needed to win in a plurality contest falls.[14]

Approval voting does not produce this "snowball effect" because, at least in principle, the "acceptability" of each candidate is insensitive to the number of candidates running. To be sure, a new entrant might draw some approval votes away from other candidates, but practically speaking the effects caused by new entrants in approval voting elections would certainly not be the massive shifts one sometimes sees in plurality elections when new candidates enter.

The mischief caused by "ideological" candidates, who make a single issue the basis of their campaign, and stalking horses, who enter to prevent certain contenders from winning, or making a runoff, would be attenuated under approval voting. This form of agenda manipulation is particularly evident in presidential primaries in which single-issue candidates or "favorite sons"—who have virtually no chance of winning their party's presidential nomination—run either to highlight particular causes or keep at least part of a state's delegation ostensibly uncommitted until the party convention to maximize their bargaining power.

In sum, Condorcet candidates seem very much more vulnerable under plurality voting than under approval voting. It is somewhat harder to ascertain the effects of runoffs in each case, but the theoretical results indicate that voting is less sincere, Condorcet candidates are guaranteed election in fewer cases, and the results are more manipulable than under ordinary systems.[15]

Footnotes to Chapter 3

1. Marquis de Condorcet, *Essai sur l'application de l'analyse à la probabilité dés decisions rendues à la pluralité des voix* (Paris, 1785); and Jean-Charles de Borda, "Mémoire sur les election au scrutin," *Histoire de l'Académie Royale des Sciences* (Paris, 1781). A translation, with commentary, of Borda's original work can be found in Alfred de Grazia, "Mathematical Derivation of an Election System," *ISIS* **44**, 135–136 (June 1953), 42–51.

2. Duncan Black, *The Theory of Committees and Elections* (Cambridge: Cambridge University Press, 1958).

3. For a review of the literature on the paradox of voting, and Arrow's Impossibility Theorem that describes conditions underlying it, see Jerry S. Kelly, *Arrow Impossibility Theorems* (New York: Academic Press, 1978); Steven J. Brams, *Paradoxes in Politics: An Introduction to the Nonobvious in Political Science* (New York: Free Press, 1976), Ch. 2; Peter C. Fishburn, *The Theory of Social Choice* (Princeton: Princeton University Press, 1973); and P. C. Fishburn, "Paradoxes of Voting," *American Political Science Review* **68**, 2 (June 1974), 537–546.

4. Peter C. Fishburn, "Condorcet Social Choice Functions," *SIAM Journal on Applied Mathematics* **33**, 3 (November 1977), 469–489; P. C. Fishburn, "Dimensions of Election Procedures: Analyses and Comparisons," *Theory and Decision* (forthcoming); Jeffrey T. Richelson, "A Comparative Analysis of Social Choice Functions," *Behavioral Science* **20**, 5 (September 1975), 331–337; J. T. Richelson, "A Comparative Analysis of Social Choice Functions, II," *Behavioral Science* **23**, 1 (January 1978), 38–44; J. T. Richelson, "A Comparative Analysis of Social Choice Functions, III," *Behavioral Science* **23**, 3 (May 1978), 169–178; J. T. Richelson, "A Comparative Analysis of Social Choice Functions, I, II, III: A Summary," *Behavioral Science* **24**, 5 (Septem-

ber 1979), 355; J. T. Richelson, "A Comparative Analysis of Social Choice Functions, IV," *Behavioral Science* **26**, 4 (October 1981), 346–353; Philip D. Straffin, Jr., *Topics in the Theory of Voting*, UMAP Expository Monograph Series (Boston: Birkhäuser Boston, 1980); Hannu Nurmi, "Majority Rule: Second Thoughts and Refutations," *Quality and Quantity* **14**, 6 (December 1980), 743–765; H. Nurmi, "On the Properties of Voting Systems," *Scandinavian Political Studies* **4** (1981), 19–32; H. Nurmi, "Review Article: Voting Procedures," *British Journal of Political Science* (forthcoming); Prakash P. Shenoy and David B. Smith, "Voting Schemes for the Financial Accounting Standards Board" (mimeographed, 1981); and William H. Riker, *Liberalism against Populism: A Confrontation between the Theory of Democracy and the Theory of Social Choice* (San Francisco: W. H. Freeman, 1981). Properties of different runoff systems are compared in Jeffrey T. Richelson, "Running off Empty: Run-off Point Systems," *Public Choice* **35**, 4 (1980), 457–468; and the effects of different spatial modeling assumptions are considered in John Chamberlin and Michael D. Cohen, "Toward Applicable Social Choice Theory: A Comparison of Social Choice Functions under Spatial Model Assumptions," *American Political Science Review* **72**, 4 (December 1978), 1341–1356. At a less technical level, good comparisons of different voting systems, with illustrations from recent United States presidential elections, can be found in Richard G. Niemi and William H. Riker, "The Choice of Voting Systems," *Scientific American* (June 1976), pp. 21ff; and Martin Gardner (written by Lynn Arthur Steen), "Mathematical Games (From Counting Votes to Making Votes Count: The Mathematics of Elections)," *Scientific American* (October 1980), pp. 16ff.

5. Ken-ichi Inada, "A Note on the Simple Majority Decision Rule," *Econometrica* **32**, 4 (October 1964), 525–531.

6. Peter C. Fishburn, "Simple Voting Systems and Majority Rule," *Behavioral Science* **19**, 3 (May 1974), 166–176; P. C. Fishburn and William V. Gehrlein, "An Analysis of Simple Two-stage Voting Systems," *Behavioral Science* **21**, 1 (January 1976), 1–23; P. C. Fishburn and W. V. Gehrlein, "An Analysis of Voting Procedures with Nonranked Voting," *Behavioral Science* **22**, 3 (May 1977), 178–185; W. V. Gehrlein and P. C. Fishburn, "Coincidence Probabilities for Simple Majority and Positional Voting Rules," *Social Science Research* **7**, 3 (September 1978), 272–283; W. V. Gehrlein and P. C. Fishburn, "Effects of Abstentions on Voting Procedures in Three-Candidate Elections," *Behavioral Science* **24**, 5 (September 1979), 346–354; W. V. Gehrlein and P. C. Fishburn, "Constant Scoring Rules for Choosing One among Many Alternatives," *Quality and Quantity* **15**, 2 (April 1981), 203–210; P. C. Fishburn and W. V. Gehrlein, "Majority Efficiencies for Simple Voting Procedures: Summary and Interpretation," *Theory and Decision* **14**, 2 (June 1982), 141–153; Raphael Gillett, "The Asymptotic Likelihood of Agreement between Plurality and Condorcet Outcomes," *Behavioral Science* **25**, 1 (January 1980), 23–32; and W. V. Gehrlein, "Condorcet Efficiency and Constant Scoring Rules," *Mathematical Social Sciences* **2**, 2 (March 1982), 123–130.

7. Robert J. Weber, "Comparison of Voting Systems" (mimeographed, 1977); R. J. Weber, "Multiply-Weighted Voting Systems" (mimeographed,

1977); R. J. Weber, "Reproducing Voting Systems" (mimeographed, 1977); Robert F. Bordley, "A Pragmatic Scheme for Evaluating Election Schemes," *American Political Science Review* (forthcoming); and Samuel Merrill, III, "A Comparison of Multicandidate Electoral Systems in Terms of Optimal Voting Strategies," *American Journal of Political Science* (forthcoming).

8. A plurality runoff system often has a provision that does not require a second ballot when some candidate is supported by a sufficiently large proportion of the voters on the first ballot, in which case the candidate with the most first-ballot votes is elected. Such a system is a hybrid of an ordinary system and a runoff system, as defined in this chapter.

9. A modified runoff system, as described in the preceding footnote, may, of course, require only one ballot.

10. The new terminology in this assumption can be explained by interpreting what follows "if either" as "the union of all sets $\{x,y\}$—such that $\{x,y\}$ belongs to Γ_1—is included in, or the same as, $M(P)$." The nontechnical reader may skip this assumption and the discussion below since it is essentially a technical condition needed to prove subsequent theorems and has little substantive significance.

11. Peter C. Fishburn and Steven J. Brams, "Approval Voting, Condorcet's Principle, and Runoff Elections," *Public Choice* **36**, 1 (1981), 89–114.

12. Based on casual observations but no systematic data that we could locate.

13. William V. Gehrlein and Peter C. Fishburn, "The Effects of Abstentions on Election Outcomes," *Public Choice* **33**, 2 (1978), 69–82.

14. The modern record for number of candidates running in a congressional election is 31, which occurred in the primary races for Maryland's Fifth Congressional District after the incumbent seat was declared vacant because of the incumbent's illness. Ben A. Franklin, "31 on Ballot Tomorrow for House Seat in Maryland," *New York Times*, April 6, 1981, p. B15. The Republican winner easily triumphed against 12 opponents with 63 percent of the vote, but the Democratic winner won with only 30 percent against 19 opponents. "Scott and Hoyer Nominated in Maryland 5th District," *Congressional Quarterly Weekly Report* **39**, 5 (April 11, 1981), 645.

15. These results have been extended to the election of committees in which more than one person is to be elected to office. See Peter C. Fishburn, "An Analysis of Simple Voting Systems for Electing Committees," *SIAM Journal on Applied Mathematics* **41**, 3 (December 1981), 499–502; and Jeffrey B. Sidney, "Single Ballot Non-Ranked Voting Systems for Committee Selection" (mimeographed, 1981). Expected-utility calculations that a voter might make in the election of a committee are illustrated in Dale T. Hoffman, "A Model for Strategic Voting," *SIAM Journal on Applied Mathematics* **42**, 4 (August 1982), 751–761. The use of approval voting in the selection of multiple propositions—such as those that might come before a zoning board where majority support is required for passage—is analyzed in Roger L. Faith and James M. Buchanan, "Towards a Theory of Yes-No Voting," *Public Choice* **37**, 2 (1981), 231–245.

Chapter 4
The Reconstruction of an Election under Alternative Rules[1]

4.1. Introduction

In this chapter we offer an interlude from the purely theoretical results of Chapters 2 and 3. This break serves not only the purpose of making this theory less austere and perhaps more palatable but also shows how the theory can be wedded to reality. Although the results so far established do not apply, strictly speaking, to elections that run more than two ballots, some of the analysis of runoff elections in the previous chapter can be adapted to more extended elimination contests.

Such a contest was held on December 6, 1976, and involved four candidates seeking the post of Majority Leader of the United States House of Representatives. This contest attracted wide media attention and was examined in detail by Oppenheimer and Peabody.[2] Although we shall not give another blow-by-blow account of this election, we shall use information from this and journalistic accounts to supplement the quantitative analysis of ballot data that provides the main basis for the conclusions we reach on the merits of different voting systems.

We shall proceed by first demonstrating how ballot data and related information from an election can be used to reconstruct plausible preference orders for the voters. Next, we shall show how such a reconstruction supports three ends. First, it provides a check on qualitative impressions about voter and candidate intentions and strategies in the actual election. Second, it allows one to estimate the probable effects that other voting systems would have had on strategies and outcomes in the election. Third, the analysis of alternative voting systems enables normative comparisons to be made among the systems compared and thereby generates information that can be useful to officials who might wish to consider changes in the extant voting rules.

The reconstruction approach and its consequences will be illustrated through an analysis of the 1976 Majority Leader election. The reconstruction will be based on the ballot data, plausible assumptions about voter behavior, and an assumption of single-peaked preferences (to be defined later) that seems reasonably accurate in the context examined. Elementary integer programming techniques provide the algebraic tools that we shall use.

Several consequences flow from this analysis. One is that an allegation made by some journalists and political scientists about the voting behavior of supporters of a defeated candidate is almost certainly false. Moreover, as we shall show, another loser, who was acknowledged to be a strong candidate, was with little doubt the Condorcet candidate—the one who would have defeated every other candidate in a series of pairwise contests (see Chapter 3). We conclude that single-ballot approval voting, among the four systems analyzed (including the one actually used), would have almost surely elected the Condorcet candidate; by contrast, the other systems would have been less likely to elect this candidate.

Hence, to the extent that the election of a Condorcet candidate is taken to be a desideratum of a voting procedure, single-ballot approval voting looks attractive in the type of contest under consideration. Thereby some of the arguments of Chapter 3 on Condorcet properties of approval voting can be extended to the legislative context—if not in voting on bills, at least in contests like the 1976 House Majority Leader race that seem presently vulnerable to the election of non-Condorcet candidates. The sincerity and strategy-proofness of approval voting are also pertinent in this race, for elimination systems that involve a series of runoffs seem even more manipulable than the two-ballot runoff systems studied in Chapter 3.

4.2. Background on the 1976 House Majority Leader Election

The House Democratic Caucus, consisting of 248 returning members and 48 newly elected freshmen, met on December 6, 1976, about a month after Election Day, to select new leaders in the upcoming 95th Congress. Thomas P. "Tip" O'Neill, Jr., of Massachusetts, who had been Majority Leader in the previous Congress, ran unopposed for Speaker of the House. Four candidates ran for the post of Majority Leader that O'Neill vacated:

Philip Burton of California, a liberal and previous Democratic Caucus chairman, was ambitious, abrasive, and generally acknowledged to be the early front-runner.

Richard Bolling of Missouri, an intellectual and aging moderate with broad support, had once been a protégé of Sam Rayburn.

Table 4.1
Vote Totals in 1976 Election for House Majority Leader*

Candidate	Ballot 1	Ballot 2	Ballot 3
Burton	106	107	147
Bolling	81	93	–
McFall	31	–	–
Wright	77	95	148
Total	295	295	295

*Source: Steven J. Brams and Peter C. Fishburn, "Reconstructing Voting Processes: The 1976 House Majority Leader Election," *Political Methodology* 7, 3–4 (1981), 97, Table 1; reprinted with permission.

John J. McFall of California, a self-effacing moderate and the previous Democratic Whip, was a person widely believed not qualified to move up to Majority Leader.

James C. Wright, Jr., of Texas, a deputy whip under McFall and the most conservative of the candidates, had risen through the ranks and, though a late-starter, waged a shrewd and vigorous campaign.

According to Oppenheimer and Peabody, "It would be the closest, most volatile, and least predictable contest for the office of House Majority Leader in the 100-year history of Congress; all the candidates except McFall could easily have won."[3] A similar assessment was offered in the *New York Times* prior to the election.[4]

The election in fact went three ballots. McFall withdrew after the first ballot and Bolling was eliminated on the second ballot. On the third and climactic ballot, Wright beat Burton 148 to 147 votes and thereby became the new Majority Leader in what the *New York Times* called a "stunning one-vote upset victory."[5] The vote totals on all three ballots are shown in Table 4.1 for the 295 Democratic representatives voting in this election.

4.3. Best/Worst Analysis: A Preliminary Appraisal

The first thing that can be said about the vote totals in Table 4.1 with respect to voter behavior is that they are fully consistent with the presumption of sincere voting, whereby each voter votes for his most preferred available candidate *on each ballot*. At least on the first ballot, the sincerity assumption seems reasonable since the low candidate would *not* have been forced to withdraw (though he, in fact, did) and members, therefore, could vote their preferences with greater equanimity. On the second ballot, after McFall's withdrawal, voting may have been insincere—which is a possibility we shall assess in Section 4.4—but on the third ballot between the two finalists, there would be no incentive for members to vote insincerely.

Under sincere voting, every candidate except Burton—who was beaten by Wright on the third ballot—could have been a Condorcet candidate (preferred by a majority of the 295 voters to each of the other three candidates). Given that voting was sincere and that no voter was indifferent between any two candidates, the data of Table 4.1 yield the following voter counts for the indicated partial or total preference orders of the candidates:

Number of Voters	Partial or Total Preference Order
106	Burton first, other three in any order
x	Bolling over McFall, Bolling over Burton over Wright
y	Bolling over McFall, Bolling over Wright over Burton
1	McFall over Burton, Burton over Wright and Bolling
18	McFall over Wright, Wright over Burton and Bolling
z	McFall over Bolling over Burton over Wright
w	McFall over Bolling over Wright over Burton
77	Wright first, other three in any order

where $x + y = 81$, $z + w = 12$, $x + z = 40$, and $y + w = 53$. For example, under the given assumptions, one $(107 - 106)$ McFall voter on the first ballot voted for Burton on Ballot 2, 18 $(95 - 77)$ McFall supporters voted for Wright on Ballot 2, and $z + w = 12$ $(93 - 81)$ McFall supporters voted for Bolling on Ballot 2. Since Burton gained 40 of the 93 $(147 - 107)$ Representatives who voted for Bolling on Ballot 2, $x + z = 40$.

The next task is to assign feasible integer values to x, y, z, and w to determine the best and worst that each candidate could have done in a pairwise contest with each other candidate. After doing this, an additional assumption that further constrains the assignments will be made.

On the basis of the foregoing data, the best and worst that each candidate could have done against every other candidate in a head-to-head contest is shown in Table 4.2. For example, in the best of all possible worlds for Burton, as shown in the first row, Burton would defeat Bolling 202 to 93 (all votes except Bolling's second-ballot votes could have gone to Burton), defeat McFall 264 to 31 (all votes except McFall's first-ballot votes could have gone to Burton), and lose to Wright by one vote (the actual result on Ballot 3). In the worst of all possible worlds for Burton, as shown in the first column, he is beaten 188 to 107 by Bolling, 189 to 106 by McFall, and 148 to 147 by Wright.

Table 4.2

Best and Worst Possible Outcomes for Each Candidate in Pairwise Contests with Others*

	Candidates	Burton	Bolling	(worst) McFall	Wright
	Burton	–	202/93	264/31	147/148
(best)	Bolling	188/107	–	264/31	200/95
	McFall	189/106	214/81	–	218/77
	Wright	148/147	202/93	264/31	–

*Source: Steven J. Brams and Peter C. Fishburn, "Reconstructing Voting Processes: The 1976 House Majority Leader Election," *Political Methodology* **7**, 3–4 (1981), 99, Table 2; reprinted with permission.

It is clear from the second, third, and fourth rows of the array that either Bolling or McFall or Wright could have been a Condorcet candidate, even though the data themselves do not lend strong support to the claim that any particular candidate is preferred by a majority of voters to each of the others.

4.4. Single-Peaked Preferences

Additional information given by Oppenheimer and Peabody, however, renders this conclusion implausible. Among other things, they note that "if Bolling had been in the runoff, everyone agreed he would have beaten either Wright or Burton,"[6] though this statement is qualified in their longer treatment;[7] that McFall was probably hurt by having been revealed as a recipient of some of Tongsun Park's money;[8] and that at best McFall's supporters were "hoping" for 40 votes.[9]

The most plausible and simplest explanation for Bolling's popularity—in particular, the presumption that he was the Condorcet candidate—arises from the assumption of "single-peaked" voter preferences over an underlying ideological order.[10] From most liberal to most conservative, this scale is Burton–Bolling–McFall–Wright; it is supported by several comments made by Oppenheimer and Peabody and in a *New York Times* assessment. Although all voters would not be expected to conform to the single-peakedness assumption, it seems reasonable for most. Under this assumption, the possible strict preference orders (from most preferred to least preferred) that could be held by voters are as follows:

O_1: Burton, Bolling, McFall, Wright
O_{21}: Bolling, Burton, McFall, Wright
O_{22}: Bolling, McFall, Burton, Wright
O_{23}: Bolling, McFall, Wright, Burton

O_{31}: McFall, Wright, Bolling, Burton
O_{32}: McFall, Bolling, Wright, Burton
O_{33}: McFall, Bolling, Burton, Wright
O_4:   Wright, McFall, Bolling, Burton.

Since there would appear to be little reason for strategic voting on Ballot 1 (as noted earlier, McFall was generally perceived to be low man and therefore likely to be eliminated first), we shall assume that first-ballot voting was sincere. From the first-ballot totals (see Table 4.1), the single-peakedness assumption then implies that

106 voters had order O_1
81 voters had the O_2 orders (O_{21}, O_{22}, O_{23})
31 voters had the O_3 orders (O_{31}, O_{32}, O_{33})
77 voters had order O_4.

Without any further assumptions on the breakdown of the O_2 and O_3 orders, these figures reveal that Bolling would have beaten Burton by at least 189 (81 + 31 + 77) to 106, Bolling would have beaten McFall by at least 187 (81 + 106) to 108 (31 + 77), and Bolling would have beaten Wright by at least 187 (81 + 106) to 108 (31 + 77).

With McFall's withdrawal after Ballot 1, his 31 votes would, on the second ballot, go to either Wright (O_{31}) or Bolling (O_{32} and O_{33}), assuming sincere voting on Ballot 2 and single-peaked orders as described previously. In point of fact, Burton gained 1 vote on Ballot 2 and Bolling and Wright gained, respectively, 12 and 18 votes on Ballot 2. Except for the one vote gained by Burton, these figures conform to the previous assumptions and, in particular, lend strong support to the single-peakedness assumption which, if correct, would have Burton gaining no votes on Ballot 2.

By contrast, Oppenheimer and Peabody are nonplussed at the Ballot 2 results:

The closeness of the Wright–Bolling vote [on Ballot 2] was surprising. A switch of two votes and Bolling would have been in the runoff. *Even more confounding was the new Burton total.* It was hard to believe that he had increased his total by only one vote. There was speculation that Burton had, in fact, shifted some votes to Wright in order to have a more conservative—and hence weaker—opponent on the final ballot.

Later Burton strongly denied that he was involved in any vote switching: . . . [italics ours].[11]

The *Washington Post* also reported this charge of vote-switching.[12] According to the single-peakedness analysis, however, the "new Burton total" was not in the least confounding and there is no hint of vote switching. Indeed, this analysis accords very well with the actual data and exonerates Burton on the vote-switching allegation. If, in fact, some of Burton's supporters had voted strategically for Wright on

Ballot 2—which could have been a clever tactical move—the foregoing analysis suggests that Burton's total would have decreased, rather than increased, in going from Ballot 1 to Ballot 2.

While the assumption of single-peakedness "works" in the sense of parsimoniously explaining the data, other explanations are certainly possible. For example, it has been suggested that the ties of McFall and Burton to the California delegation may have been crucial to the second-ballot totals: members of this delegation who voted for McFall on the first ballot would presumably find Burton distasteful to their interests and those of the state. Consequently, they would not support him after McFall's withdrawal, which is also consistent with Burton's lack of movement on the second ballot.

We would not discredit situation-specific explanations of voting behavior, which also might include personal friendships, committee ties, pressure-group influences, campaign commitments, and the like. The main point rather is that the single-peakedness assumption works as a *general* explanation; it may be reinforced—or perhaps, on occasion, contravened—by particularistic circumstances, but these should not diminish the power of ideology, as an overarching *and* plausible factor underlying the voting of Democratic Representatives in this election, to explain the outcome that occurred.

Although there could have been some vote changes between Ballots 1 and 2 among the original supporters of Burton, Bolling, and Wright, these changes would appear to have been negligible. Moreover, the single-peakedness analysis suggests that the initial McFall supporters voted sincerely on Ballot 2. Those who favored Bolling next (O_{32} and O_{33}) had virtually no motivation to vote otherwise since Bolling needed every vote he could muster on Ballot 2 in order to get into the runoff on Ballot 3 (where, by acknowledgment, he would have won). Those who favored Wright next (O_{31}) would have been strongly motivated to vote for Wright to get him into the runoff against Burton; even if Wright had been low man on Ballot 2, Wright supporters could have taken consolation in the fact that their third choice (Bolling) rather than their last choice (Burton) would almost surely have been the new House Majority Leader.

For these reasons, we believe that the votes cast on Ballot 2 are, with very few exceptions, sincere. Accordingly, in discussing the Burton–Bolling–Wright situation further, we shall presume that, approximately,

107 voters have order P_1 = (Burton, Bolling, Wright)

93 voters have order P_{21} = (Bolling, Burton, Wright)

or order P_{22} = (Bolling, Wright, Burton)

95 voters have order P_3 = (Wright, Bolling, Burton).

These four P orders, taken from the Ballot 2 totals (see Table 4.1), are the possible strict preference orders on the three candidates that are single-peaked over the underlying ideological order, Burton–Bolling–Wright. Since there is no reason to suppose that voting on Ballot 3 was other than sincere (147 for Burton, 148 for Wright), about 40 (147 − 107) voters held order P_{21} and about 53 (148 − 95) voters held order P_{22} at the time of the final ballot.

We shall also assume in what follows that the voters were aware of Bolling's imminent victory if he should get into the runoff. Finally, it will be assumed that with virtually any kind of reasonable voting system on Ballot 1, McFall would have the low total and thus drop out of contention—if not immediately, then after the second ballot when the low candidate would have been forced to withdraw.

4.5. Different Voting Systems

We shall now compare the likely effects of four voting systems on the Ballot 2 contest among Burton, Bolling, and Wright. McFall will not be considered further. The four systems are the same as those extensively analyzed in Chapter 3, but here we assume only the three candidates in the race *after* the first ballot:

OP: *ordinary plurality*. Each voter casts a single vote for exactly one of the three candidates. The candidate with the largest total wins. A tie between the top two candidates is resolved by a runoff. A tie among all three results in a new (first) ballot.

OA: *ordinary approval*. This is the same as OP except that a voter can vote for either one or two candidates. Each candidate voted for by a two-candidate voter receives a full vote from that voter. (The total number of votes cast can therefore range from 295 to 590.)

RP: *runoff plurality*. This is the actual system used. A voter votes for one candidate on the first ballot, and the top two candidates go into the runoff. Ties are resolved by new ballots among all the candidates involved.

RA: *runoff approval*. The same as RP except that a voter can vote for either one or two candidates on the first ballot.

In discussing these voting systems, we shall first indicate plausible totals on the first (or only) ballot under each system and then suggest what systems would have favored which candidates. Plausible first-ballot totals are given in Table 4.3. Here m is the number of the 95 voters whose first choice is Wright but who vote for their second choice (Bolling) under system OP, and n is the number of the same 95 Wright supporters who vote for Wright *and* Bolling under system OA.

Table 4.3

Plausible First-Ballot Totals for Each of Four Voting Systems*

System	Burton	Bolling	Wright	Total
OP	107	93 + m	95 − m	295
OA	107	93 + n	95	295 + n
RP (actual)	107	93	95	295
RA	102	93	202	497

*Source: Steven J. Brams and Peter C. Fishburn, "Reconstructing Voting Processes: The 1976 House Majority Leader Election," *Political Methodology* 7, 3–4 (1981), 103, Table 3; reprinted with permission.

The figures for OP and OA indicate that 107 Burton and 95 Bolling supporters vote sincerely and, in the case of OA, do not vote for a second candidate.

The figures for RA are based on the assumption that Bolling supporters vote only for Bolling on the first ballot but that all 202 (107 + 95) voters who have either Burton or Wright as their first choice vote for both Burton *and* Wright on the first ballot. We shall defend the reasonableness of these figures in ensuing paragraphs.

Under the presumption that Bolling would almost surely defeat either Burton or Wright in a head-to-head contest, and assuming a rough estimate as given by Oppenheimer and Peabody of each candidate's strength prior to the voting,[13] we have tentatively ranked the candidates in terms of the probability that each of the four systems would favor them, as shown in Table 4.4. Because of Burton's initial relative strength, he would surely be most favored under OP. Given the perception of Wright as the underdog, it seems likely under OP that

Table 4.4

Ranking of Candidates According to Probability That Four Voting Systems Favor Them*

System	Most Probable Winner to Least Probable Winner
OP	Burton, Bolling, Wright
OA	Bolling, Burton, Wright
RP	Bolling, Burton, Wright
RA	Burton, Wright, Bolling

*Source: Steven J. Brams and Peter C. Fishburn, "Reconstructing Voting Processes: The 1976 House Majority Leader Election," *Political Methodology* 7, 3–4 (1981), 104, Table 4; reprinted with permission.

some of Wright's supporters would vote for Bolling (their second choice), though probably not enough (it would require $m \geq 14$) to swing the win away from Burton to Bolling.

On the other hand, it seems plausible under OA that 14 or more of the 95 Wright supporters would vote for Bolling as well as Wright to ensure that they get at least their second choice if not their first choice. Hence, OA gives Bolling, the Condorcet candidate, a good chance of winning, Burton less chance, and Wright almost no chance under OA because Bolling supporters would have no good reason to cast second approval votes for the perceived underdog. On the other hand, they would be unlikely to vote also for the favored candidate, Burton, because they would do so at the expense of decreasing Bolling's chances.

Although the prior indications under RP were that Bolling would most likely win, his supporters were clearly concerned that he might lose on the first ballot here (Ballot 2 initially) and thus not go onto the runoff ballot. This is of course what happened. Given the expectation that Bolling would not get into the runoff, it appeared that Burton would probably defeat Wright. Hence, system RP favors Bolling most and Wright least, despite the actual results that were observed.

Under system RA, Bolling would have almost no chance since the Burton and Wright supporters could easily perceive that they could keep him out of the runoff by casting second approval votes for each other's candidate. As under RP, Burton has a better chance than Wright under RA if these two go onto the runoff ballot, so Burton is ranked ahead of Wright.

It is the foregoing type of reasoning that leads us to rank the four voting systems in terms of their desirability for each candidate: (1) Burton's best bet is OP, his next best RA—while his worst chance would be with OA since in this case it seems likely that the Wright supporters would swing the election to Bolling; (2) Bolling's best bets appear to be OA and RP—under both of which he could pick up support from Wright—then OP, with RA clearly in last place; (3) Wright's best bet would be RA—under which he has to contend seriously only with Burton—followed by the actual system RP, then OA and OP which give him almost no chance of winning.

The fact that RP gave all candidates at least a fighting chance, which Wright in the end was able to capitalize on, might be used as an argument in its favor. Although this made for an exciting election, however, it is questionable whether this is a proper criterion for choosing among the systems. In particular, since Bolling was a clear favorite over each of Burton and Wright, and appeared to be an excellent consensus candidate since all voters had him as either their first or second choice (presuming single-peaked preferences), it seems tempting to conclude that system OA, which probably would have yielded Bolling as the winner, is a better system than RP. In the case at hand, ordinary approval voting affords each voter the opportunity to vote for his second choice as well as his first choice. Thus, if he feels that his first choice does not have a good chance of winning, he can express his approval for his second choice and thereby have more say in the election without abandoning his first choice.

Under OP, by contrast, a voter would be tempted to abandon his first choice for strategic reasons and vote insincerely. Although the voter would be less likely under runoff plurality than under ordinary plurality to vote insincerely (on the first ballot), RP runs the "risk" of bypassing the strongest overall candidate. This of course is just what happened on December 6, 1976.

The worst system, in our opinion, is runoff approval voting, especially when preferences are single-peaked. Because of the first-ballot strategic possibilities that are opened up by RA—most notably, fostering the candidacies of ideologically distant but weak candidates on the first ballot—the generally most-favored candidate (Bolling) is a decided underdog. This is the opposite effect of ordinary approval voting and one we consider very undesirable.

In sum, we believe the empirical analysis demonstrates that OA is the best method of selection, followed by the actual method used, RP; OP and RA seem to be distinctly inferior because they provide almost no assurance that a Condorcet candidate (if one exists) will be selected. Of course, as was seen, RP is not foolproof, and neither is OA—unless the preferences of all voters are dichotomous (Section 3.2)—but they are certainly better than the other two systems with respect to the Condorcet criterion and probably sincerity and strategy-proofness as well.

4.6. Conclusions

In this chapter we have used a combination of deductive and inductive methods, based on actual ballot data and reasonable assumptions about voter behavior and preferences, to reconstruct plausible preference orders for voters. (For different kinds of reconstruction using public election voting and survey data, see Section 6.6 and Chapter 9.) The reconstructed orders were then used to assess the likely effects of different voting systems on voter strategies and election outcomes.

Of four voting systems examined, two seem indisputably inferior. These are the ordinary plurality system (OP) and runoff approval voting (RA). Both systems, but especially RA, are unduly susceptible to manipulation by strategic voting and appear less likely to elect a Condorcet candidate than the other systems in the type of contest under consideration.

In the particular election examined, the actual system used—runoff plurality voting (RP)—and the ordinary approval voting (OA) system appear to be competitive. System RP has the advantage of familiarity and, in addition, may appeal to some people because of the excitement of sequential ballots. Moreover, it gives the appearance of eliminating the weakest candidate after the first ballot. However, as we have shown, the "weakest candidate" may in fact be a Condorcet candidate who could beat each of the others in pairwise contests but is eliminated even when all voters vote sincerely on the first ballot. Also, RP is susceptible to strategic manipulation that may help an "extreme" candidate win a plurality on the first ballot and then succeed on the second ballot if his opponent is not a Condorcet candidate. In this case, supporters of that candidate may shift some of their first-ballot votes to the other extreme candidate in an effort to block the centrist candidate from the runoff. Although there is good reason to believe that this did not occur in the 1976 House Majority Leader election, it is certainly possible in similar elections.

Since OA "encourages" voters to vote for their second choice when they perceive that their first choice has little chance of winning, it allows a fairly broad expression of preferences without forcing voters to vote insincerely—and tends to elect Condorcet candidates when they exist. In addition, OA is not susceptible to the type of manipulation just noted for RP, and it is more efficient than RP since it requires only one ballot. Although OA may not offer the suspense afforded by a second ballot under RP, we believe this should not be a serious deterrent to its use.

In closing, we feel compelled to point out a major difficulty attending this kind of retrospective analysis. It stems from the fact that in elections in which it is reasonable to assume that candidates (as well as voters) are politically astute, they can be expected to estimate their prospects under the extant election rules. If they judge these rules to be unfavorable to their candidacies, they may decide not to run for election. Thus, as Shepsle has pointed out to us,[14] there is no assurance that the field of candidates would have remained constant in the 1976 race had one of the three alternative systems we analyzed been used. Some of the candidates who threw their hats into the ring may have opted out; by the same token, new candidates may have entered.

Since one cannot restage a hypothetical past, it will never be known whether Bolling would have prevailed under OA. But we *suspect* he would have entered because he probably would have been the Condorcet candidate in any plausible field of entrants. Given the propensity of

OA to find Condorcet candidates (if they exist), we conjecture that the rules of this system would have sustained his candidacy, even if some of the entrants would have changed.

Footnotes to Chapter 4

1. This chapter is based largely on Steven J. Brams and Peter C. Fishburn, "Reconstructing Voting Processes: The 1976 House Majority Leader Election," *Political Methodology*, **7**, 3–4 (1981), 95–108.

2. Bruce I. Oppenheimer and Robert L. Peabody, "The House Majority Leader Contest, 1976" (mimeographed, 1977); B. I. Oppenheimer and R. L. Peabody, "How the Race for Majority Leader Was Won—by One Vote," *Washington Monthly* **9** (November 1977), 46–56.

3. B. I. Oppenheimer and R. L. Peabody, "How the Race for Majority Leader Was Won—by One Vote," *Washington Monthly* **9** (November 1977), 47.

4. James M. Naughton, "4 Seeking House Leadership Press Claims in the Election Today," *New York Times*, December 6, 1976, pp. 1, 28.

5. David E. Rosenbaum, "O'Neill Is Speaker, Rep. Wright of Texas Wins Majority Post," *New York Times*, December 7, 1976, pp. 1, 33.

6. B. I. Oppenheimer and R. L. Peabody, "How the Race for Majority Leader Was Won—by One Vote," *Washington Monthly* **9** (November 1977), 47.

7. B. I. Oppenheimer and R. L. Peabody, "The House Majority Leader Contest, 1976" (mimeographed, 1977).

8. B. I. Oppenheimer and R. L. Peabody, "How the Race for Majority Leader Was Won—by One Vote," *Washington Monthly* **9** (November 1977), 53.

9. B. I. Oppenheimer and R. L. Peabody, "How the Race for Majority Leader Was Won—by One Vote," *Washington Monthly* **9** (November 1977), 54.

10. A full explanation of this and the related condition of "value restrictedness," with examples, is given in Steven J. Brams, *Paradoxes in Politics: An Introduction to the Nonobvious in Political Science* (New York: Free Press, 1976), pp. 37–41; see also Peter C. Fishburn, *The Theory of Social Choice* (Princeton: Princeton University Press, 1973), pp. 100–144. Single-peakedness means, roughly, that there exists a single dimension underlying the preferences of voters (e.g., a liberalism-conservatism scale) along which alternatives (e.g., candidates) can be ordered. Single-peaked preferences preclude the existence of a paradox of voting. This constraint on individual preferences was originally noted by Francis Galton, "One Vote, One Value," *Nature* **75** (February 28, 1907), 414, and discussed extensively in Duncan Black, *The Theory of Committees and Elections* (Cambridge: Cambridge University Press, 1958), pp. 14–35.

11. B. I. Oppenheimer and R. L. Peabody, "How the Race for Majority Leader Was Won—by One Vote," *Washington Monthly* **9** (November 1977), 56.

12. Mary Russell, "Representative Wright Is Elected House Majority Leader," *Washington Post*, December 7, 1976, pp. A1, A6.

13. B. I. Oppenheimer and R. L. Peabody, "How the Race for Majority Leader Was Won—by One Vote," *Washington Monthly* **9** (November 1977), 53–54.

14. Kenneth A. Shepsle (personal communication to S. J. Brams, November 14, 1978).

Chapter 5
Power and Equity:
Which System Is Fairest?

5.1. Introduction

In previous chapters, we compared approval voting to other single-ballot voting systems that may restrict the numbers of candidates one is allowed to vote for, and to runoff election systems in which the two candidates with the most first-ballot votes go onto the runoff ballot. Approval voting seems to be competitive and often superior to other systems in its ability to elicit honest or sincere responses from voters, its relative invulnerability to strategic manipulation, and its propensity to elect Condorcet or majority candidates. With respect to the last criterion, it was shown in Chapter 4 that approval voting would almost surely have found the probable Condorcet candidate in an important congressional leadership contest in 1976.

We turn in this chapter to another criterion for comparing and evaluating voting systems—equity. This notion, based upon the distribution of voting power of individuals under different systems in best and worst cases, raises several questions germane to approval voting:

1. To what extent does a voter's ability to affect the outcome of an approval voting election ("efficacy") depend on how many candidates he votes for?
2. To what extent does a voter's "power" depend on his specific preferences for the candidates?
3. To what extent does approval voting treat voters equitably?

We shall assume that the number $m \geq 3$ of candidates under consideration refers only to serious contenders; fringe candidates who have no chance of winning will be disregarded. In addition, we shall focus on large electorates and presume that voters' preferences are more or less evenly distributed over the different preference orders for the m candidates. If a final winner is assumed to be chosen randomly from a set of two or more candidates who are tied with the largest vote total, then the results lend themselves to a probabilistic interpretation. In effect, these results can be viewed as average-effects answers to the foregoing questions.

When there are $m = 3$ candidates, it will be shown that (1) voting for either one or two candidates is equally efficacious, (2) all voters are equally powerful, whatever their preferences, and (3) voters are treated equitably under approval voting. However, when $m \geq 4$, (1) voting for about half the candidates is most efficacious, (2) voters' relative powers depend on their preferences, and (3) nontrivial inequities exist among voters. We shall also argue that, whereas plurality voting grants equal power to every voter, it is more inequitable than approval voting for voters with different types of preferences.

The analysis of equity in the first part of the chapter is limited to dichotomous voters, but this restriction is later relaxed. As will be shown, even when more general preference orders are considered, plurality voting tends to be less equitable than approval voting.

Unlike previous chapters, the focus of this chapter is on averages, or generic measures, of the phenomena examined. This seems appropriate inasmuch as what can be expected over a broad range of possibilities seems most useful to investigate first. However, we shall also comment on situation-specific aspects of approval voting, particularly those involving three candidates in which the preferences of voters are not dichotomous.

To prepare for the subsequent analysis, we shall first define a measure of the difference between potential outcomes of an election. This measure is then used to define the "efficacy" of a voting strategy, which itself is a measure of the ability of the strategy to affect the outcome of an election. The notion of efficacy is next used to construct a measure of a voter's "power," which ultimately depends on his utilities for the candidates. This will then lead into a discussion of both average inequities and optimal strategies for utility-maximizing voters.

5.2. Efficacy

Recall from Section 2.3 that a strategy S of a voter is a subset of candidates; a voter uses S when he votes for every candidate in S and does not vote for any other candidate. The set of all m candidates will be ruled out as a strategy since its effect on the outcome is the same as the effect of an abstention. Hence, a strategy is necessarily a *proper* subset of candidates (not the entire set). The *outcome* of an election is the subset of candidates who have the largest vote total.

To assess the relative abilities of different strategies to affect the outcome under approval voting, define a measure $p(A,B)$ of the difference between two potential outcomes, or subsets of candidates, A and B:

$$p(A,B) = 1 - \frac{|A \cap B|}{|A \cup B|}.$$

Here $|X|$ is the number of candidates in X; thus, $|A \cup B|$ is the number of distinct candidates in either A or B (the union of these sets), and $|A \cap B|$ is the number in both A and B (the intersection of these sets). The $p(A,B)$ measure goes from 0, when the two outcomes, A and B, are identical, to 1 when they are disjoint.

Consider a focal voter, with the votes of all other voters fixed. Let A be the outcome when the focal voter abstains, and let B be the outcome when he uses strategy S. By using S instead of abstaining, the focal voter might either create new tied winners (making B the larger set: $A \subset B$, or A is included in B) or break old ties (making B the smaller set: $B \subset A$), but he can affect the outcome in no other way.

Assume that each candidate in an outcome has an equal chance of winning (random tie-breaking). Then it is not difficult to prove that, given the fixed votes of voters other than the focal voter,

$p(A,B)$ = Pr (an x belonging to S wins when the focal voter uses S)
　　　　 − Pr (an x belonging to S wins when the focal voter abstains),

where "Pr" denotes "probability that." Thus, under random tie-breaking, $p(A,B)$ is the amount by which the focal voter's vote for S *increases* the probability that some candidate in S will win.

To define the "efficacy of strategy S" for the focal voter, assume that all combinations of other voters' votes are equally weighted. To count these combinations, let m and n be, respectively, the number of candidates ($m \geq 3$) and the number of other voters who do not abstain. Now there are $2^m - 2$ nonempty proper subsets of candidates, excluding voting for all and voting for no candidates. Thus, each other voter has $2^m - 2$ nonabstention strategies from which to choose. Since there are n other voters, there are

$$H(m,n) = (2^m - 2)^n$$

possible ways that the others can vote.

To define the efficacy of S, let h, varying from 1 to $H(m,n)$, index the ways that others might vote. For each h, let $A_h(S)$ and $B_h(S)$ be, respectively, the outcomes that obtain when the focal voter abstains and when he uses S. The *efficacy of strategy S* is then defined as the average value of $p(A_h(S),B_h(S))$ over all h.

Because the ways that others might vote are weighted equally, every S that contains the same number of candidates has the same efficacy.

Therefore, when S contains k candidates, the efficacy of S is given by

$$E_k(m,n) = \sum_{h=1}^{H(m,n)} p(A_h(S),B_h(S))/H(m,n).$$

In effect, $E_k(m,n)$ is the average of all $p(A,B)$—the averaging being over all combinations of voting strategies of the n other voters—in which the focal voter votes for k ($1 \le k \le n$) candidates versus abstains ($k = 0$).

It is easily seen that $E_k(m,n) = 0$ if and only if $k = 0$: the abstention strategy is the only one that has zero efficacy. Moreover, since the focal voter can never produce a totally different outcome by not abstaining [$A_h(S) \cap B_h(S)$ is never empty], $p(A_h(S),B_h(S)) < 1$ for all h, and the efficacy of a nonabstention strategy is therefore always strictly between 0 and 1.

As defined here, $E_k(m,n)$ is simply the average change—over all ways that others might vote—that the focal voter can effect by voting for k candidates rather than abstaining. However, given both that ties are broken randomly and that each of the n other voters votes independently and has probability $1/(2^m - 2)$ of using each of the $2^m - 2$ nonabstention strategies, then

$E_k(m,n) = $ Pr (an x belonging to S wins when the focal voter uses S)
$-$ Pr (an x belonging to S wins when the focal voter abstains).

This is the same interpretation we offered earlier for $p(A,B)$, but now the votes of the n other voters are assumed not to be fixed but rather to vary over all possible strategy combinations, making $E_k(m,n)$ the amount by which the focal voter's vote for S increases the probability, *on the average*, that some candidate in S will win.

However one interprets $E_k(m,n)$—as an (undefined) increase, or as a probabilistic increase, given random tie-breaking and independent voting—it must approach zero for all fixed k and m as n gets large since the proportion of h values for which $p(A_h(S),B_h(S)) > 0$ approaches zero as n gets large. In other words, one voter has almost no ability to change the outcome by his vote in a large electorate. This does not, however, say anything about the *relative* effects of votes for different numbers of candidates on the outcome. Hence, to assess relative efficacies and provide an answer to the first question posed in Section 5.1, consider the ratios of efficacies, defined by

$$r_k^j(m,n) = \frac{E_j(m,n)}{E_k(m,n)}$$

for j,k belonging to $\{1,2, \ldots ,m - 1\}$. The limit of this ratio as the number of voters gets large is

$$r^j_k(m) = \lim_{n \to \infty} r^j_k(m,n),$$

about which we shall have more to say in Section 5.3.

Although we shall not prove it here, it is not hard to show that $r^1_2(3,n) > 1$ for all n. Thus, in a three-candidate election, a vote for one candidate ($j = 1$) is more efficacious than a vote for two candidates ($k = 2$). However, as a consequence of Theorem 5.1 (given below), $r^1_2(3) = 1$, so that votes for one candidate and for two candidates are approximately equally efficacious in a three-candidate race in a large electorate.

For large electorates, therefore, there is no essential difference in the efficacies of one-candidate and two-candidate voting strategies. In other words, in virtually all public elections and in most voting bodies (small committees, with less than ten or so members, excepted), an individual who votes for one candidate has practically the same ability to affect the outcome—small as it may be—as an individual who votes for two candidates in a three-candidate election.

The general limit result for $m \geq 3$ is given by the following theorem, whose proof is given elsewhere.[1]

Theorem 5.1. $r^j_k(m) = j(m - j)/[k(m - k)]$ *for all* $m \geq 3$ *and all* j,k *belonging to* $\{1,2, \ldots , m - 1\}$.

Thus, for large electorates and $m \geq 4$, efficacy is essentially single-peaked and symmetric about $m/2$, where $j(m - j)$ is maximized. That is, it increases with increasing k until about $m/2$, and then begins to decline from this peak in the same manner as it increased. Values of $|S|$ that are equidistant from $m/2$ have approximately equal efficacies, and values of $|S|$ closest to $m/2$ have the largest efficacies.[2]

To view this in a slightly different way, suppose m and n are fixed with n large. Let $c(m,n)$ equal $E_1(m,n)/(m - 1)$. Then, since $E_k(m,n)/E_1(m,n)$ is approximately equal to $k(m - k)/(m - 1)$, Theorem 5.1 says that

$$E_k(m,n) = k(m - k)c(m,n) \qquad \text{for } k = 1,2, \ldots ,m - 1,$$

with negligible error when n is large. This means that the $E_k(m,n)$ are approximately directly proportional to the values of $k(m - k)$. Note that this approximation applies also to the abstention strategy since it gives $E_0(m,n) = 0$.

To illustrate values of efficacy for large electorates, consider first four-candidate elections. The above approximation says that

$$E_1(4,n) = 3[c(4,n)],$$
$$E_2(4,n) = 4[c(4,n)],$$
$$E_3(4,n) = 3[c(4,n)],$$

and for five-candidate elections it says that

$$E_1(5,n) = 4[c(5,n)],$$
$$E_2(5,n) = 6[c(5,n)],$$
$$E_3(5,n) = 6[c(5,n)],$$
$$E_4(5,n) = 4[c(5,n)].$$

Thus, when $m = 4$, one-candidate strategies and three-candidate strategies are about equally efficacious, whereas two-candidate strategies are about 33 percent more efficacious than the others. And for $m = 5$, two-candidate and three-candidate strategies are about 50 percent more efficacious than one-candidate and four-candidate strategies. For $m = 7$, a three-candidate strategy is about twice as efficacious as a one-candidate strategy.

More generally, in large electorates, votes for different numbers of candidates are not, generally speaking, equally efficacious. As we have shown, strategies which contain very few candidates, and those which contain most of the candidates, are not as efficacious as those which contain about half of the candidates. This finding demonstrates that Riker's claim, based on a single example, that "indifferent voters or the voters with a broad tolerance for positions"—who would approve of most candidates (three out of four in Riker's example)—"dominate in the choice" is not generally true.[3] In fact, it is voters with medium, not broad or narrow, tolerance who will in general be most efficacious.

5.3. Situation-Specific Effects and Power

Since three-candidate elections are common in politics and also of theoretical importance in themselves, we shall look at them in more detail before turning to other situations and offering a definition of power. For $m = 3$ candidates, enumerative computations for small values of the number n of other voters yield the efficacies and efficacy ratios shown in Table 5.1.

Note that E_1, E_2, and r_2^1 decrease as n increases, except that $r_2^1(3,1) = r_2^1(3,2)$. These latter values say that voting for one out of three candidates is 40 percent more efficacious than voting for two candidates if there are either one or two other voters. By comparison, voting for one candidate is 100 percent more efficacious if there are no other voters (because the focal voter ensures the election of his presumed

Table 5.1

Efficacies and Efficacy Ratios in
Three-Candidate Elections
with Small Numbers of Other Voters

Number of Other Voters: n	Efficacy of Voting for One: $E_1(3,n)$	Efficacy of Voting for Two: $E_2(3,n)$	Efficacy Ratio: $r_2^1(3,n)$
0	2/3	1/3	2.00
1	7/18	5/18	1.40
2	35/108	25/108	1.40
3	177/648	135/648	1.31

favorite rather than putting him in a tie with another candidate) and 31 percent more efficacious if there are three other voters.

To understand the basis of these values better, consider the figures for $n = 3$. Let the set of candidates be $X = \{a,b,c\}$, and suppose that each of the other three voters has equal probability ($\frac{1}{6}$) of using each of the six nonabstention strategies, and that ties in outcomes are broken randomly. Then $E_1(3,3) = 177/648 = 0.273$ says that the focal voter can increase the probability that candidate a is elected by an increment of 0.273 if he votes for a instead of abstaining. Since a has probability $\frac{1}{3}$ of being elected when the focal voter abstains (by the symmetry of the probabilistic model over the candidates), the focal voter can increase a's probability of election by 82 percent—from 0.333 to 0.606 ($= 0.333 + 0.273$)—by voting for a. In like manner, since $E_2(3,3) = 135/648 = 0.208$, the focal voter can increase the probability that either a or b is elected by 31 percent—from $\frac{2}{3}$ (if he abstains) to 0.875 ($= 0.667 + 0.208$)—by voting for both a and b. These figures show also that a's probability of election is 0.333 if the focal voter abstains, about 0.437 (half of 0.875) if he votes for a and another candidate, and 0.606 if he votes only for a.

So far we have considered a measure of the difference it makes to the outcome of an approval-voting election to vote for a specific number of candidates. This measure is based on equal weights for all ways that voters other than the focal voter might vote. Although the equal-weighting assumption is appropriate from a generic viewpoint, it is obviously not the whole story. As we shall presently show, there are situations that clearly violate it.

Suppose a primary election involves ten candidates who represent all sorts of political philosophies, many of which are attractive only to very small proportions of the electorate. Thus, of the ten, perhaps only two or three are conceded to have any chance of winning. Now, according to the previous analysis, a vote for five candidates is nearly three times as efficacious as a vote for one candidate. However, this is virtually meaningless in the present situation and can be very misleading if taken seriously. For example, if the five-candidate voter either votes for all the favorites or votes for none of the favorites—according, say, to the polls (see Chapter 7)—then his vote has no chance of affecting the outcome, whereas the one-candidate voter has some chance of affecting the outcome if he votes for one of the favorites. Clearly, what matters here, as far as influencing the outcome is concerned, is how many of the favorites a voter votes for in the election.

Thus, in an election among $m \geq 3$ candidates, of whom only a specific $m^* < m$ are acknowledged to have any chance of winning, the measure of efficacy proposed earlier makes sense only if it is applied to the reduced set of m^* candidates that constitutes the viable contenders, with k in $E_k(m^*,n)$ denoting the number of the m^* candidates in the focal voter's strategy. Since a vote for all m^* contenders has the same net effect as a vote for no contenders, $E_{m^*}(m^*,n) = E_0(m^*,n) = 0$.

If $m^* \geq 4$, as is often the case in primary elections, the preceding analysis demonstrates that there may be serious discrepancies in the efficacy of voting for different numbers of candidates. This would appear to make approval voting liable to the charge that a voter's ability to affect the outcome can depend on how many of the m^* contenders he votes for in an election.

To be sure, since all voters have the same set of voting strategies, and since approval voting is an anonymous social choice procedure,[4] it could be argued that all voters are equally powerful. Although this is true on one level, it ignores the fact that different voters may be motivated to vote for different numbers of candidates (as determined, in part, by their particular preferences), and it is not at all clear that individuals who vote for different numbers of candidates should be considered equally powerful.

To pursue this further, suppose that three voters use strategies $\{a\}$, $\{b\}$, and $\{a,b\}$, respectively. It might then be argued that the first two voters have equal power, whereas the third has twice the power of the first or the second since his vote is equivalent to the sum of the votes of the first two voters. Suppose, however, that $X = \{a,b,c\}$ and that a fourth voter uses strategy $\{c\}$. Then, since the votes of the third and fourth voters cancel each other out—their combined vote is tantamount to an abstention—it might be thought that these voters are equally powerful. But then the $\{c\}$ voter is twice as powerful as the $\{a\}$ or $\{b\}$ voter. It all seems a bit confusing!

We maintain that the arguments of the preceding paragraph are fallacious, or misleading at best, precisely because they do not account properly for the voters' abilities to affect the outcome of the election. To return to the previous example, suppose in fact that $X = \{a,b,c\}$, and that there are exactly four voters such that:

voter 1 votes for a;
voter 2 votes for b;
voter 3 votes for a and b;
voter 4 votes for c.

The outcome is therefore $\{a,b\}$, whereas the outcomes that would obtain if exactly one voter abstains would be $\{b\}$ if 1 abstains, $\{a\}$ if 2 abstains, $\{a,b,c\}$ if 3 abstains, and $\{a,b\}$ if 4 abstains. Hence, everyone except voter 4 affects the outcome by his particular vote. By using the measure p applied in turn to each voter's abstention outcome versus the actual outcome $\{a,b\}$, we submit that a reasonable measure of the powers of each of the four voters in this example is given by $p(A,B)$: $\frac{1}{2}$, $\frac{1}{2}$, $\frac{1}{3}$ and 0 for voters 1, 2, 3, and 4, respectively, which are relatively equivalent to 3, 3, 2, and 0.

Thus, voter 3—the only voter to vote for two candidates—has neither twice the power of voter 1 nor the same power as voter 4; rather, his power lies between those of voters 1 and 2 and voter 4. Clearly, if there are other voters whose votes help to produce an outcome different from $\{a,b\}$, or if the votes of one or more of the four voters changes, then their relative powers may also change.

When this situation-specific reasoning is generalized to account for all nonabstaining ways that others might vote, it is natural to propose $E_k(m,n)$—the earlier measure of efficacy—as the "power" of a voter who votes for k of m candidates when there are n other voters. In other words, we define the *power* of a voter who uses a particular strategy as the efficacy of that strategy. The conclusions of the preceding analysis then apply in an obvious way to power so conceived. In particular, if $m = 3$ and the electorate is large, then all nonabstaining voters have approximately equal power, whereas if $m \geq 4$ and n is large, voters with values of $k = |S|$ near to $m/2$ have greater power than voters with $|S|$ further away from $m/2$.

5.4. Power and Equity for Dichotomous Voters

Since the concept of power-as-efficacy is broad and undifferentiated, we shall later consider a refinement that takes into account the voters' specific preferences for the candidates. But first we want to show how power considerations impinge on the equity of approval voting and then compare it to plurality voting.

Recall from Definition 2.1 in Section 2.2 that the preferences of a voter are dichotomous if he can divide the set of candidates into two nonempty and disjoint subsets M and L (most-preferred and least-preferred) such that he is indifferent among all candidates in M, indifferent among all candidates in L, and prefers every candidate in M to every candidate in L. In Section 2.4 (Corollary 2.1), we showed that a dichotomous voter's only admissible strategy under approval voting is to vote for all candidates in M.

Since dichotomous voters have a unique admissible strategy, it is natural to define their power to be $E_{|M|}(m,n)$. Regardless of the membership of M, then, all dichotomous voters who vote for $k = |M|$ candidates will have the same power.

When $m = 3$, a dichotomous voter with $k = 1$ has more power than one with $k = 2$, although their powers tend to equalize as n gets large. However, for $m = 4$ (see Section 5.2), a dichotomous voter with $k = 2$ has about 33 percent more power than one with k belonging to $\{1,3\}$, and for $m = 5$ a dichotomous voter with k belonging to $\{2,3\}$ has about 50 percent more power than one with k belonging to $\{1,4\}$. Thus, in an approval voting election among four or more candidates, it "pays" a dichotomous voter to have about half the candidates in his preferred subset, for he will then maximize his effect on the outcome of the election. On the other hand, he is better off in a three-candidate race if he has only one candidate in his preferred subset.

To see this in a different way, suppose that the independent-voters model with equiprobable strategy choices holds along with random tie-breaking. Suppose further that, by convention, a dichotomous voter gets a utility of 1 if one of his preferred candidates is elected, and a utility of 0 if one of his nonpreferred candidates is elected. Then the increase or gain in expected utility that accrues from the vote of a dichotomous voter is simply $E_k(m,n)$. Hence, when $m \geq 4$, dichotomous voters with values of k near to $m/2$ stand to gain more than dichotomous voters who favor either fewer or more of the candidates.[5]

This analysis shows that approval voting gives rise to an inherent inequity among certain types of voters when there are four or more candidates. In view of this, it is appropriate to ask whether other simple voting systems also suffer from a similar type of inequity. We shall answer this question only for single-ballot plurality voting, the most commonly used of multicandidate voting systems.

Under plurality voting, each voter can vote for only one candidate, so there is only one efficacy number for each (m,n) pair, which we denote as $E(m,n)$. It is defined as the average value of $p(A_h,B_h)$ over all ways—indexed by h—that n other voters can vote under the plurality system, where A_h is the outcome that obtains if the focal voter abstains and B_h is the outcome that obtains if he votes for a specific candidate.

Thus, $E(m,n)$ is similar to $E_1(m,n)$ for approval voting, though the two are not identical because of specific differences in the ways others can vote under the two systems. If it is assumed that the n other voters vote independently and each has probability $1/m$ of using each of the nonabstention strategies for plurality voting, and if it is assumed further that ties in outcomes are broken randomly, then

$$E(m,n) = \text{Pr}(x \text{ wins the election when the focal voter votes for } x)$$
$$- \text{Pr}(x \text{ wins the election when the focal voter abstains}),$$

where the latter probability is $1/m$ by the assumptions just given.

Because of the equiprobability assumption, every voter in a plurality-voting election has the same power, namely $E(m,n)$, when there are m candidates and n other voters. But plurality voting is *not* inherently equitable for voters with different types of preferences. In fact, as we shall demonstrate, plurality voting is less equitable than approval voting for dichotomous voters, which is an argument we shall extend in Section 5.5 to nondichotomous voters.

As before, suppose that a dichotomous voter gets a utility of 1 if one of his preferred candidates is elected, and a utility of 0 otherwise. Since the admissible strategies under plurality voting for a dichotomous voter are precisely the single-candidate subsets of M (Corollary 2.3 in Section 2.4), suppose the voter votes for one of the $k = |M|$ candidates in M, say x.

Then, given the assumption used to define $E(m,n)$, his vote for x as compared to an abstention will increase x's chances for election by $E(m,n)$, and, by the symmetry among candidates, it will decrease the chances for election of each of the other $m - 1$ candidates by $E(m,n)/(m - 1)$. Since there are $k - 1$ candidates in M besides x, his increase or gain in expected utility that accrues from his vote is

$$E(m,n) - (k - 1)E(m,n)/(m - 1) = \frac{(m - k)E(m,n)}{m - 1}.$$

Clearly, a dichotomous voter's expected-utility gain under plurality voting is very sensitive to the number of candidates k in his preferred subset. For example, if $m = 5$, then a dichotomous voter with a single preferred candidate ($k = 1$) stands to gain four times as much as a dichotomous voter with four more-preferred candidates ($k = 4$). We conclude that plurality voting is inherently inequitable for dichotomous voters.

To buttress the case further for approval over plurality voting if voters are dichotomous, assume that n is large so that the approximation of $E_k(m,n)$, given in Section 5.2 after Theorem 5.1, applies under approval voting. Then, under approval voting, the ratio of the largest expected-utility gain [at $k = (m - 1)/2$ for odd m, and $k = m/2$ for even

m] to the smallest expected-utility gain [at $k = 1$ or $k = m - 1$] for dichotomous voters is

$$\frac{m + 1}{4} \text{ if } m \text{ is odd,}$$

$$\frac{m^2}{4(m - 1)} \text{ if } m \text{ is even.}$$

Under plurality voting, the ratio of the largest (at $k = 1$) to smallest (at $k = m - 1$) expected-utility gains for dichotomous voters is $m - 1$. These ratios are as follows for m from 3 to 10:

m:	3	4	5	6	7	8	9	10
approval voting:	1	1.33	1.5	1.8	2	2.29	2.5	2.78
plurality voting:	2	3	4	5	6	7	8	9

Thus, according to ratios of largest to smallest expected-utility gains, inequities under plurality voting far outstrip those under approval voting for dichotomous voters. There are, of course, other ways to compare inequities,[6] but it seems safe to say that any reasonable measure will yield the same conclusion.

5.5. Optimal Voting Strategies

So far we have investigated the power of voters and the equity of voting systems only in the case in which voter preferences are dichotomous. To analyze these concepts in more general settings, we again assume that a voter's power depends on the effect his vote has on the outcome of an election. Although an individual's voting power has been conceived of in various ways—including his ability to influence the agenda of alternatives to be considered, and his influence on how other people vote—power-as-efficacy is probably the most common conception in the literature.[7] Indeed, Webster's defines efficacy as "the power to produce an effect," and power as the "ability to act or produce an effect," making these concepts virtually synonymous.

We have followed this usage previously in equating efficacy with power, but power, as Nagel has argued, should also take account of an individual's preferences.[8] "Producing an effect," after all, has an empty ring unless it is one that the voter desires. For dichotomous voters who prefer about half the candidates, they can be both efficacious and satisfy their desires by voting for all their preferred candidates, but the determination of optimal strategies for other voters requires a different formulation.

This formulation is probabilistic and assumes that a focal voter's preferences are characterized by a von Neumann–Morgenstern utility function u on the candidates,[9] and that he votes to maximize his expected utility. As before, we assume n is large, ties are broken randomly, and that each of the n other voters votes independently and has probability $1/(2^m - 2)$ of using each of his $2^m - 2$ nonabstention strategies.

We showed earlier that a voter can maximize his efficacy by voting for about half the candidates. His optimal (i.e., expected-utility maximizing) strategy, however, may be very different from this strategy, as we shall next demonstrate. Hoffman and Merrill have independently derived similar results; in doing so, they consider goals other than expected-utility maximization.[10]

Let $u_1, u_2, \ldots, u_m$ denote the focal voter's von Neumann–Morgenstern utilities for the m candidates, indexed so that $u_1 \geq u_2 \geq \ldots \geq u_m$, and let $\bar{u} = \sum u_i/m$, his average utility. Assume that $u_1 > u_m$, or that $u_1 > \bar{u} > u_m$.

If the focal voter votes for k candidates, he increases the probability of election for *each* of these by $E_k(m,n)/k$, and decreases the probability of election of each of the other $m - k$ candidates by $E_k(m,n)/(m - k)$. Therefore, since $u_1 \geq \ldots \geq u_m$, his maximum gain in expected utility, G_k, when he votes for k candidates rather than abstains is

$$G_k = \sum_{i=1}^{k} u_i E_k(m,n)/k - \sum_{i=k+1}^{m} u_i E_k(m,n)/(m - k)$$

$$= \frac{m E_k(m,n)}{k(m - k)} \left(\sum_{i=1}^{k} u_i - k\bar{u} \right).$$

Substituting for $E_k(m,n)$ the approximation for large n given at the end of Section 5.2, we obtain

$$G_k = mc(m,n) \left(\sum_{i=1}^{k} u_i - k\bar{u} \right).$$

It follows (with negligible error) that $G_{k+1} > G_k$ for $1 \leq k < m - 1$ if and only if $u_{k+1} > \bar{u}$. (The reason is that as long as $u_{k+1} > \bar{u}$, a positive value, $u_{k+1} - \bar{u}$, is added into the summation, in parentheses, in the above equation, making G_k larger as k increases.) Consequently, the focal voter maximizes his expected-utility gain by voting for all candidates whose utilities exceed $\bar{u}$. This rule, which is invariant under so-called positive affine transformations of u, was derived under other assumptions by Merrill and Weber.[11]

Henceforth, let $G_u(m,n)$ denote a voter's *maximum* expected utility gain when he has utility function u, so that, when

$$u_1 \geq u_2 \geq \ldots \geq u_k > \bar{u} \geq u_{k+1} \geq \ldots \geq u_m,$$

$$G_u(m,n) = \frac{mE_k(m,n)}{k(m-k)} \left(\sum_{i=1}^{k} u_i - k\bar{u} \right).$$

We now consider how much $G_u(m,n)$ can vary when all voter utility functions are normalized in a consistent manner.

To assess the variability in G_u for all u when the focal voter votes optimally for k candidates, again assume that the maximum utility he derives from the election of a candidate is 1, the minimum utility is 0. Under this normalization, G_u can be viewed as the fraction of the total variation in u (from 0 to 1) that the individual can gain by voting optimally instead of abstaining.

Under appropriate indexing of the candidates, the set U_k of all normalized utility functions that correspond to an optimal vote for k candidates is the set of all u that satisfy

$$1 = u_1 \geq u_2 \geq \ldots \geq u_k > \bar{u} \geq u_{k+1} \geq \ldots \geq u_m = 0.$$

It is proved elsewhere[12] that

$$1/m \leq \bar{u} \leq 1/2 \text{ for all } u \text{ belonging to } U_1,$$

$$1/(m - k + 1) < \bar{u} \leq k/(k + 1) \text{ for all } u \text{ belonging to}$$
$$U_k, k = 2, \ldots, m - 1,$$

where the bounds on $\bar{u}$ are the best possible. The first bounds are for the special case of $k = 1$ and demonstrate that if the focal voter's optimal strategy is to vote for just one candidate, his average utility can never exceed $\frac{1}{2}$. As k increases, however, and the voter's optimal strategy is to vote for more and more candidates, the upper bound on the voter's average utility increases and approaches one for large k.

Bounds can also be established for G_u which are the best possible:

$$\frac{m}{2(m - 1)} E_1(m,n) \leq G_u(m,n) \leq E_1(m,n) \text{ for all } u \text{ belonging to } U_1,$$

$$\frac{m}{2k(m - k)} E_k(m,n) < G_u(m,n) \leq E_k(m,n) \text{ for all } u \text{ belonging to}$$
$$U_k, k = 2, \ldots, m - 1.$$

The last inequality shows that the ratio of the maximum gain to the minimum gain for all u belonging to U_k is $2k(m - k)/m$. When $m = 3$ and k is either 1 or 2, this ratio equals $\frac{4}{3}$. Hence, in a three-candidate election, one voter may stand to gain about 33 percent more in expected utility than another voter who votes for the same number of candidates.

For $m \geq 4$, the ratio $2k(m - k)/m$ is maximized by integral k near $m/2$; the maximum is

$$m/2 \text{ if } m \text{ is even,}$$

$$(m - 1)(m + 1)/2m \text{ if } m \text{ is odd.}$$

For example, when $m = 4$, the ratio is 2, which means that one voter can enjoy as much as twice the utility gain of another voter when they both maximize utilities by voting for $k = 2$ candidates. Therefore, within U_k—even when voters choose optimal strategies—there can be very significant differences between expected-utility gains for voters with different utility functions.

If E_k in the preceding inequalities for G_u is replaced by the approximation $k(m - k)c(m,n)$ for large n given at the end of Section 5.2, the lower bound on G_u becomes $mc(m,n)/2$ for every k, and the upper bound becomes $k(m - k)c(m,n)$. Hence, the ratio of maximum to minimum gain (when a voter votes optimally for about half the candidates) is $m/2$ for m even and $(m - 1)(m + 1)/(2m)$ for m odd. Thus, the variation in this ratio is essentially linear in m.

Since the lower bound on G_u of $mc(m,n)$ does not depend on k, it may be true that a voter, choosing his optimal strategy of voting for about half the candidates, cannot guarantee a higher expected-utility gain than one choosing a nonoptimal strategy. On the other hand, an optimal strategy does in general allow for the *possibility* of greater gains since the upper bound, $k(m - k)c(m,n)$, is maximized when k is near $m/2$.

When a voter's efficacy and expected-utility gain are considered jointly and $m \geq 4$, a worst-off voter under approval voting is one who has $u_1 = 1$, $u_2 = \cdots u_{m-1} = \frac{1}{2}$ (or $1/2 - \epsilon$), and $u_m = 0$. A best-off voter is one with $u_1 = \cdots = u_k = 1$ and $u_{k+1} = \cdots = u_m = 0$, where $k = m/2$ if m is even, and k is either $(m - 1)/2$ or $(m + 1)/2$ if m is odd. For both the worst-off and best-off voters, the average utility $\bar{u}$ is (approximately) $\frac{1}{2}$, but a voter with the first utility function would vote only for his top candidate (if all but u_1 is less than $\frac{1}{2}$), whereas a voter with the second utility function would vote for the top $m/2$ candidates. Each would derive the same utility of 1 if his top candidate(s) won, but the maximum expected-utility gain, $G_u(m,n)$, and the upper bound on this gain, $E_k(m,n)$, is clearly greater in the second case, for in this case a voter's vote potentially could be efficacious in electing half the candidates (i.e., the $m/2$ with $u_i = 1$).

In Section 5.4 we compared the ratio of maximum to minimum expected-utility gains for a voter with dichotomous preferences under approval and plurality voting. The ratio for plurality voting remains the same when voters' preferences are not necessarily dichotomous, as shown elsewhere,[13] and is equal to

$$(k + 1)(m - k)/(m - k + 1)$$

for utility functions in U_k. By contrast, as we showed earlier in this section, the ratio of maximum to minimum expected-utility gains for approval voting is

$$2k(m - k)/m.$$

These two ratios are equal when either $k = 1$ or $k = m/2$; the plurality ratio exceeds the approval ratio when $k > m/2$; and the approval ratio exceeds the plurality ratio when $1 < k < m/2$.

Since the plurality ratio is as great as the approval ratio for all k, and strictly greater for some k, when m is either 3 or 4, approval voting is more equitable than plurality voting—in the gains sense—for three-candidate and four-candidate elections. When $m \geq 5$, it is possible to have $1 < k < m/2$, so the approval ratio may exceed the plurality ratio. For example, when $m = 5$, the plurality ratio divided by the approval ratio is 1 for $k = 1$, $\frac{15}{16}$ for $k = 2$, $\frac{10}{9}$ for $k = 3$, and $\frac{25}{16}$ for $k = 4$.

A comparison of largest to smallest expected-utility gains for *all* utility functions of U_k yields the following ratios:

m:	3	4	5	6	7	8	9	10
approval voting:	1.33	2	2.40	3	3.43	4	4.44	5
plurality voting:	2	3	4	5	6	7	8	9

Note that the approval voting ratios are consistently higher than those given in Section 5.4 when voter preferences are assumed to be dichotomous, yet they are still less than the plurality ratios for each m.

Thus, in the general case—when voter preferences are not necessarily dichotomous—plurality voting is *more inequitable* in the gains sense than approval voting. Consequently, though plurality voting may appear to be more equitable than approval voting because it forces all voters to vote in the same way,[14] the foregoing analysis demonstrates just the opposite to be true: plurality voting creates greater disparities in expected-utility gains—regardless of the number of candidates and the preferences of voters—when voters choose optimal voting strategies under each system.

5.6. An Asymmetric Example

To conclude on a different note, consider a situation in which a focal voter does not necessarily perceive the world in the symmetric way presumed earlier. If, instead, he views some candidates to be ahead, and some behind, we shall illustrate how he can fashion his approval voting strategy to reflect his perceptions.[15]

Assume that, regardless of the number of candidates, the focal voter believes that only a, b, and c have a chance of winning. He might vote for other candidates, but he knows that such votes cannot affect the outcome. Assume, further, that his preference order is abc, and that his normalized utilities for these candidates are respectively 1, v, and 0, where $0 < v < 1$. With respect to $\{a,b,c\}$, he must decide whether to vote only for a, or for both a and b.

Given that n is large, there are various ways in which the focal voter's decision could make a difference in the outcome. However, by far the most likely of these are the following, based on the votes of the other voters:

1. a and b are tied, and b has at least as many votes as c;
2. b is one vote ahead of a, and b has more votes than c;
3. b and c are tied, and c has at least two more votes than a;
4. c is one vote ahead of b, and two or more ahead of a.

In the first two events, the focal voter is better off voting for a; in the latter two he is better off voting for both a and b.

Under normal circumstances, the focal voter's subjective probabilities for events 1 and 2 will be virtually identical, and the same will be true for events 3 and 4. If s_i is his subjective probability for event i, and tie breaking is done randomly, the focal voter's expected utility from voting for a only, minus his expected utility from voting for both a and b, will be approximately $[(3 + v)s_1 + vs_3]/2 - [(1 + 3v)s_1 + 3vs_3]/2$. (The calculations leading to this result are straightforward and will not be shown.) This difference is positive if and only if $v < s_1/(s_1 + s_3)$. Therefore, an approximately optimal decision rule will be to vote for a but not b if

$$v < 1/(1 + s_3/s_1),$$

and to vote for both a and b if

$$v > 1/(1 + s_3/s_1).$$

An attractive feature of this rule is that it does not require separate assessments of s_1 and s_3—which are likely to be very small—but asks only for an assessment of the ratio s_3/s_1.

It would, of course, be very interesting to evaluate the extent to which voters adhere to this rule—without prior guidance in its use—in an approval-voting election among three prime contenders. More generally, it would seem worthwhile to attempt to find out why voters do or do not vote for just first, versus both first and second, choices in such an election. In the absence of knowledge on this point, we shall suggest in the next four chapters, as we did for elections analyzed previously, plausible assumptions one might make to approximate approval voting results in multicandidate races.

5.7. Conclusions

The efficacy of a voting strategy is a measure of that strategy's ability, on the average, to change the outcome of an election from what it would be if the voter in question abstained. In large electorates, the most efficacious approval voting strategies are for a focal voter to vote for either the top one or top two candidates in three-candidate contests, approximately the top half of all candidates in more populous contests, given that all possible ways that other voters can vote are equiprobable and ties are broken randomly.

We defined the power of a voter who uses a particular strategy to be the efficacy of that strategy, which does not take account of the voter's specific preferences for the candidates. When cardinal utilities are associated with the preferences of a voter, his utility-maximizing strategy in large electorates is to vote for all candidates whose utilities exceed his average utility over all the candidates.

A voter's optimal strategy can lead to substantially different expected-utility gains, depending on his utilities for the various candidates. However, plurality voting gains are even more disparate—despite the fact that every voter is restricted to voting for just one candidate—so approval voting is more equitable. When there is situation-specific information about the standing of candidates—indicating who is viable and what the most likely outcomes are—it is possible to derive optimal strategies based on this information, and a voter's utility function, that reflect the perceived asymmetric positions of the candidates.

The results on equity, we believe, offer strong evidence that approval voting is fairer to the individual voter than plurality voting. Not only is he likely to be more efficacious under approval voting, but when he is not he cannot suffer as severe deprivations—that is, power losses—as under plurality voting. While these differences between the two voting systems are most pronounced when voter preferences are dichotomous, they are still substantial when voters have general preference orders. Thus, we conclude that the voter, in being able to exercise power more effectively under approval voting because of the greater number of options available to him, is also treated more fairly under this system than under plurality voting.

Footnotes to Chapter 5

1. Peter C. Fishburn and Steven J. Brams, "Efficacy, Power, and Equity under Approval Voting," *Public Choice* **37**, 3 (1981), 425–434.

2. The most efficacious strategies also maximize the likelihood that a Condorcet candidate will be selected, linking efficacy to the Condorcet results of Chapter 3. See William V. Gehrlein and Peter C. Fishburn, "Constant Scoring Rules for Choosing One among Many Alternatives," *Quality and Quantity* **15**, 2 (April 1981), 203–210.

3. William H. Riker, *Liberalism Against Populism: A Confrontation Between the Theory of Democracy and the Theory of Social Choice* (San Francisco: W. H. Freeman, 1981), p. 110.

4. Peter C. Fishburn, "Symmetric and Consistent Aggregation with Dichotomous Voting," in *Aggregation and Revelation of Preferences*, edited by Jean-Jacques Laffont (Amsterdam: North-Holland, 1979), pp. 201–218.

5. There is, of course, an element of interpersonal utility comparison in this type of analysis. In scaling all voters' utilities from 0 to 1, gains in expected utility are relative to the differences in utility between voters' most-preferred and least-preferred candidates. If utilities were not normalized in this way, then gain could be defined as the difference in expected utility accruing from a strategy, divided by (maximum utility) − (minimum utility). The present treatment does not differentiate between voters who feel they have a great deal to win or lose according to the results of an election and those who have only a cursory interest in the outcome.

6. Dale T. Hoffman, "Relative Efficiency of Voting Systems: The Cost of Sincere Behavior" (mimeographed, 1979); and Robert J. Weber, "Comparison of Voting Systems" (mimeographed, 1977).

7. John F. Banzhaf, "Weighted Voting Doesn't Work: A Mathematical Analysis," *Rutgers Law Review* **19**, 2 (Winter 1965), 317–343; Peter C. Fishburn and William V. Gehrlein, "Collective Rationality versus Distribution of Power for Binary Social Choice Functions," *Journal of Economic Theory* **15**, 1 (June 1977), 72–91; William F. Riker, "Some Ambiguities in the Notion of Power," *American Political Science Review* **48**, 3 (September 1964), 787–792.

8. Jack H. Nagel, *The Descriptive Analysis of Power* (New Haven: Yale University Press, 1975).

9. John von Neumann and Oskar Morgenstern, *Theory of Games and Economic Behavior*, 3d Ed. (Princeton: Princeton University Press, 1953); and Peter C. Fishburn, *Utility Theory for Decision Making* (New York: John Wiley and Sons, 1970).

10. D. T. Hoffman, "Relative Efficiency of Voting Systems: The Cost of Sincere Behavior (mimeographed, 1979); Samuel Merrill, III, "Strategic Voting in Multicandidate Elections under Uncertainty and Under Risk," in *Power, Voting, and Voting Power,* edited by Manfred J. Holler, (Würzburg: Physica-Verlag, 1982), pp. 179–187; S. Merrill, III, "Decision Analysis of Multicandidate Voting Systems," UMAP Module 384 (Newton, MA: Education Development Center, n.d.); S. Merrill, III, "Strategic Decisions under One-Stage Multicandidate Voting Systems," *Public Choice* **36**, 1 (1981), 115–134; and S. Merrill, III, "A Comparison of Multicandidate Electoral Systems in Terms of Optimal Voting Strategies," *American Journal of Political Science* (forthcoming). Merrill compares a variety of voting systems (under the assumption of

optimal voting strategies), including ranking systems like the Borda method, in the aforementioned papers and makes empirical estimates of the performance of candidates in the 1972 Democratic Party primaries under different systems in "Decision Analysis of Multicandidate Voting Systems," and "Strategic Decisions under One-Stage Multicandidate Voting Systems" (see Section 8.3 for a discussion of these elections).

11. Samuel Merrill, III, "Approval Voting: A 'Best Buy' Method for Multicandidate Elections?" *Mathematics Magazine* **52,** 2 (March 1979), 98–102; R. J. Weber, "Comparison of Voting Systems" (mimeographed, 1977).

12. Peter C. Fishburn and Steven J. Brams, "Expected Utility and Approval Voting," *Behavioral Science* **26,** 2 (April 1981), 136–142.

13. P. C. Fishburn and S. J. Brams, "Expected Utility and Approval Voting."

14. In a sense, all voters under approval voting vote in the same way, too: they vote for and against—by not voting—all the candidates. Under "direct approval voting," voters would actually disapprove of (by voting "no") those candidates they did not approve of (for whom they vote "yes"), which Morin argues would clarify the purpose of an approval voting election (personal communication to Brams, September 21, 1980), though it is formally equivalent to approval voting. See Richard A. Morin, *Structural Reform: Ballots* (New York: Vantage Press, 1980).

15. For other asymmetric examples, see S. Merrill, III, "Approval Voting: A 'Best-Buy' Method For Multicandidate Elections?"; Dale T. Hoffman, "A Model for Strategic Voting," *SIAM Journal on Applied Mathematics* **42,** 4 (August 1982), 751–761.

Chapter 6
Deducing Condorcet Candidates from Election Data

6.1. Introduction

The theoretical results on power and equity in the previous chapter describe attributes of voting systems but give little insight into their performance in practice. Similarly, the earlier findings on sincerity, strategy-proofness, and Condorcet candidates facilitate theoretical comparisons among different systems but do not demonstrate whether, in a particular election, a Condorcet candidate was or could have been elected if voting was sincere.

In Chapter 4, by contrast, we tried to show, in a detailed reconstruction of an intriguing House election, that the extant voting rules prevented the selection of the likely Condorcet candidate, but other rules—particularly, approval voting—probably would have reversed this anti-majoritarian bias. Yet, this case study was just that—an analysis of a unique event from which it is difficult to generalize, except perhaps in the relatively few elections that use elimination rules similar to the House's.

These rules, and the multiple ballots they engendered, generated more information about voting behavior than is usual in single-ballot or runoff elections. Moreover, other information about the preferences of House members in this election could be surmised from extensive reporting on this election that supplemented the ballot analysis and provided grounds for a more refined assessment of the actual and hypothetical results.

In later chapters, we shall attempt to reconstruct preference and voting-behavior information about other elections, including recent presidential elections, and draw conclusions about the probable results under alternative rules. But in this chapter we want to lay the groundwork for inferring from election totals, and approval voting ballot data, whether or not a voting system produced a Condorcet candidate. Complementing this theoretical analysis, we shall examine survey and election data from a mayoral election in Boston that will illustrate how some of the theoretical findings can be applied to empirical data. We shall also consider how voting for different numbers of candidates under approval voting affects conclusions that can be drawn about the likelihood that a Condorcet candidate was elected.

6.2. Deductions from Election Totals

In Section 3.2 (Theorem 3.1) we showed that approval voting invariably elects a Condorcet candidate if and only if the preferences of all voters are dichotomous. When the preferences of some voters are trichotomous or multichotomous, we also showed (Section 3.6, Theorem 3.5) that ordinary approval voting better ensures the election of a Condorcet candidate than any other nonranked voting system, including runoff systems, given that such a candidate exists—that is, when there is no paradox of voting caused by cyclical majorities.

In Chapter 3 we started from assumptions about the preferences of voters and deduced consequences that they have for election outcomes. Throughout we assumed that voters, while they might vote insincerely, would choose only admissible strategies—that is, those not dominated by any other strategies.

Now we shall reverse this orientation in this chapter and, starting from election returns, ask whether they imply that the winner must be a Condorcet candidate. In fact, the assumptions to be described shortly imply that it is never possible to conclude that a plurality winner must be a Condorcet candidate, except under very restrictive conditions. The conditions are less restrictive under approval voting, but the winner may be a Condorcet candidate if they are not met (i.e., the conditions are sufficient but not necessary).

Let $m \geq 3$ denote the number of candidates, identified as $a_1, a_2, \ldots,$ a_m. For simplicity, and to adhere to the most interesting practical cases, we consider only the cases $m = 3$ and $m = 4$. As before, a voting system is specified by a nonempty subset s of $\{1, 2, \ldots, m - 1\}$. Under system s, each voter votes for k candidates, for any k belonging to s. There are three systems for $m = 3$: plurality voting, or $s = \{1\}$; "vote for two," or $s = \{2\}$; and approval voting, or $s = \{1,2\}$. For $m = 4$, there are seven systems: $\{1\}$, $\{2\}$, $\{3\}$, $\{1,2\}$, $\{1,3\}$, $\{2,3\}$, and $\{1,2,3\}$; the first describes plurality voting, the last approval voting.

To determine if the winner under system s must be a Condorcet candidate, information on several parameters is required: (i) the types of preference orders over $\{a_1, \ldots, a_m\}$ that voters may have, (ii) the types of voting strategies they may use as a function of their preference orders and s; and (iii) the nature of the election data that are available for analysis. We shall describe each of these in turn.[1]

First, we assume that a voter can have any nontrivial weak preference order on $\{a_1, \ldots, a_m\}$. He thus partitions the alternatives into two or more indifference sets that are ordered by strict preference. A voter with order $a_1 a_2 a_3 a_4$ prefers a_1 to a_2 to a_3 to a_4; one with order $(a_1 a_2)(a_3 a_4)$ is indifferent between a_1 and a_2, and between a_3 and a_4, and prefers a_1 and a_2 to a_3 and a_4. As assumed in Section 2.4, where we used slightly different notation for the candidates, parentheses enclose indifferent candidates.

Second, a voter will be assumed to use any voting strategy that is admissible for the given system s and his preference order P, as defined by Theorem 2.2 in Section 2.4. Roughly speaking, strategy S—which is a nonempty subset of $\{a_1, \ldots, a_m\}$—is admissible if $|S|$ belongs to s and there is no strategy T such that $|T|$ belongs to s and T dominates S. For example, with $s = \{1,2,3\}$ and $P = a_1(a_2 a_3)a_4$, the voter's admissible strategies are $\{a_1\}$, $\{a_1,a_2\}$, $\{a_1,a_3\}$, and $\{a_1,a_2,a_3\}$. However, if $s = \{2\}$, his admissible strategies are $\{a_1,a_2\}$, $\{a_1,a_3\}$, $\{a_1,a_4\}$, and $\{a_2,a_3\}$. Surprisingly, the latter two strategies involve voting for one's worst candidate (a_4), or not for one's best (a_1), respectively. One might choose the former strategy because voting for a_2 or a_3 instead of a_4 could result in a_1's defeat; one might choose the latter strategy because voting for a_1 instead of a_2 or a_3 could ensure a_4's victory.

Third, the election data used are what one would expect to be publicly available, namely the number n of voters and the number n_i of votes for candidate a_i, $i = 1, \ldots, m$. For plurality voting, $\Sigma n_i = n$, but under approval voting Σn_i could lie anywhere between n and $(m - 1)n$, should every voter approve of all but one candidate. Voters' preferences, and the numbers who choose each feasible strategy, are not assumed to be known, except to the extent that they can be deduced from n and the n_i.

The results to be given in Section 6.3 critically depend on the preceding assumptions. Because of the varieties of strategies that are allowed and the paucity of detail about how people voted, the likelihood of concluding that the winner is a Condorcet candidate, as will be seen, is often very small if not zero. Needless to say, more detailed data and/or less liberal strategy assumptions could increase this likelihood substantially, as we shall show in subsequent sections.

6.3. Results for Three and Four Candidates

Consider first the case of an election involving just three candidates. Assume, with no loss in generality, that a_1 is the winner, with $n_1 > n_2 \geq n_3$, when $m = 3$. Then, as Theorem 6.1 shows, one can conclude from the election returns above that a_1 is a Condorcet candidate only if approval voting is used.

Theorem 6.1. *If* s = {*1*} *or* s = {*2*}, *then it is impossible to conclude with certainty that* a₁ *is a Condorcet candidate. If* s = {*1,2*}, *then* a₁ *must be a Condorcet candidate if and only if*

$$n_1 > n/2 + \min\{n_2, n_1 + n_2 + n_3 - n\}. \tag{6.1}$$

Inequality (6.1) is illustrated in Figure 6.1, where $p_i = n_i/n$, the proportion of voters who voted for a_i. For presentational compactness, the abscissa (horizontal axis) and ordinate (vertical axis) are $p_1 + p_3$ and $p_2 + p_3$. As in the theorem, we assume that $p_1 > p_2 \geq p_3$. The large four-sided area represents all p that satisfy $1 \leq \Sigma p_i \leq 2$ and $p_1 > p_2 \geq p_3$. The upper four-sided region, including the two lower dashed boundaries, is the region in which inequality (6.1) is false. The lower four-sided region, excluding its upper boundaries, is where (6.1) holds.

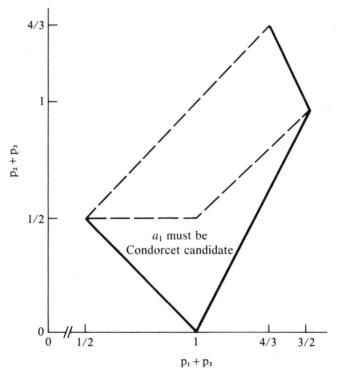

Figure 6.1 Region in which a_1 must be a Condorcet candidate under approval voting when $m = 3$ and $n_1 > n_2 \geq n_3$. (Source: Peter C. Fishburn, "Deducing Majority Candidates from Election Data," *Social Science Research* **9**, 3 [September 1980], 219; Figure 1; reprinted with permission.)

To illustrate Theorem 6.1, assume there are 100 voters, and $n_1 = 40$, $n_2 = 35$, and $n_3 = 25$. Because

$$40 < 100/2 + \min\{35,0\} = 50 + 0 = 50,$$

it cannot be asserted *from the vote totals alone* that a_1 is a Condorcet candidate, though in fact he may be. That is, the preference orders of the voters may be such that a_1 would defeat both a_2 and a_3 in separate pairwise contests, but the totals and the assumption that all voters use only admissible approval voting strategies are insufficient to establish this claim.

Now, in the previous example, it was implicitly assumed that each voter cast one approval vote—necessarily for his most-preferred candidate—since the number of votes cast (100) was equal to the number of voters. (Equivalently, the number of voters casting two approval votes, $n_1 + n_2 + n_3 - n$, was 0.) Altering this example, assume that a_1 receives double the number of approval votes he got before (40), but the other candidates stay the same: $n_1 = 80$, $n_2 = 35$, and $n_3 = 25$. Still, since

$$80 < 100/2 + \min\{35,40\} = 50 + 35 = 105,$$

one cannot conclude that a_1 is a Condorcet candidate, even though his vote total (80) now substantially exceeds the combined vote total (60) of the other two candidates. In fact, only when $n_1 = 86$, with $n_2 = 35$ and $n_3 = 25$ as before, is the inequality reversed:

$$86 > 100/2 + \min\{35,46\} = 50 + 35 = 85.$$

In other words, a_1's approval vote total (86) must be 43 percent more than a_2 and a_3's combined total (60) before one can be assured from the returns alone that he is a Condorcet candidate. Indeed, as shown in Figure 6.1, as long as $p_2 + p_3$ is greater than $\frac{1}{2}$, $p_1 + p_3$ must be greater than 1 for it to be *possible* to conclude that a_1 is a Condorcet candidate. Obviously, a_1 must do extremely well, compared with a_2 and a_3, to ensure that he is a Condorcet candidate under approval voting.

No victory, whatever the magnitude, can provide this assurance if plurality voting, or "vote for (exactly) two," is the voting system in use. For example, assume a_1 receives 100 percent of the plurality vote in an election. If a_2 were the first choice of 51 percent of a_1's supporters, but they had (foolishly) voted for a_1—their second choice—for strategic reasons, then a_2 would be the Condorcet candidate, despite a_1's unanimous election. Hence, nothing definite can be concluded about whether there is a Condorcet candidate and, if so, who it is in a plurality election.

We now turn to the four-candidate case. Assume, with no loss in generality, that a_1 is the winner, with $n_1 > n_2 \geq n_3 \geq n_4$, when $m = 4$.

Theorem 6.2. *If* s *is any one of the seven voting systems for* m $= 4$ *other than* $\{1,2\}$ *and* $\{1,2,3\}$, *then it is impossible to conclude with certainty that* a_1 *is a Condorcet candidate. If either* s $= \{1,2\}$ *or* s $= \{1,2,3\}$, *then* a_1 *must be a Condorcet candidate if and only if*

$$n/2 > n_2 + n_3 + n_4.$$

For example, if s allows voters to vote for one candidate or for two candidates, and perhaps for three as well, then, when there are 100 voters, one can conclude that a_1 is a Condorcet candidate if and only if the combined vote total of the other three is less than 50. Since $s = \{1,2\}$ implies that $\Sigma n_i \le n \le 2\Sigma n_i$, and $s = \{1,2,3\}$ implies that $\Sigma n_i \le n \le 3\Sigma n_i$, there is a sense in which $s = \{1,2\}$ is more likely than $s = \{1,2,3\}$ to allow the conclusion that the winner is a Condorcet candidate. This is so because, with $n = 100$, it would seem more likely that $n_2 + n_3 + n_4 < 50$ under $s = \{1,2\}$ than under $s = \{1,2,3\}$, for the former system allows no more than 200 votes *in toto* while the latter system (approval voting) allows as many as 300 votes *in toto*.

6.4. Modified Assumptions and Disaggregated Data

As noted earlier, the assumptions on which Theorems 6.1 and 6.2 are based are not very generous in allowing the conclusion that the winner must be a majority candidate. For $m = 3$, only the approval voting system permits this conclusion, and then only if the winner has votes from more than half the voters (50 in the previous example) plus the smaller of the number of votes received by the second-place candidate (35 in the example) and the number of voters who voted for two candidates (0, 40, and 46 in the example). When $m = 4$, one can conclude that the winner is a Condorcet candidate if the combined votes for the three losers is less than $n/2$, and then only if system $s = \{1,2\}$ or $s = \{1,2,3\}$ is used.

In view of the lack of results for plurality voting, can anything be concluded about the winner's being a Condorcet candidate under plurality voting when the earlier assumptions we posited are modified? Suppose first that the strategic voting assumption is dropped: assume instead that all voters vote sincerely, i.e., for a most-preferred candidate. Then, as before, one cannot conclude that the winner must be a Condorcet candidate even if he receives every vote but one, for it could be true that everyone who votes for a_1 is indifferent between a_1 and a_2, but a_2 is preferred by one voter, making him the Condorcet candidate. (Only if a_1 received every vote could he be assured of being a Condorcet candidate, but not necessarily a strict, or unique, one.)

Suppose next that the original strategic voting assumption is retained, and change only the presumed types of allowable preference orders, assuming that no voter is ever indifferent between any two candidates. Again, it is impossible under plurality voting to conclude that the winner must be a Condorcet candidate because of insincere voting on the part of one or more voters. However, taking the two modifications together, if it is assumed that voters have strict preference orders and also vote sincerely, then plurality voting implies that the winner, a_1, must be a Condorcet candidate if and only if $n_1 > n_2 + \ldots + n_m$, or $n_1 > n/2$. In other words, a candidate is assuredly Condorcet under plurality voting if and only if he receives more than half the votes, given sincere voting and strict preferences on the part of all voters.

The ballot data assumed in Section 6.2 were the aggregate number of nonabstaining voters and the aggregate number of votes received by each candidate; Condorcet candidates were inferred on the basis of the preferences of the nonabstaining voters. To carry the analysis a step further, we shall now posit a richer data base that disaggregates the totals for each candidate.

In particular, we shall assume that $n(S)$, the number of voters who voted for all the candidates in S but for no other candidates, is known for each nonempty proper subset S of candidates. We shall also assume, as before, that voters are concerned and hence no voter votes for all the candidates. Thus, the number of voters n on which majorities are based is the sum of the $n(S)$ over the nonempty proper subsets of candidates.

In Section 6.5 we shall give the basic assumptions underlying the analysis of disaggregated data, including what voters' approval voting ballots reveal about their preferences. We shall use these assumptions to derive conclusions about majorities as functions of the ballot data, which are then illustrated in this section and Section 6.6.

The empirical example discussed in Section 6.7 is based on data from a Boston mayoral election, whose analysis strongly suggests that the winner among the five candidates was a Condorcet candidate. The effects of the numbers of candidates that voters vote for on the likelihood of being able to conclude that the winner of an approval voting election must be a Condorcet candidate will then be briefly examined.

6.5. Analysis of Approval Voting Ballot Data[2]

We begin with specific assumptions about voters' preferences and the ways that they vote. These vary in their restrictiveness and allow one to derive different conclusions about Condorcet candidates from approval voting ballot data.

It will be assumed that a voter partitions the set X of candidates into two or more indifference classes $X_1, \ldots, X_K$ such that he is indifferent among all candidates in each X_i, and prefers all candidates in X_i to all candidates in X_j whenever $i < j$. Thus, X_1 is his most-preferred subset, and X_K is his least-preferred subset.

We shall say that a voter uses strategy S included in X when he votes for all candidates in S and votes for no candidate in the complement of S. Three increasingly restrictive assumptions about the voting behavior of nonabstaining voters will be considered:

A1. Each voter uses an admissible strategy (Section 2.4);
A2. Each voter uses a sincere admissible strategy (Section 2.5);
A3. Each voter uses a strongly sincere admissible strategy (to be defined).

Suppose a voter's ordered indifference classes are $X_1, \ldots, X_K$. Then a sincere admissible strategy S is *strongly sincere* if, for all X_i, all members of X_i are contained in S whenever $X_i \cap S \neq \emptyset$. That is, whenever S contains at least one member of X_i (the intersection is not empty), it contains all members of X_i. Although it is reasonable to expect voters to use strongly sincere admissible strategies in most situations, there are cases in which it may be to a voter's advantage to use a strategy that is not strongly sincere or even insincere.

When X contains exactly three candidates, it is easily seen that A1, A2, and A3 are equivalent. For example, if a voter's preference order is $a_1 a_2 a_3$, his admissible strategies are $\{a_1\}$ and $\{a_1, a_2\}$, both of which contain his most-preferred candidate a_1 and neither of which contains his least-preferred candidate, a_3, satisfying the definition of admissibility under approval voting. These strategies are sincere because if the voter votes for a_2, he also votes for a_1; and strongly sincere because whenever a_1 or a_2 is included in strategy S, all members in the indifference class it represents, X_1 and X_2 (i.e., one member in each), are contained in S.

There are, however, admissible strategies that are not sincere (satisfy only A1) when $K \geq 4$—an example is $\{a_1, a_3\}$ when the voter has preference order $a_1 a_2 a_3 a_4$. And there are sincere admissible strategies that are not strongly sincere (satisfy only A1 and A2) when some X_i for $1 < i < K$ contains two or more candidates.

The approval voting ballot data indicate voters' strategies without necessarily revealing their complete preference orders. For example, if $X = \{a_1, a_2, a_3\}$ and $S = \{a_3\}$, then under A1 a_3 must be preferred to a_1 and a_2, but whether a_1 is preferred to a_2, or a_2 is preferred to a_1, or a_1 is indifferent to a_2, cannot be ascertained. Hence, to examine what must be true of the data in order to conclude with certainty that one candidate has a majority over another candidate, it is necessary to consider preference orders that can give rise to each strategy. Accordingly, we shall say that a preference order on X is *consistent* with strategy S and assumption Ak if S satisfies Ak for that preference order.

Definition 6.1. Given ballot data $n(S)$ for all nonempty S that are properly included in X, and given candidates x,y belonging to X, write $x >_k y$ if and only if more voters prefer x to y than prefer y to x for every possible assignment of preference orders to voters that are consistent with their strategies and assumption Ak.

For example, $x >_2 y$ means that x must have a majority over y regardless of voters' preference orders so long as their orders adhere to A2 for the strategies revealed by the ballot data. In the following theorem, "iff" means "if and only if," $X\backslash\{y\}$ is the set of all candidates except y, and $|A|$ is the number of elements in set A.

Theorem 6.3. *Given* x,y *belonging to* X *and* n(S) *for each nonempty* S *properly included in* X, *let* n *be the sum of the* n(S). *Then, when* $|X| \geq$ 3,

$$x >_1 y \text{ iff } n(\{x\}) + n(X\backslash\{y\}) > n/2;$$

$$x >_2 y \text{ iff } n(\{x\}) + n(X\backslash\{y\}) + \sum_{\substack{\{\text{all } S \text{ such that } x \text{ belongs} \\ \text{to } S, \, y \text{ does not belong to } S, \\ 1 < |S| < |X| - 1\}}} n(S)/2 > n/2;$$

$$x >_3 y \text{ iff } \sum_{\substack{\{\text{all } S \text{ such that } x \text{ belongs} \\ \text{to } S, \, y \text{ does not belong to } S\}}} n(S) > n/2.$$

Theorem 6.3 can be applied to each pair $\{x,y\}$ when x wins the election to determine whether x must be a Condorcet candidate. Consider, for example, a three-candidate election among a_1, a_2, and a_3 when there are 100 voters with ballot data $(n_1, n_2, n_3, n_{12}, n_{13}, n_{23}) = (38, 20, 9, 10, 15, 8)$, where $n_i = n(\{a_i\})$ and $n_{ij} = n(\{a_i,a_j\})$. Then a_1 must have a majority over a_2 since $n_1 + n_{13} = 53 > 50 = n/2$. However, one cannot conclude that a_1 must have a majority over a_3 since $n_1 + n_{12} < 50$.

Since there must be at least four candidates before differences arise among A1, A2, and A3, we present an example that illustrates these differences. With $X = \{a_1, a_2, a_3, a_4\}$, suppose again that $n = 100$ and, under the notational convention of the preceding paragraph, let

$$
\begin{aligned}
n_1 &= 42, \\
n_2 &= 31, \\
n_{12} &= 5, \\
n_{13} &= 2, \\
n_{14} &= 6, \\
n_{123} &= 2, \\
n_{124} &= 3, \\
n_{134} &= 9,
\end{aligned}
$$

with all other $n(S) = 0$. Since $n_1 + n_{134} > 50$, $a_1 >_1 a_2$, but one cannot conclude that a_1 has a majority over either a_3 or a_4 on the basis of A1. However, $a_1 >_2 a_3$ since $n_1 + n_{124} + (n_{12} + n_{14})/2 > 50$, whereas it is not true that $a_1 >_2 a_4$ since $n_1 + n_{123} + (n_{12} + n_{13})/2 < 50$. Finally, since $n_1 + n_{12} + n_{13} + n_{123} > 50$, $a_1 >_3 a_4$, and therefore a_1 must be a Condorcet candidate when A3 holds.

We next contrast Theorem 6.3 with Theorem 6.1 to show what can be gained from more detailed ballot data. We shall do this for $X = \{a_1, a_2, a_3\}$, with n_i and n_{ij} as before. In addition, let N_i be the total votes for a_i, so that $N_1 = n_1 + n_{12} + n_{13}$, $N_2 = n_2 + n_{12} + n_{23}$, and $N_3 = n_3 + n_{13} + n_{23}$. Assume that a_1 has the most votes. Given the more detailed data used above, Theorem 6.3 says that a_1 must be a Condorcet candidate if and only if

$$
n_1 + n_{12} > n/2;
$$

$$
n_1 + n_{13} > n/2.
$$

On the other hand, given only the N_i totals, along with n, Theorem 6.1 says that one can conclude that a_1 must be a Condorcet candidate if and only if

$$
N_1 > n/2 + \min\{N_3, N_1 + N_2 + N_3 - n\};
$$

$$
N_1 > n/2 + \min\{N_2, N_1 + N_2 + N_3 - n\}.
$$

When each N_i is replaced by its expression in n_i and the n_{ij}, these inequalities reduce to

$$
n_1 + n_{12} > n/2 + n_{23} + \min\{n_3, n_{12}\},
$$

$$
n_1 + n_{13} > n/2 + n_{23} + \min\{n_2, n_{13}\},
$$

which obviously imply the initial pair of inequalities in this paragraph.

Although we shall not make a detailed comparison of the two pairs of inequalities, it should be clear that there are numerous ways in which one could conclude that a_1 must be a Condorcet candidate when the more detailed data are available but not when only the aggregated N_i data are available. Suppose, for example, that n_1, n_{12}, and n_{13} account for 40, 20, and 15 percent of the ballots, respectively, so that $n_1 + n_{12} = 0.60n > n/2$ and $n_1 + n_{13} = 0.55n > n/2$. Then, if only the aggregated data were available, one could never conclude that a_1 is a Condorcet candidate since either $n_{23} + \min\{n_3, n_{12}\}$ must account for at least 10 percent of the ballots, or $n_{23} + \min\{n_2, n_{13}\}$ must account for at least 5 percent of the ballots. In Section 6.6 we shall apply Theorem 6.3 to actual election data to illustrate its usefulness.

6.6. An Empirical Example and Probabilistic Analysis

Consider the five-candidate election in 1959 for mayor of Boston that has been analyzed in detail by Levin.[3] The actual election was conducted in two stages. The first stage was a plurality election that included five candidates: Powers, Collins, Piemonte, Hennigan, and McMorrow. The second stage was a runoff election between Powers and Collins, who had the most votes (34 and 22 percent, respectively) in the primary. Collins won the runoff with 114,074 votes to Powers's 90,035, despite the fact that Powers was the plurality winner in the first election by a substantial margin.

Although this election was not conducted by approval voting, it is possible to reconstruct plausible approval voting patterns from the ballot data and Levin's survey data. We do not claim total accuracy for the reconstruction but rather present it to illustrate what might have occurred under approval voting. As will be seen, the assumptions to be made tend to exaggerate the figures for Collins and Powers relative to the others because of their entry in the runoff, but the exaggeration may not be too great in view of the fact that both candidates were the prime contenders. In addition, the assumptions limit approval voting strategies to no more than two candidates, although this seems not a severe restriction since it appears that most voters in a five-candidate election would not vote for more than two candidates.[4]

We shall assume that a voter would have voted in an approval voting election if and only if he voted either in the primary or runoff election. The following two assumptions then govern the approval voting strategies:

1. A voter who voted for only one candidate (i.e., either abstained in the first election or runoff, or else voted for the same candidate in both) would have voted only for that candidate under approval voting.
2. A voter who voted for two different candidates in the first election and runoff would have voted for exactly those two in an approval voting election.

These assumptions, and Levin's election and survey data, yield the following approximate percentages, or $100[n(S)/n]$, for the indicated strategies:

Strategy	$100[n(S)/n]$
Powers	29
Collins	46
Piemonte	1
Hennigan	1
McMorrow	1
Powers & Collins	3
Powers & Piemonte	3
Powers & Hennigan	2
Powers & McMorrow	1
Collins & Piemonte	6
Collins & Hennigan	4
Collins & McMorrow	3
Total	100

Although no conclusions about a Condorcet candidate are possible under A1, either of the very plausible A2 and A3 hypotheses implies that Collins was the Condorcet candidate. For example, A2 gives Collins $>_2$ Powers since $46 + (6 + 4 + 3)/2 > 50$, Collins $>_2$ Piemonte since $46 + (3 + 4 + 3)/2 > 50$ (this is the closest comparison for Collins), and so forth.

Hence, despite the vulnerability of the earlier reconstruction assumptions, there are reasonable grounds to believe that Collins would have defeated each of the other candidates by a substantial margin in pairwise contests. (By contrast, recall that in the reconstruction of the House Majority Leader election in 1976 in Chapter 4, the approval voting winner would probably have been different from the person actually chosen in the elimination contest that occurred.) In view of this, it is interesting to note that Collins came close to missing the runoff since Piemonte, who came in third in the primary, got 20 percent of the first election vote compared to Collins's 22 percent.

The previous figures for approval voting strategies give the following percentages of electorate support for each candidate in the hypothetical approval voting election:

Powers	38
Collins	62
Piemonte	10
Hennigan	7
McMorrow	5

The discrepancy between Piemonte's 10 percent here and his 20 percent in the first election is due mainly to the reconstruction assumptions and the fact that fewer than half the total number of people who voted in the runoff election voted in the first election. Because of the runoff effect on the analysis, the figures for Piemonte, Hennigan, and McMorrow in an approval voting election would probably have been somewhat greater than those given above, whereas the figures for Powers and Collins might have been slightly less than their estimated 38 and 62 percent approval, respectively.

To conclude this section, we shall illustrate Theorem 6.3 further by examining the effect of the numbers of candidates that voters vote for on the likelihood of being able to conclude that the winner of an approval voting election is a Condorcet candidate. We shall focus on the three-candidate case and let $X = \{a_1, a_2, a_3\}$, $n_i = n(\{a_i\})$, and $n_{ij} = n(\{a_i, a_j\})$.

A probabilistic choice model will be used to analyze the effect of strategy sizes. The model assumes that voters vote independently according to the following choice probabilities:

$p/3$ is the probability that a voter uses $S = \{a_i\}$ for $i = 1,2,3$;

$(1 - p)/3$ is the probability that a voter uses $S = \{a_i, a_j\}$ for

$$(i,j) = (1,2), (1,3), (2,3).$$

Thus, $p = \Pr\{|S| = 1\}$ and $1 - p = \Pr\{|S| = 2\}$.

Let $P_n(p)$ be the probability that the resultant ballot data imply that there must be a Condorcet candidate, given n voters, and let $n^* = (n + 1)/2$ if n is odd, and $n^* = n/2 + 1$ is n is even. Then, by Theorem 6.3 and the symmetry of the choice probabilities in a_1, a_2, and a_3,

$$\begin{aligned}
P_n(p) &= \Pr\{n_1 + n_{12} \geq n^*, n_1 + n_{13} \geq n^*\} \\
&\quad + \Pr\{n_2 + n_{12} \geq n^*, n_2 + n_{23} \geq n^*\} \\
&\quad + \Pr\{n_3 + n_{13} \geq n^*, n_3 + n_{23} \geq n^*\} \\
&= 3\Pr\{n_1 + n_{12} \geq n^*, n_1 + n_{13} \geq n^*\}.
\end{aligned}$$

For example, $n^* = 2$ when $n = 3$ so that

$$\begin{aligned}
P_3(p) &= 3[\Pr\{n_1 = 3\} + \Pr\{n_1 = 2\} + \Pr\{n_1 = n_{12} = n_{13} = 1\}] \\
&= 3[(p/3)^3 + 3(p/3)^2(1 - p/3) + 6(p/3)((1 - p)/3)^2] \\
&= p(4p^2 - 3p + 6)/9.
\end{aligned}$$

$P_3(p)$ increases from 0 at $p = 0$ to a maximum (of $\frac{7}{9}$) at $p = 1$. It can be proved that this type of increase is true for every n. Hence, the likelihood of being able to conclude that the winner is a Condorcet candidate in a three-candidate approval voting election tends to increase as the proportion of voters who vote for one rather than two candidates increases.

Theorem 6.4. $P_n(p)$ *increases in* p *for every positive integer* n.

Theorem 6.4 can be extended to larger numbers of candidates, as illustrated elsewhere.[5] Basically, as voters contract the lists of candidates they approve of, the probability that the ballot data imply that the winner must be a Condorcet candidate increases.

6.7. Conclusions

The orientation of this chapter has been toward data analysis: starting from vote totals for each candidate in an election, we have given conditions under which one can conclude, on both deterministic and probabilistic grounds, that the winner in an election is a Condorcet candidate.

In fact, however, there are virtually no conditions, in three- or four-candidate elections, that permit one to conclude that a Condorcet candidate has been elected when plurality voting is used. By contrast, if the lead of the winning candidate is sufficiently large in an approval voting election, one can draw such a conclusion, but the winner's lead in general has to be a big one.

When the election results by candidate are disaggregated, and approval voting ballot data are available on how many voters voted for each subset of candidates, less stringent conditions can be given that enable one to conclude that the winner is a Condorcet candidate, given reasonable assumptions about what voters' ballots reveal about their preferences. These conditions vary according to assumptions one makes about the sincerity of voting.

Ballot data were not available for the Boston mayoral election that we analyzed, but the aggregate returns on a plurality election and a runoff, coupled with survey data, allowed the approximation of approval voting ballot data. Somewhat surprisingly, even though the winner of the runoff finished a poor second in the plurality election with only 22 percent of the vote, the data supported the conclusion that he was probably a Condorcet candidate. When unequivocal support is lacking, we showed that the likelihood of being able to certify that the winner is a Condorcet candidate increases as voters tend to vote for fewer candidates.

In our opinion, these results nicely complement the theoretical results in Chapter 3 on Condorcet candidates and the empirical study in Chapter 4. In Chapter 7 we shall turn to a discussion of polls, and their possible effects on voting strategies, and analyze a senatorial election in which polls played a prominent role.

Footnotes to Chapter 6

1. The subsequent results in this section and the first part of Section 6.4 are based on Peter C. Fishburn, "Deducing Majority Candidates from Election Data," *Social Science Research* **9**, 3 (September 1980), 216–224. Proofs of Theorems 6.1 and 6.2 are given in this article.

2. The analysis in this section and Section 6.6 is based on Peter C. Fishburn and Steven J. Brams, "Deducing Simple Majorities from Approval Voting Ballot Data," *Social Science Research* **10**, 3 (September 1981), 256–266. Proofs of Theorem 6.3 and 6.4 are given in this article.

3. Murray B. Levin, *The Alienated Voter: Politics in Boston* (New York: Holt, Rinehart, and Winston, 1960).

4. Steven J. Brams and George Sharrard, "Analysis of Pilot Study Questions on Preference Rankings and Approval Voting" (mimeographed, 1979).

5. P. C. Fishburn and S. J. Brams, "Deducing Simple Majorities from Approval Voting Ballot Data."

Chapter 7
Polls and the Problem of Strategic Information in Elections[1]

7.1. Introduction

In the analysis up to now, we have assumed that voters use available and relevant information to make rational choices. They vote insincerely, for example, because there is a reason—they can effect a better outcome by not voting for all their most-preferred or acceptable candidates. In plurality voting, in particular, the practice of voting for a second choice is not uncommon in elections wherein one's first choice would appear not to be a serious contender.

In Chapter 4, we suggested that there might have been some strategic voting in the 1976 House Majority Leader race, but probably not a great deal, especially on the first ballot, since subsequent opportunities to influence the outcome could be anticipated that would allow more informed strategic choices, based on the information about the respective strengths of candidates revealed on the first ballot. In Chapter 5 we showed that efficacy and power considerations dictate voting for about half the candidates—or those, if cardinal utilities are assigned to the candidates, who have utilities greater than the mean—under approval voting. However, when more information is available about the relative standings of the candidates, this information may induce a voter to deviate in a specific instance from his optimal overall strategy that assumes all ways of voting by the other voters are equiprobable.

In this chapter, we shall suggest how polls introduce information about the standing of candidates in an election to which voters may react strategically. In particular, we assume voters adjust, if necessary, their sincere voting strategies to differentiate between the top two candidates in a poll, voting for the more preferred of the two. Such adjustments under plurality voting inevitably lead to insincere voting, but under approval voting differentiation between the top two candidates can always be accomplished—either by contracting or expanding the candidates approved of—by sincere voting.

Under both systems, the adjustments may defeat Condorcet candidates. We shall give the necessary and sufficient conditions for this pathological effect to occur for plurality voting; the situation is more complex for approval voting, wherein a Condorcet candidate's position may be reinforced, undermined, or unaffected by polling, and where cycling over candidates may also occur. Using a United States Senate election, we shall illustrate the favorable impact that polling under approval voting might have had on the probable Condorcet candidate's election, but a general comparison of the consequences of polling under plurality and approval voting requires further investigation.

7.2. Concerns about Public Opinion Polling

Public opinion polling is a fact of life in major elections in the United States. Although there are restrictions on the publication of poll results in some countries (e.g., in France, no poll information can be revealed seven days before a presidential election), polling is commonplace in virtually all democracies today. Yet there exist almost no theoretical models that offer insight into how voter reactions to the strategic information that polls provide may affect individual voting decisions, and how these in turn impinge upon election outcomes.

Lacking such models, it is difficult to say, for example, whether a ban on poll information before an election is in the public interest. In our view, the answer to this and related questions depends on what criteria one uses for determining better or worse public choices, and whether a voting system encourages these when the public is given access to poll information.

But this has not been the focus of debate over the use of polls, which have been vehemently attacked since the modern era of scientific opinion polling began in the 1930's. Rather, at least in the United States, the biggest controversy has been over Election-Day projections by the television networks of winners in presidential elections. In particular, early projections by the networks in some elections are thought by some to have influenced both turnout and voting decisions in states where the polls had not yet closed.[2]

This problem, which surfaces every four years and evokes cries of outrage—particularly from people in western states whose polls close last—is not, in our opinion, the most significant problem with election polling. The enduring and far more serious problem, we believe, is that polls introduce information about the standing of candidates during the course of a campaign to which voters may react strategically. Their reactions to this information, which is now widely disseminated not only in national elections but also in many state and local elections, may change outcomes, sometimes in what appear to be pathological ways.

We shall show this to be true under both plurality and approval voting, pointing out that each system gives rise to somewhat different pathologies. We shall also show that runoff systems, which pit the two top vote-getters in the initial election against each other in a second election, act like a final poll that highlights the two leading contenders.

Polls are not the only source of new information about the standing of candidates. Though based on different constituencies, presidential caucuses and primaries in the United States provide a continual updating on the candidates and their performance, somewhat akin to polls, that may lead to bandwagon or underdog effects, or jockeying between candidates for the lead (or often nonlead when candidates seek to lower expectations, and thereby do better than predicted, to give the appearance of a build-up in momentum).

No practical voting system would appear to be impervious to the introduction of new information, and the concomitant strategic adjustments that this information engenders, first in individual choices and ultimately in social choices. But some systems may be less vulnerable than others, and we shall offer in the concluding section of this chapter a preliminary assessment of the strengths and weaknesses of the different systems analyzed.

In subsequent sections, we shall consider only situations in which the preferences of voters are such that there is a single Condorcet candidate. We shall then show, by example, how the introduction of poll information may lead voters to change their voting strategies in ways that prevent the election of the Condorcet candidate under each of the voting systems to be examined. The fact that each of the voting systems is not vulnerable to exactly the same weaknesses will make possible a comparison of their pathologies.

To be sure, the introduction of poll information that dethrones the Condorcet candidate in one situation may be reversed in another. That is, given different voters with different preferences, the Condorcet candidate's election may be helped, not hurt, by poll information, so it is inaccurate to view polls as pathological, or even mainly so. Ultimately, it would be desirable to know how frequently, on the average, the election of the Condorcet candidate is either fostered or retarded by different voting systems when poll information becomes publicly available. Although this is a difficult question to answer without a good deal more analytic work, perhaps supplemented by computer simulations, some general results on plurality voting will be given.

In the absence of work that would facilitate comparisons among different systems, we shall focus on problems that polls may cause in upsetting the election of Condorcet candidates. But situations in which the election of the Condorcet candidate is helped by a poll will also be described and illustrated. Before pursuing both the benign and less-than-benign effects of polls, however, models describing how voters might adjust their voting strategies to poll information are needed. The particular model used varies somewhat for each of the voting systems to be considered.

7.3. Plurality Voting

Under plurality voting, each voter can vote for one candidate, and the candidate with the most votes wins. Before the poll, we assume that each voter votes sincerely because, in the absence of poll information, there is no reason to vote otherwise.

The poll, we assume, accurately indicates the support of the candidates, based on sincere voter choices. This assumption will be illustrated by

EXAMPLE 1. Suppose there are nine voters with the following preference scales for the set of three candidates $\{a,b,c\}$:

   I. 4: *acb*
  II. 3: *bca*
 III. 2: *cab*.

Since the four voters in class I prefer a to c to b, the poll would indicate a to have 4 votes (44 percent), whereas b and c would have 3 and 2 votes (33 and 22 percent), respectively.

We make the following assumption about the effects of the poll on sincere voter choices:

Poll Assumption (Plurality): After the poll, voters will adjust their voting strategies to differentiate between the top two candidates, as indicated by the poll, if they prefer one of these candidates to the other and their sincere pre-poll strategies did not involve voting for exactly one of these choices. Given that they are not indifferent between the top two candidates in the poll, they will vote after the poll for the one of these two they prefer.

Since class I and class II voters chose one of the top two candidates, only the two class III voters, who voted for c, would change their votes. Because they prefer a to b, it would appear to be in their interest to vote (insincerely) for a, thereby distinguishing him from the other top contender, by giving him their votes. The result would be that a would win with 6 votes, with b getting 3 votes and c none.

In fact, however, it is c who is the Condorcet candidate: he is preferred to a by class II and III voters (5 to 4), and to b by class I and III voters (6 to 3). Yet the poll not only does not make him victorious but instead magnifies a's plurality victory (4 votes) by inducing c's supporters, thinking that their candidate is out of the running, to throw their support to a, giving him a two-thirds majority (6 votes).

Example 1 can be generalized to yield the following proposition:

Proposition 7.1. *Under plurality voting, the Condorcet candidate will always lose if he is not one of the top two candidates identified by the poll.*

This is so because sincere votes for all the other candidates—including the Condorcet candidate, assuming one exists—shift to the top two candidates identified by the poll, making one the majority winner (except for ties). Even if the Poll Assumption (Plurality) were modified to differentiate, say, the top three—instead of the top two—candidates, Proposition 1 would still obtain with "three" in place of "two."

By making only the top two candidates contenders, the Poll Assumption (Plurality) forces the effective elimination of all other candidates, even though *their* plurality totals may be close to those of the contenders. To be sure, they might be given serious consideration in a tight race, though had c been considered in the running in Example 1, a would still have won: the poll would have had no effect, for even if c's supporters had stuck with him, a still would have won with a plurality of votes.

Surprisingly, even if the Condorcet candidate wins without a poll, and hence is one of the top three candidates in a poll that differentiates the top three, he may be hurt by the poll after strategic adjustments. To illustrate this point, consider

EXAMPLE 2. Add a fourth candidate, d, to the previous three in Example 1, and assume that there are twelve voters with the following preference scales:

    I. 3: *acbd*
    II. 3: *bcad*
    III. 4: *cabd*
    IV. 2: *dabc*.

After the poll establishes that a, b, and c are the top three candidates, the two class IV voters would be motivated to switch to their second choice, a, who would thereby increase his total from 3 to 5 votes—and win with a plurality after the poll. Yet c is the Condorcet candidate, who, by staying the same at 4 votes, is hurt, relative to a, by the poll and, in fact, would lose to a in a plurality contest after the poll, though c was the plurality winner before the poll.

Thus, the Poll Assumption (Plurality), which induces strategic adjustments in favor of the top two candidates, may also have a deleterious effect on the Condorcet candidate when it is modified to elevate a larger number of candidates (possibly including the Condorcet candidate, who might even be the pre-poll plurality winner) to the status of "contenders." However, when one of the top two contenders distinguished by the Poll Assumption (Plurality) is the Condorcet candidate, this candidate will always be elected.

Proposition 7.2. *Under plurality voting, the Condorcet candidate will always win if he is one of the top two candidates identified by the poll.*

By definition, the Condorcet candidate will defeat all other candidates in pairwise contests, including the other top candidates identified in the poll. Therefore, the Condorcet candidate will necessarily win when voters adjust their strategies to distinguish between him and a non-Condorcet candidate.[3]

It should be noted that the Condorcet candidate need not be the plurality winner in the poll, but could instead place second, for Proposition 7.2 to hold. If the Condorcet candidate places second, and the poll has the effect of turning him into a majority winner, then it is proper to say that the poll is instrumental in electing the Condorcet candidate.

So far we have shown that a poll that distinguishes the top two candidates, and causes voters to make strategic adjustments according to the Poll Assumption (Plurality), will either hurt the Condorcet candidate if he is not one of the top two (Proposition 7.1), or elect him if he is (Proposition 7.2). Curiously, if more than two candidates are distinguished as serious contenders by the poll—contrary to the Poll Assumption (Plurality)—the Condorcet candidate may be hurt *even if he is among those so elevated*, as Example 2 demonstrated.

Henceforth, we shall assume that the effects of a poll are governed solely by the Poll Assumption (with some modifications for approval voting noted in the next section): only the top two candidates in the poll are set apart from the rest, with voters making strategic adjustments to differentiate between them. This assumption probably understates, at least in the case of plurality voting, the upsetting effects of polls on the election of Condorcet candidates, for Proposition 7.2, which establishes when Condorcet candidates are invariably elected, depends on it. If there are more than two serious contenders, then there appear to be no simple Condorcet election guarantees that result from strategic adjustments caused by a poll.

7.4. Approval Voting

As indicated in Section 2.5, a voter is assumed to vote sincerely under approval voting if and only if, whenever he votes for some candidate, he votes for all candidates preferred to that candidate. In the absence of poll information, there seems no reason for a voter to vote insincerely—that is, not to vote for *all* candidates, above a certain minimum whom he considers acceptable (see Section 2.5). We assume that a poll will never induce insincere voting but rather may change the cutoff point between acceptable and unacceptable candidates:

Poll Assumption (Approval): After the poll, voters will adjust their voting strategies to distinguish between the top two candidates, as indicated by the poll, if they prefer one of these candidates to the other and their sincere, pre-poll strategies did not involve voting for exactly one of these choices. Given that they are not indifferent between the top two candidates in the poll, they will vote after the poll for their preferred candidate *and all candidates preferred to him (if any).*

This assumption is identical to the Poll Assumption (Plurality), except for the last (underscored) phrase. However, the *consequences* of the two Poll Assumptions for the voter who makes strategic adjustments—insincere voting under the plurality system, (continuing) sincere voting under the approval system—are strikingly different.

We shall now show that the certainty of Propositions 7.1 and 7.2 about, respectively, the nonelection and election of the Condorcet candidate under plurality voting is replaced by uncertainty under approval voting. Specifically, two examples will demonstrate the following:

Proposition 7.3. *Under approval voting, a non-Condorcet candidate may be helped, and the Condorcet candidate hurt, by a poll, whether or not the Condorcet candidate is one of the top two candidates identified by the poll.*

EXAMPLE 3: CONDORCET CANDIDATE ONE OF TOP TWO IN POLL. Suppose there are 65 voters with the following preference scales:[4]

   I. 10: *abc*
  II. 10: *acb*
 III. 9: *bac*
  IV. 10: *bca*
   V. 15: *cab*
  VI. 11: *cba*.

If each voter considers his top two choices acceptable, the results are: *c*–46; *a*–44; *b*–40. (Note: *c* also wins under plurality voting—or approval voting, if all voters vote only for their top choice—getting 26 votes to a's 20 and b's 19. Moreover, besides being the approval and plurality winner, c is the Condorcet candidate, defeating both a and b 36 to 29; b again comes in last, losing to a in a pairwise contest 35 to 30.)

After the poll, identifying c and a as the top two candidates, the six classes of voters will make the following divisions between acceptable and unacceptable candidates:

    I.   10: ab/c
   II. 10: a/cb
  III. 9: ba/c
  IV. 10: bc/a
   V. 15: c/ab
  VI. 11: cb/a.

Now b, the former last-place candidate, wins with 40 votes, c—the Condorcet candidate—gets 36 votes, and a gets 29 votes. Clearly, the poll drastically alters the election outcome, elevating the last-place candidate (b) to first place, and, in the process, toppling the Condorcet candidate (c).

A few observations are in order about this example:

   i. Because the Condorcet candidate is one of the top two choices under plurality voting, a poll under plurality voting would ensure his victory (Proposition 7.2).

  ii. Under approval voting, the Condorcet candidate can be defeated by strategic adjustments of two different kinds: if voters vote for their single favorite candidate (plurality voting), the strategic adjustments induce some to vote for two candidates (*expansion* of strategies); if voters vote for their top two candidates, as assumed above, adjustments under approval voting induce some to vote for one candidate (*contraction* of strategies).[5] Whether voters expand or contract their approval strategies, the Condorcet candidate can be defeated if he is not one of the top two in the poll.

 iii. Strategic adjustments *after the first poll* may lead to new instabilities. In Example 3, the first adjustments, which pushed b and c to the top, cause *re*adjustments in the previous divisions for voters in classes II, IV, and VI:

    I.   10: ab/c
   II. 10: ac/b
  III. 9: ba/c
  IV. 10: b/ca
   V. 15: c/ab
  VI. 11: c/ba.

A new poll, then, based on the above divisions, would show that c—the Condorcet candidate—wins with 36 votes, and a and b tie with 29 votes each, which creates a cycle: c wins before the poll, b wins after the poll, and c wins after readjustments to the first adjustments, which would be reflected in a second poll. This example illustrates the inherent disequilibrium that may characterize outcomes influenced by *continual polling* under approval voting. We shall say more about this example later.

EXAMPLE 4: CONDORCET CANDIDATE NOT ONE OF TOP TWO IN POLL. In Example 3 we showed that a non-Condorcet candidate (b) may be helped, and the Condorcet candidate (c) hurt, by strategic adjustments after a poll if the Condorcet candidate is one of the top two candidates identified by the poll. In the present example, we shall show that this problem can arise when the Condorcet candidate is not one of the top two candidates identified by the poll.

Suppose there are five voters with the following preference scales:

I. 2: acb
II. 2: bca
III. 1: cab.

If each voter considers only his top choice acceptable, the results are: a–2; b–2; c–1. Yet c is the Condorcet candidate, defeating both a and b 3 to 2, while a beats b 3 to 2.

After the poll, identifying a and b as the top two candidates, the three classes of voters will make the following divisions (only the class III voter adjusts his approval strategy—through expansion):

I. 2: a/cb
II. 2: b/ca
III. 1: ca/b.

Now a becomes the winner with 3 votes, so a non-Condorcet candidate (a) is helped, and the Condorcet candidate (c), who stays the same with 1 vote, is hurt compared to him.

Recall in Example 3 that readjustments made after the adjustments to the poll would, in a new poll, reelect the Condorcet candidate, attesting to the instability of outcomes that continual polling may produce. There is no such instability in Example 4, however, since a and b (with 2 votes) remain the top two candidates after the poll, making readjustments unnecessary.

Examples 3 and 4 demonstrate the truth of Proposition 7.3: a Condorcet candidate may be hurt by a poll, essentially independent of his standing in it, under approval voting. But this truth has another, brighter side.

Proposition 7.4. *Under approval voting, the Condorcet candidate may be helped, and a non-Condorcet candidate hurt, by a poll, whether or not the Condorcet candidate is one of the top two candidates identified by the poll.*

EXAMPLE 5. To demonstrate this proposition if the Condorcet candidate is one of the top two identified by the poll, suppose there are nine voters with the following preference scales:

 I. 4: *abc*
 II. 3: *bac*
 III. 2: *cba.*

If each voter considers only his top choice acceptable, *a* and *b* emerge as the top two candidates, with 4 and 3 votes, respectively, leading to the following divisions after the poll:

 I. 4: *a/bc*
 II. 3: *b/ac*
 III. 2: *cb/a.*

Now the Condorcet candidate, *b*, who previously finished in second place with 3 votes, moves up to first place with 5 votes, and the other two candidates, *a* and *c*, stay the same with 4 and 2 votes, respectively.

EXAMPLE 6. To demonstrate Proposition 7.4 if the Condorcet candidate is not one of the top two identified by the poll, suppose there are four voters with the following preference scales:

 I. 2: *abcd*
 II. 1: *acbd*
 III. 1: *dcba.*

If each voter considers his top three choices acceptable, *b* and *c* emerge as the top candidates, with 4 votes each, leading to the following divisions after the poll:

 I. 2: *ab/cd*
 II. 1: *ac/bd*
 III. 1: *dc/ba.*

Now the Condorcet candidate, *a*, who previously finished in third place, moves up to first place with 3 votes, against 2 votes for *b* and *c* and 1 for *d*. In sum, the Condorcet candidate may be helped (Proposition 7.4), as well as hurt (Proposition 7.3), by a poll under approval voting, but unlike plurality voting this movement up and down does not depend on whether he is one of the top two in the poll (Propositions 7.1 and 7.2).

Example 3 illustrated how, under approval voting, one candidate may be elected before a poll, a second candidate after adjustments are made on the basis of the poll, and then the first candidate reelected after readjustments are made to the first adjustments. By contrast, in Example 5, a and b would be interchanged as the top two candidates as a result of the poll,' but, because the voters would not change their divisions that differentiate them, the result after the poll would remain stable if another poll were conducted.

Continual polling, however, may, without displacing the top candidate, still effect changes. Example 6 illustrates this point. After the poll reveals a to be in first place with 3 votes, with b and c tied for second place with 2 votes each, it is reasonable to suppose that the voters would distinguish their most-preferred candidate *among the top three* from the other two by making the following divisions:

 I. 2: a/bcd
 II. 1: a/cbd
 III. 1: dc/ba.

Note that these divisions reinforce a's victory: he retains his 3 votes, but b drops to 0 votes and c drops to 1 vote; d retains his 1 vote, but altogether a has a majority of the approval votes cast (3 out of 5), which he did not have before (3 out of 8).

Readjustments reflecting these results would in turn induce the following divisions:

 I. 2: a/bcd
 II. 1: a/cbd
 III. 1: d/cba.

Now a's victory would be further reinforced, with c dropping out and only d remaining in the contest against a. Voters would make no further readjustments, for they already are distinguishing their top two candidates, so a's victory would stabilize at 3 votes, with d receiving 1 vote.

If these poll results were the returns from presidential caucuses or primaries, one might say that a bandwagon had developed for a. But, in fact, a's ballooning vote total would be entirely attributable to continual (sincere) strategic adjustments, not insincere voting for the expected winner that "bandwagon effect" usually connotes.

In Example 3, after the $c \rightarrow b \rightarrow c$ cycle following the readjustments, c wins twice more after further readjustments due to continual polling before the process stabilizes at 36 votes for c (the Condorcet candidate), 29 for a, and 19 for b. Yet, continual polling does not inevitably lead, in the "long run," to an equilibrium outcome under approval voting, as the following (and final) example demonstrates:

EXAMPLE 7. Suppose there are nine voters with the following preference scales:

   I. 4: *abc*
   II. 3: *bca*
   III. 2: *cba*.

If the four voters in class I vote only for *a*, and the five voters in classes II and III vote for both *b* and *c*, *b* and *c* show up as the top two candidates, with 5 votes each on the poll. This leads to the following divisions after the poll:

   I. 4: *ab/c*
   II. 3: *b/ca*
   III. 2: *c/ba*.

Now *b* and *a* top the field, with 7 and 4 votes, respectively, leading to the following divisions after a second poll:

   I. 4: *a/bc*
   II. 3: *b/ca*
   III. 2: *cb/a*.

Because *b* and *a* would still lead after the poll (though *b*'s total would drop to 5 votes), one would expect this result to stabilize.

Recall, however, that voters in class II originally approved of both *b* and *c* (before polling). Now consider a provisional change in the Poll Assumption (Approval), based on the following reasoning: with *a* and *b* now the poll leaders, class II voters calculate that they have nothing to lose by voting for *c* as well as *b*; *c* may not be able to win, but if he should have a chance, they would prefer him to *a*. Given this logic, if the three class II voters indicate in the poll that they also approve of *c*, it would be {*b,c*} rather than {*a,b*} who would show up in the poll as the top two candidates. But this is the original poll result, so more polling, presumably, would simply repeat the {*b,c*} → {*a,b*} → {*b,c*} cycle of top candidates, with no equilibrium. Instead, *b* would oscillate in and out of the single top spot, with *a* and *c* alternating places as the other leading contender.

To be sure, in this example we assumed that readjustments to the results of the first poll would not leave the division of the class II voters intact, even though this division already differentiated the top two candidates in the poll. Instead, we assumed that, contrary to the Poll Assumption (Approval), the class II voters would revert to their original strategy of voting for their top two choices, which, while maintaining the distinction that the poll indicates they should make between *b* and *a*, would also allow them to express the fact that they find two of the candidates acceptable.

It is not apparent *a priori* whether this poll assumption, or the original assumption (used in the previous examples in this section), would better mirror strategic adjustments that voters might make. Both assumptions seem plausible: either voters might revert to their original approval strategies, or stick with their last strategy, if both strategies differentiated between the top two candidates in the poll. The latter assumption reflects a kind of inertia voters might have; the former, a disposition of voters to return to their first judgments about which candidates are acceptable.

In either case, continual polling can have various effects under approval voting, summarized by the fifth (and last) proposition:

Proposition 7.5. *Under approval voting, adjustments caused by continual polling may (i) have no effect on the outcome, (ii) reinforce or undermine a particular outcome, or (iii) induce cycling.*

The general conditions under which each of these effects occurs under approval voting are not evident. But the examples certainly demonstrate that each is possible for reasonable assumptions about voter reactions to polls, rendering the outcome sensitive to the time at which polling ceases and the election is held.

7.5. Runoff Systems and an Empirical Example

All the previous results for plurality voting and approval voting would appear to hold if elections under these two systems are followed by a runoff between the top two vote-getters. That is, the polls before the election and the runoff would still cause the same adjustments and readjustments.

There is a difference, however: *in an election with a runoff, the first election constitutes, in effect, the final poll.* This is so because the first election sets apart the top two vote-getters, forcing voters to choose between them in the runoff if they did not do so previously. Because voters cannot also vote for other candidates, as under approval voting, a runoff will lead to exactly the same consequences as a poll that induces adjustments under plurality voting with no runoff. Thus, when there is a Condorcet candidate, he will be elected if and only if he is one of the top two vote-getters in the election before the runoff (cf. Propositions 7.1 and 7.2). Prior to both the election and runoff, however, continual polling will have the same effects as it would without a runoff under both plurality and approval voting.

There was no runoff in the 1970 United States Senate election in New York, whose plurality results were:

James Buckley: 39 percent;
Richard Ottinger: 37 percent;
Charles Goodell: 24 percent.

Polling prior to the election revealed Goodell to be the low man; he undoubtedly suffered in the election returns because of adjustments his supporters made in favor of Buckley and Ottinger, as the Poll Assumption (Plurality) would suggest.

Goodell, however, was probably the Condorcet candidate. He was backed by the Republican Party and the Liberal party, whereas the more liberal Ottinger had the endorsement of the Democratic Party, and the more conservative Buckley had the endorsement of the Conservative Party. It is generally acknowledged that Goodell could have beaten both Buckley and Ottinger in separate face-to-face contests.

It is reasonable to assume that most Buckley (B) and Ottinger (O) supporters had the following preference scales:

Buckley (39): *BGO*
Ottinger (37): *OGB*.

Goodell (G) supporters probably divided about equally between B and O on the second choices:

Goodell (12): *GBO*
Goodell (12): *GOB*.

Under approval voting, it seems plausible that perhaps half the Buckley and Ottinger supporters would have also voted for Goodell, and half the Goodell supporters would have voted for their second choices. These assumptions yield:

Buckley: 45
Ottinger: 43
Goodell: 62.

With G and B the top two candidates in an approval-voting poll, voters according to the Poll Assumption (Approval) would make the following adjustments:

Buckley (39): *B/GO*
Ottinger (37): *OG/B*
Goodell (12): *G/BO*
Goodell (12): half *G/OB* and half *GO/B*.

These adjustments would yield the following: G–61; O–43; B–39. But now, with G and O in the lead, readjustments would induce the following: G–63; B–45; O–37.

These swings between Ottinger and Buckley, and Goodell's large approval vote, seem somewhat unrealistic,[6] but they do indicate that Goodell, as the Condorcet candidate, probably would have been helped by continual polling under approval voting (as well as by approval voting itself). Whereas such polling under plurality voting undoubtedly hurt him, it would have probably helped him under approval voting by inducing some Buckley and Ottinger supporters to vote for him, too.

Plurality voting followed by a runoff would have elected either Buckley or Ottinger. By comparison, a runoff under approval voting, which would have picked up Goodell as one of the top two candidates, would have led to his election as the Condorcet candidate (Proposition 7.2).

Clearly, one election in which the likely Condorcet candidate was defeated under plurality voting but probably would have triumphed under approval voting—and had his victory reinforced by approval polls—does not attest to the latter system's superiority, even with respect to the Condorcet criterion. Before summarizing the advantages and disadvantages of each voting system when voters adjust their strategies to take account of poll information, it is worth noting that in some settings voters might be able to take account of such additional information—beyond the aggregate candidate totals as revealed by a poll—as voter preference scales and numbers of candidates that different classes of voters deem acceptable.

Potentially, this would enable voters to calculate optimal strategic adjustments in the resulting voting game, but the difficulties of making these game-theoretic calculations (see Section 8.5) would appear formidable and may well deter voters from making the effort. Alternatively, an understanding of the possible adverse effects that polls may induce for their favorite candidate may lead voters to refuse to react strategically, or even participate in the voting process.

7.6. Conclusions

For voters who do make the strategic adjustments we have postulated, the effects of polling are clear under plurality voting: the Condorcet candidate is helped if he is one of the top two in the poll, hurt otherwise. Unfortunately for Goodell in 1970, he was not one of the top two and suffered accordingly. But even if he had been considered a serious contender, the fact of his being the Condorcet candidate among three candidates would not necessarily have induced strategic adjustments that favored him. As shown earlier, the Condorcet candidate may lose if there are more than two top contenders.

The situation is more complex for approval voting, with no necessary and sufficient condition governing the election of the Condorcet candidate. Instead, the Condorcet candidate may win or lose after a poll, irrespective of whether he is one of the top two candidates in the poll. This fact can be a boon to a Condorcet candidate, like Goodell, who runs third in the polls (though he probably would not have under approval voting) but still need not have victory elude him. But the Condorcet candidate who shows up first or second in the polls, and then is displaced after strategic adjustments, will have good reason to feel outraged and embittered, especially because his election would have been guaranteed by strategic adjustments under plurality voting.

The saving grace of approval voting in this kind of situation may be the instability of the polling effects it induces, which does not occur under plurality voting. As several of the previous examples demonstrated, continual polling may lead, if not immediately then eventually, to the Condorcet candidate's advantage, even enhancing his lead. This possibility deserves further investigation, because it could tip the balance in favor of approval voting if its propensity to find Condorcet candidates not among the top two more than offsets its disadvantage in not guaranteeing the Condorcet candidate's election when he is one of the top two.

To recapitulate, polling effects as we have modeled them—and sequential-election results as well, as in presidential caucuses and primaries—may not be salutary: they may undermine the Condorcet candidate under both plurality and approval voting, and these pathologies are not mitigated by runoff elections. Indeed, in an election with a runoff, the first election can be considered a kind of final poll, but one which cannot help a candidate other than one of the top two, as with polling under plurality voting.

Yet the pathologies of polls, at least under approval voting—and perhaps other voting systems not considered here (e.g., ranking systems)—are not always permanent, with new poll information, and voters' reactions to it, having the potential to turn the defeat of the Condorcet candidate into victory. These fluctuations that continual polling under approval voting may create, compared with the stable changes that polls under plurality voting induce, leave open the question of whether polling effects in general favor Condorcet candidates more under one system than the other.

Footnotes to Chapter 7

1. This chapter is based largely on Steven J. Brams, "Strategic Information and Voting Behavior," *Society* **19**, 3 (September/October 1982): 4–11.

2. A study of the effects of vote projections on late California voters in the 1964 presidential election found this not to be true, but the effects of projections, especially on turnout, seem to have been substantial in the 1980 presidential election, perhaps in part because Ronald Reagan's landslide victory over Jimmy Carter deviated from expectations about a close race. See Harold Mendelsohn, "Election-Day Broadcasts and Terminal Voting Decisions," *Public Opinion Quarterly* **30**, 2 (Summer 1966), 212–225; and John E. Jackson

and William H. McGee III, "Election Reporting and Voter Turnout" (mimeographed, 1981). Turnout decline on the West Coast in the 1980 election is disputed in Laurily K. Epstein and Gerald Strom, "Election Night Projections and West Coast Turnout," *American Politics Quarterly* **9**, 4 (October 1981), 479–491, where other references to the literature—and continuing debate on this issue—are given. Theoretical and empirical effects of polling are reviewed in Steven J. Brams, *Paradoxes in Politics: An Introduction to the Nonobvious in Political Science* (New York: Free Press, 1976), pp. 65–78. Quantitative calculations making use of poll information are developed in Dale T. Hoffman, "A Model for Strategic Voting," *SIAM Journal on Applied Mathematics* **42**, 4 (August 1982), 751–761.

3. Winning, however, does not imply that the Condorcet candidate will be helped compared to the other top candidates, as the following example illustrates:

   I. 10: *abc*
  II.   5: *bac*
 III.   4: *cba*.

Although the Condorcet candidate wins decisively before the poll, after the poll he just edges out *b* 10 to 9 because the four class III *c* supporters switch to *b*.

4. This example was given in Steven J. Brams, *The Presidential Election Game* (New Haven: Yale University Press, 1978), pp. 219–220; and S. J. Brams, *Comparison Voting,* Innovative Instructional Unit (Washington, DC: American Political Science Association, 1978), pp. 47–48, which will appear in slightly revised form in *Modules in Applied Mathematics: Political and Related Models*, Vol. 2, edited by Steven J. Brams, William F. Lucas, and Philip D. Straffin, Jr. (New York: Springer-Verlag, 1982). It was originally suggested to S. J. Brams by Philip D. Straffin, Jr.

5. Contraction of strategies seems more defensible than expansion of strategies because it does not involve voting, after strategic adjustments, for candidates not previously approved of by a voter.

6. William C. Stratmann estimates that, under approval voting, Goodell would have won with about 59 percent of the vote (i.e., approval from about 59 percent of the voters) to about 55 percent each for Buckley and Ottinger. Personal communication to S. J. Brams, September 21, 1977, based on work reported in W. C. Stratmann, "The Calculus of Rational Choice," *Public Choice* **18** (Summer 1974), 93–105.

Chapter 8
Recent Empirical Examples and Theoretical Extensions

8.1. Introduction

A number of elections have already been analyzed to try to ascertain the probable effects of approval voting: the 1980 New Hampshire presidential primaries (Section 1.3); the 1976 House Majority Leader contest (Chapter 4); the 1959 Boston mayoral race (Section 6.6); and the 1970 United States Senate election in New York (Section 7.5), in which we also looked at possible polling effects. In this chapter, we shall examine what seems almost a reprise of the Senate race in New York, ten years later, and then turn our attention to presidential elections. We shall report on a reconstruction of the first of two recent three-way presidential elections (1968), reserving the second (1980) for a more detailed statistical analysis in Chapter 9.

Next we shall return to the theme of Chapter 7, showing how information on the spatial positions of candidates along a left-right continuum may affect voter choices under plurality and approval voting. But spatial positions and poll data are not the only kinds of information that voters might utilize. If voters have information about each other's preferences, they can make game-theoretic calculations, which we shall illustrate with an example. Finally, we shall discuss a monotonicity paradox that afflicts certain voting systems, including runoff systems and a preferential voting system.

8.2. The 1980 New York Senate Race: A Reprise of 1970?

Ironically, there was a kind of reenactment of the 1970 New York Senate race (Section 7.5) in 1980, involving Alphonse D'Amato (Republican Party–Conservative Party candidate), Elizabeth Holtzman

(Democratic Party candidate), and Jacob Javits (Liberal Party candidate). D'Amato beat Holtzman 45 to 44 percent, with Javits, the incumbent, coming in a distant third with 11 percent of the vote after he failed to gain the Republican Party endorsement in New York.

Based on an ABC News exit poll on election day, De Maio and Muzzio calculated how many of each candidate's supporters would have voted for one of the other two candidates had the choice they actually made not been in the race.[1] They estimated that under approval voting Holtzman would have won with 60 percent approval, D'Amato would have finished second with 56 percent approval, and Javits would have come in last with 49 percent approval, with Holtzman the probable Condorcet candidate because twice as many Javits voters would have favored her over D'Amato. Remarkably, while trailing the other two, Javits would have more than quadrupled his plurality total of 11 percent, indicating the strong residual support he had in the electorate.

But even garnering only 11 percent in the actual election, Javits was almost certainly a spoiler, notwithstanding his claim that D'Amato "would have won anyway."[2] This claim is simply not substantiated by the strong disposition of Javits voters toward Holtzman, which would have been reflected in the approval voting results. Despite the fact that many of Javits's supporters seem to have deserted him for strategic reasons in the final days of the campaign—he was trailing the other two candidates in the polls, but not nearly by the margin registered on Election Day—his presence in the race almost certainly undermined the election of the apparent Condorcet candidate, Holtzman.

Thus, for the second time in ten years, the majority preferences of New York state voters seem to have been deflected, resulting in the election of a non-Condorcet United States Senator. The fact that Buckley lost in 1976 to Daniel Patrick Moynihan, a more centrist Democrat than Ottinger, supports our argument that Buckley indeed "lucked out" in 1970 because of the divided centrist vote.

D'Amato's case is somewhat different, because both he and Javits would have been beaten in pairwise contests by the liberal Democrat, Holtzman—not the more moderate Javits—in part, we think, because of Javits's age and illness, which became issues in the campaign. This election, by the way, illustrates that the Condorcet candidate, and approval voting winner, is not inevitably the person "in the middle," blandly acceptable to most voters. The strongest candidate may be attractive precisely because he articulates an ideology with broad appeal, as Ronald Reagan's 1980 election victory, analyzed in Chapter 9, demonstrates.

It is worth noting in the two Senate races that a runoff election between the top two vote-getters almost surely would have elected

Holtzman in 1980, but it would not have elevated Goodell to winning status in 1970 because he would not have made the runoff. By contrast, approval voting would probably have elected both of the likely Condorcet candidates, Goodell and Holtzman.

These senatorial elections in 1970 and 1980 illustrate how polls may hurt the trailing candidate—both of whom showed up better in the polls than in the election returns—due undoubtedly to the fact that some of their supporters decided in favor of their second choices to prevent their worst choices from being elected. Yet, as these elections demonstrate, the polls may be insufficient to dissuade voters to abandon a hopeless choice (Javits), or support the Condorcet choice (Goodell). Quite the contrary, the polls may induce the voters to desert a Condorcet candidate like Goodell, who does not appear viable in a three-candidate race.

Approval voting would not force this switch because it is, in principle, insensitive to the numbers of candidates running—a voter can vote for all "acceptable" candidates, however many. Thus, for example, it would have allowed Javits's supporters to vote for other acceptable candidates (e.g., Holtzman) as well. Thereby, we believe, elections like the 1970 and 1980 senatorial races would, under approval voting, better express not only the majority sentiment for the presumed Condorcet candidates (Goodell and Holtzman) but minority sentiments as well (e.g., for Javits, whom nearly half the voters considered acceptable, even if he would not have won).

8.3. Approval Voting and Presidential Elections[3]

Polling is extensive in presidential elections, beginning even before the earliest caucuses and primaries of a presidential election. In this section, we shall begin an analysis of the probable effects of approval voting in presidential elections, focusing on the 1968 general election because it involved a significant third-party candidate. Mirroring the theme of Chapter 7, we shall argue that the polls in this election probably caused considerable strategic voting, especially by the third-party candidate's supporters. Although approval voting would not have changed the outcome in this election, it would have given rather different election results, just as it would have given a different cast to the 1980 presidential election, as we shall show in Chapter 9 using different data and analytic techniques.

It should be borne in mind, as we indicated in Section 4.6, that all attempts to reconstruct election outcomes under different procedures assume that the candidates, campaign, and other aspects of the election are held constant. This is a major simplifying assumption that needs to be understood in interpreting—with caution—the results.

As a practicable reform, Kellett and Mott have made a strong case that approval voting be adopted in presidential primaries, which, at least in the early stages, often involve several candidates running for their party's nomination.[4] When Kellett and Mott asked a sample of 225 Pennsylvania voters to "vote for any candidates whose nomination you can support" in the 1976 presidential primary (eight Democratic candidates and eight Republican candidates were listed on two sample ballots), 72 percent of those voting chose to support two, three, or four candidates.

A case for approval voting in national party conventions can also be made. (See point 7 in Section 1.2 for a specific proposal that links approval voting with candidate commitments made in primaries.) As in primaries, the main effect would probably be to give comparatively more support to moderates that most delegates find acceptable, comparatively less to extremists who are only acceptable to ideological factions in their party.

If there had been approval voting in the 1972 Democratic convention, it seems at least doubtful that George McGovern would have been his party's nominee. Not only did he not have strong support from his party rank and file,[5] but he also was accorded little chance of winning in the general election.

McGovern's support in the preceding Democratic presidential primaries seems definitely to have been helped by plurality voting, as Joslyn has demonstrated.[6] Although Joslyn did not try to show how McGovern would have fared under approval voting, Merrill did estimate the 1972 Democratic results if voters had used optimal strategies under several different voting systems.[7] Based on thermometer-scale ratings of the candidates (to be discussed below) taken from the University of Michigan's Center for Political Studies 1972 American National Election Study survey, Merrill estimated that Hubert Humphrey would have been approved of by 64.1 percent of Democratic voters to McGovern's 58.0 percent, lending support to the contention that McGovern was not the strongest choice of the Democratic Party in 1972.

Humphrey was also the strongest candidate under the two other rules studied by Merrill (Borda and cardinal rating), losing to McGovern only under plurality voting in a field of four candidates that also included Edmund Muskie and George Wallace. Although McGovern was the strongest plurality candidate in the race, garnering 33.0 percent support to Humphrey's 29.4 percent, his support was considerably narrower than Humphrey's, who would have more than doubled his plurality total under approval voting. These estimates, of course, do not replicate voting in individual state primaries, but they are indicative, we believe, of the broad-gauged support that Humphrey enjoyed and McGovern did not. Barry Goldwater, the 1964 Republican Party nominee, also seems to have been a candidate of limited appeal who, like McGovern, lost in a landslide to his opponent (Lyndon Johnson) in the general election.

Although most general elections are, for all intents and purposes, two-candidate contests, since 1900 there have been several serious bids by third-party candidates in presidential elections.[8] The most notable challenges in the first quarter of the century were in 1912, when Theodore Roosevelt won 27.4 percent of the popular vote, and in 1924, when Robert La Follette won 16.6 percent of the popular vote.

More recently, Harry Truman faced defections from both wings of the Democratic Party in 1948. The Progressive candidate, Henry Wallace, and the States' Rights candidate, Strom Thurmond, each captured 2.4 percent of the popular vote. Nevertheless, Truman was able to win 49.6 percent of the popular vote to Republican Thomas Dewey's 45.1 percent.

The most serious challenge by a minor-party candidate since World War II was that of George Wallace in the 1968 presidential election. We shall shortly analyze this election in some detail to try to assess the possible effects of approval voting in a presidential election. In Chapter 9, we shall look at another serious challenge—that of John Anderson in 1980—but in 1976 there was a less significant challenge that is worth noting nonetheless.

That was by Eugene McCarthy, a former United States senator from Minnesota. Playing the spoiler role, McCarthy sought to protest what he saw to be the outmoded procedures and policies of the Democratic Party, for whose nomination he had run in 1968 and 1972. Although McCarthy garnered only 0.9 percent of the popular vote, his candidacy may have cost Jimmy Carter four states, which Gerald Ford won by less than what McCarthy polled. In the end, of course, Carter did not need the electoral votes of these states; however, if he had lost in a few states that he won by slim margins, these McCarthy votes could have made the difference in the 1976 election.

We turn now to an analysis of the third-party challenge by George Wallace's American Independence Party in 1968. As with Strom Thurmond's support twenty years earlier, Wallace's support was concentrated in the South. Although Wallace had no reasonable chance of winning the presidency, it seemed at the time that he had a very good chance of preventing both Richard Nixon and Hubert Humphrey from winning a majority of electoral votes, thereby throwing the election into the House of Representatives. There Wallace could have bargained with these candidates for major policy concessions—in particular, weaker enforcement of civil rights statutes and a halt to the busing of school children.

Wallace captured 13.5 percent of the popular vote and was the victor in five states, winning 46 electoral votes. He came close to denying Nixon, who got 43.4 percent of the popular vote to Humphrey's 42.7 percent, an electoral-vote majority.

Would this outcome have been different, or would its magnitude have significantly changed, if there had been approval voting in 1968? Presumably, all voters who voted for one of the three candidates would not have changed those votes. But how many would have cast second approval votes, and for whom would they have voted?

The best information available to answer this question was collected in the University of Michigan Survey Research Center's 1968 National Election Study. Data derived from a ''feeling thermometer'' assessment of candidates—whereby respondents are asked to indicate warm or cold feelings toward the candidates on a 100-degree scale—may be used to define an ''acceptability'' scale for candidates, from which plausible approval voting strategies of voters can be surmised.

Taking account of both the reported votes of the respondents (the survey was taken just after the election) and their feeling-thermometer assessments of the candidates, Kiewiet developed a set of ten rules for assigning approval votes to respondents.[9] After adjusting reported voting by the sample to reflect the actual voting results, he estimated that Nixon would have increased his vote total to 69.8 percent (a 58 percent increase over the 44.1 percent in the survey who reported voting for Nixon), Humphrey would have increased his vote total to 60.8 percent (a 44 percent increase over the 42.3 percent in the survey who reported voting for Humphrey), and Wallace would have increased his vote total to 21.3 percent (a 58 percent increase over the 13.5 percent in the survey who reported voting for Wallace).

Kiewiet draws several conclusions from his analysis. First, plurality voting nearly deprived Nixon of his victory: although many voters were not overly enthusiastic about Nixon, more than a two-thirds majority probably considered him at least acceptable. Second, although most of the additional approval votes Nixon and Humphrey would have received would have come from each other's supporters, Wallace supporters—according to the rules used for assigning approval votes— would have cast more than twice as many approval votes for Nixon as for Humphrey.

It is this factor which largely explains Nixon's 9 percent approval-voting edge over Humphrey. Wallace also would have benefited from approval voting. In fact, his estimated 21 percent approval voting share exactly matches the percentage who reported they would vote for him two months before the election.[10] If there had been approval voting, Wallace almost surely would not have lost most of his original supporters, and probably would have picked up some support from the major party voters as well, to capture approval votes from more than one-fifth of the electorate.

Perhaps the most interesting conclusion that can be derived from these estimates is that Nixon was undoubtedly the Condorcet candidate. Kiewiet estimates that Nixon would have defeated Wallace in a pairwise contest 81.5 percent to 18.5 percent, and would have defeated Humphrey 53.4 percent to 46.6 percent, given the propensity of Wallace voters to favor Nixon.

Several objections can be raised against Kiewiet's estimates and indeed against virtually any estimates based on assumptions about how the attitudes or "feelings" of voters would translate into voting behavior. Rather than dwelling on these, however, consider a rather different set of estimates made by Kiewiet based on more "strategic" assumptions.

These assumptions reflect the view of most voters in 1968 that only Humphrey and Nixon stood a serious chance of winning the election. After all, even at his high point in the polls, Wallace commanded the support of barely more than one-fifth of the electorate. Consistent with the poll model developed in Chapter 7, then, it is plausible to assume that voters would cast approval votes to distinguish between Humphrey and Nixon.

More specifically, Kiewiet assumed that (i) Humphrey and Nixon supporters would vote for Wallace, if they also approved of him, but would not vote for the other major-party candidate; (ii) all Wallace voters would vote for either Humphrey or Nixon, but not both, in addition to Wallace. As he put it,

In effect, a poll indicating Wallace had no chance of winning would, under approval voting, turn the election into two elections: the first, a pairwise contest between Nixon and Humphrey, wherein all voters would choose one or the other; the second, a sort of referendum for Wallace, who would receive approval votes from voters who wished to support him even if he could not win the election.[11]

In operational terms, Kiewiet postulated that Humphrey and Nixon supporters would vote for their first choice and, in addition, for Wallace if the latter's thermometer rating exceeded 50. Wallace supporters, on the other hand, were assumed always to cast a second approval vote for the majority-party candidate they gave the highest thermometer rating to, no matter what this rating was. Thereby Wallace voters were "forced" to be rational in accordance with the assumptions of the poll model.

What estimates does this set of assumptions yield? Nixon would have received 53.4 percent of the popular vote and Humphrey 46.6 percent—the same percentages given earlier had they been in a pairwise contest—and Wallace 21.3 percent. Thus, the approval voting percentages of Humphrey and Nixon would have been substantially reduced over those estimated earlier (69.8 and 60.8 percent, respectively), but Wallace would have come out exactly the same (21.3 percent estimated earlier) since the "strategic" assumptions do not alter the voting behavior of Wallace supporters for Wallace.

The two sets of estimates for Humphrey and Nixon probably bracket the percentages the candidates would actually have received had there been approval voting in 1968. In any case, Nixon would have been the clear-cut winner in the popular-vote contest because of the much broader support he, rather than Humphrey, would have received from Wallace supporters.

The Electoral College also magnified Nixon's narrow popular-vote victory because he won by slim margins in several large states. However, speaking normatively, we believe this fact should have no bearing on the outcome. Much more significant is the fact that Nixon was the first or second choice of most voters and hence more acceptable than any other candidate. This, we believe, is the proper criterion for the selection of a president—and other democratically elected officials as well.

It is also interesting to note that approval voting would probably obviate the need for a runoff election in most multicandidate presidential elections if the Electoral College were abolished. No winning candidate in a presidential election has ever received less than 40 percent of the popular vote, with the exception of Abraham Lincoln in 1860, who got 39.8 percent. It seems highly unlikely that the candidate (or candidates) who are the first choice of 40 percent of the electorate would not be approved of by as many as one-sixth of the remaining voters and thereby receive at least 50 percent support from the electorate (with the approval totals not necessarily in the same order as the plurality totals).

The legitimacy of election outcomes in the eyes of voters would surely be enhanced if the winning candidate received the support of a majority of the electorate. This would be true even if he was the first choice of fewer voters than some other candidate, because this fact would not show up in the approval-voting returns.

By comparison, a proposed popular-vote amendment to abolish the Electoral College that has considerable support provides for a runoff between the top two vote-getters if neither receives at least 40 percent of the vote.[12] This seems an unnecessary provision if more than 50 percent approve of the winning candidate. Of course, if no candidate wins even a majority of approval votes, then a runoff can still be conducted to ensure a majority winner, though disadvantages with a runoff under approval voting were pointed out in Sections 3.6 and 4.5.

But a runoff would probably not be necessary in most presidential elections unless approval voting itself produces major changes in candidate strategies and election outcomes. Beyond these changes, however, approval voting could affect a fundamental alteration in the two-party system itself by encouraging additional parties or candidates to enter the fray. (On the other hand, because the "snowball effect" under plurality voting—alluded to in Section 1.2 (point 7) and Section 3.7—would have little force under approval voting, there might actually be fewer candidates drawn into a race, though this probably applies mostly to primaries that would not directly affect the two-party system.)

Fringe candidates, it seems, would probably drain little support from centrist candidates because, for strategic reasons, fringe candidate supporters would probably also tend to vote for a centrist. Additional centrist candidates, on the other hand, might draw support away from major-party candidates if they (the new centrists) were perceived as serious contenders.

The question that is hard to answer, in the absence of experience, is whether such contenders could position themselves in such a way as to displace the major-party candidates. If so, presumably they would be motivated to run, giving voters more viable alternatives from which to choose and, in the process, weakening the two-party system. Their election, however, would probably not produce drastic changes in public policy since they would not be viable if they were unacceptable to numerous middle-of-the-road voters. In general, it seems likely that at the same time approval voting would give some additional support to strong minority candidates like George Wallace, it would also help centrist candidates—including perhaps nominees of new parties—both in winning their party's nomination in the primaries and conventions and prevailing against more extreme candidates in the general election.

8.4. The Sensitivity of Voting Systems to Numbers of Candidates

To illustrate why centrists would usually but not always be favored by approval voting, assume that there is an overriding issue in a campaign (e.g., the economy). Assume also that the attitudes of voters on this issue can be represented along a left-right continuum, which may be interpreted to measure attitudes that range from very liberal (on the left) to very conservative (on the right). For example, if the issue were the economy, liberal-conservative attitudes might be indexed by some quantitative variable like "degree of government intervention in the economy"; liberal voters would presumably favor a higher degree of government intervention, conservative voters less.

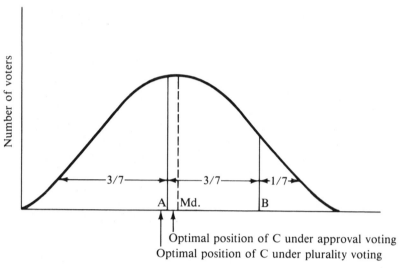

Figure 8.1 Optimal positions of candidate C under plurality and approval voting.

Assume that the two major parties nominate presidential candidates *A* and *B*, whose positions are shown along the horizontal axis in Figure 8.1. The vertical height of the voter distribution curve in Figure 8.1 indicates the number (or percentage) of voters who have attitudes at each point along the horizontal axis. Because the postulated distribution has one peak, or mode, it is characterized as *unimodal*. Since the curve has the same shape to the left and right of its median (md.), which is the point where the vertical dashed line intersects the horizontal axis, the distribution is *symmetric*.[13]

Assume that the goal of candidates is to maximize their vote totals, and voters vote (sincerely) for the candidate closest to their ideal position on the horizontal axis. Given the positions of *A* (slightly to the left of the medium) and *B* (farther to the right of the median) in Figure 8.1, and the assumed fractions of voters in each of the three regions these positions define, under plurality voting a third candidate *C* would be motivated to take a position just to the left of *A*, capturing essentially all the 43 percent ($\frac{3}{7}$) of the vote in the left region. If the other two candidates divided the remainder of the vote approximately equally (about 29 percent each)—which is not unreasonable since *A* would get most of the 43 percent in the middle, *B* all the 14 percent to his right and some in the middle—*C* would win the plurality election.[14]

In an election under approval voting, by contrast, *C*'s position just to the left of A probably would not be optimal. Instead, by moving to the right of A, he could attract support from both A and B voters. If, by positioning himself near the median, he got approval from, say, $\frac{2}{3}$ of the voters to the left of A, $\frac{9}{10}$ of the voters between A and B, and $\frac{1}{3}$ of the voters to the right of B, his approval-vote total would be about 70 percent:

$$\frac{2}{3}\left(\frac{3}{7}\right) + \frac{9}{10}\left(\frac{3}{7}\right) + \frac{1}{3}\left(\frac{1}{7}\right) = \frac{151}{210}.$$

These assumptions about C's acceptability to different segments of the electorate, while arbitrary, give not unreasonable estimates.

Given the positions of A and B, it seems unlikely that either would receive more approval votes than C, situated between them, although A might come close. This gives C the incentive under approval voting to take a position close to the median, rather than, as under plurality voting, to the side of his more moderate opponent (A in the example).

This example illustrates the sensitivity of plurality voting to the number of candidates and their positions. Approval voting is, by comparison, relatively insensitive to the other candidates in a race because—at least in principle—a candidate's acceptability does not depend on who else is in the race. Thus, it more closely satisfies "independence of irrelevant alternatives," which is a condition in the social-science literature that has been used in a different context and also widely misinterpreted.[15]

In practice, of course, if the field of candidates, say, doubled, a voter might decide to drop some old candidates and pick up some new ones (if they were closer to his ideal position) because of a narrowing of his "acceptability range" in the larger field. Nevertheless, approval voting appears to be less sensitive to new candidates who might enter a race than plurality voting, whose results are often influenced, if not upset, by new entrants.

A case in point is Javits's entry into the United States Senate race in New York in 1980 when, after losing in the Republican Party primary to D'Amato, he ran in the general election under the banner of the Liberal party. As argued in Section 7.2, Javits's entry almost surely threw the race to D'Amato, who, the polls showed, would have lost to Holtzman in a two-person contest. Javits was not "irrelevant"; while his presence would have been felt (with 49 percent approval) had there been approval voting, he probably would not have thrown the election to a non-Condorcet candidate.

The problem we have discussed in this section is not strictly a problem of information. In fact, poll information about the relative standing of candidates may alleviate this problem by inducing voters to shun the minor candidates and cast their votes for the candidates who "count."

However, this information did not stop 11 percent of New York voters from casting their lot with Javits, an almost certain loser, in the 1980 race, which underscores the persistence of the sensitivity problem.

Clearly, remedies that rely on the strategic acumen of voters to throw sincerity to the winds if it might contravene their interests are insufficient. Moreover, even when insincere voting succeeds in electing a Condorcet candidate, we consider the necessity of voters' being insincere to achieve a socially desirable result problematic.

We shall next address the question of how detailed information on voters' preferences, which permits them to calculate how others are likely to vote, may condition their own choices and affect the election outcome. This information puts voting into a game-theoretic context, which we shall illustrate with two simple examples. These will provide a springboard for discussing the equilibrium properties of outcomes, and their social acceptability, in games.

8.5. Approval Voting and Game Theory

We showed in Section 5.6 how information on the standing of candidates, perhaps as revealed by a poll, could be utilized by voters to make voting decisions to maximize their expected utilities. A poll may also, as shown in Chapter 7, induce changes in approval voting strategies. More specifically, as we argued in Section 8.3, many Wallace supporters, who realized their candidate was out of the running in the 1968 presidential election, evidently voted for their second choice under plurality voting, and probably would have voted for both Wallace and their second choice under approval voting.

These strategic calculations can be developed further using some ideas from game theory.[16] To illustrate them in a simple situation, consider a three-member committee in which the voters have the following preferences for three candidates {a,b,c}: (1) abc, (2) bac, and (3) cba. If each of the voters votes for just his first choice, a three-way tie results. Realizing this, voters 1 and 2 would have an apparent interest in supporting either a or b to prevent their worst choice, c, from winning, but which of these candidates they would settle on, given plurality voting, is hard to say.

Now voter 3, realizing his first choice, c, is unacceptable to both voters 1 and 2, would favor b over a. Indeed, he could form a coalition with voter 2, supporting b, whether voter 1 supports this choice or not.

In fact, b is the Condorcet candidate since he would be preferred to a by voters 2 and 3, and to c by voters 1 and 2. Furthermore, under plurality voting, it would seem that the optimal strategies of voters 2 and 3 are to vote for b, and for voter 1 to vote for a, given that they have complete information on each other's preferences. The reason why voter 1 would vote for *a* is that if, for whatever reason, voters 2 and 3 do not both vote for *b*, there would be some chance of *a*'s winning should he get the support of one other voter, or if there is a tie.

We said above that voter 3's strategy of voting for *b* was "optimal," but this statement can be challenged: by voting for *b*, he precludes the possibility of *c*'s winning, should, for example, voters 1 and 2 vote their sincere preferences. In this case, there would be a three-way tie, which would give *c* some chance of winning if, say, a random choice among the three candidates were made.

By contrast, voter 3 would be better able to take account of such a contingency if, given approval voting, he could vote for *both b* and *c*. Moreover, he would not have to vote insincerely for just *b* to allow for the possibility that *c* might be able to win.

Given this choice of {*b,c*} by voter 3 under approval voting, would voter 2 have any incentive to vote for his two top choices, too? The answer is "no," because if he voted for {*a,b*}, this would create a two-way tie between *a* and *b* with two votes each, given that voter 1 continues to vote only for {*a*}. And voter 1 has an incentive to do just this since he would prefer such a tie to *b*'s winning with certainty if he should cast a third and decisive approval vote for him.

Since voters 1, 2, and 3 have no incentive to switch unilaterally from their respective approval voting strategies of {*a*}, {*b*}, and {*b,c*}, the resulting outcome, *b*, is called a *Nash equilibrium*.[17] This is a stable set of strategies for the following reasons:

If voter 1 unilaterally switched to his other admissible strategy, {*a,b*}, the resulting outcome (still *b*) would not be better.

If voter 2 unilaterally switched to {*a,b*}, the resulting outcome (tie between *a* and *b*) would be worse than *b*'s winning with certainty.

If voter 3 unilaterally switched to {*c*}, the resulting outcome would be better only if *c* won in the resulting three-way tie. If it is assumed that voter 3 prefers *b*'s winning with certainty to *c*'s winning only occasionally (say, $\frac{1}{3}$ of the time), then he, too, would have no incentive to switch.

This lack of motivation to switch strategies on the part of all three voters means that the foregoing admissible approval voting strategies of {*a*}, {*b*}, and {*b,c*} induce a stable outcome, which is also the Condorcet choice. So do the admissible plurality voting strategies {*a*}, {*b*}, and {*b*}, but strategy {*b*} for voter 3 is not only insincere but provides him with no opportunity to realize his best outcome unless *both* voters 1 and 2 should unwisely vote for {*c*}. Because approval voting would assuredly lead to {*c*} if only *one* of these voters voted for {*c*}, in a sense it provides voter 3 with greater potential for gain—that is, to realize his best outcome.

We shall not try to develop this idea of "potential gain" further, but it would seem that sincere (approval) strategies like $\{b,c\}$ will in general offer a voter greater potential gain—if other voters do *not* follow their own optimal strategies—than insincere (plurality) strategies like $\{b\}$ for voter 3. This idea is related to the notion, discussed in Section 2.5, that a sincere voter cannot regret having failed to vote for a more-preferred candidate, for strategic reasons, under approval voting.

We now turn to the question of whether stable sets of admissible strategies, associated with Nash equilibria, can be insincere under approval voting in a game of complete information. As Theorem 2.3 in Section 2.5 demonstrates, if there are only three candidates, all admissible voter strategies are sincere under approval voting. Consider a voting game in which there are five voters, and their preferences for four candidates, $\{a,b,c,d\}$, are as follows:

1. 3: *abcd*
2. 2: *(bc)(ad)*.

Now the second set of two voters has the single admissible strategy $\{b,c\}$ and so will always choose it—regardless of the strategy choices of the other three voters—because it dominates all other strategies.

Assume that the first set of three voters choose their admissible but insincere strategy $\{a,c\}$. Then c will win with five votes to three votes for a and two for b. Since none of the voters, by unilaterally switching his strategy, can induce a better outcome (c would still win), the foregoing strategies of the five voters that elect c are in equilibrium.

Paradoxically, three voters (the first set) would prefer either a or b to c. Because a is preferred by a majority of voters to b (as well as to c and d), a is the Condorcet candidate.

Thus, there may be equilibrium strategies under approval voting that are not only insincere but may also result in the election of a non-Condorcet candidate. This is not to say, however, that there are not sincere approval voting strategies that would elect the Condorcet candidate—the choice of $\{a\}$ by the first set of voters would do just that—but that there are other admissible strategies, also in equilibrium, that will not elect the Condorcet candidate a. In particular, the choice of the sincere strategy $\{a,b\}$ by the first three voters will elect b, and the choice of the insincere strategy $\{a,c\}$, as just seen, will elect c; neither of these candidates is the Condorcet candidate, but both sets of strategies are in equilibrium, given the choice of $\{b,c\}$ by the second set of voters.

One lesson to be drawn from this example is that stable choices, in a game-theoretic sense, are not necessarily socially acceptable. In fact, c is a *Pareto-inferior* outcome—b is at least as good (for the second set of voters) and better for others (the first set of voters). Between b and a, however, b has some claim to being considered more acceptable—

though a is the Condorcet choice—because he is not the last choice of any voter.

Note that since both a and b are favored by different sets of voters, both outcomes are Pareto-superior. The fact that a is the Condorcet choice says only that more voters prefer a to b than vice versa.

In sum, equilibrium outcomes in a game may be Pareto-inferior, non-Condorcet, or both, and these outcomes may be the product of either sincere or insincere admissible strategies. To be sure, if all voters in the previous example had complete information about each others' preferences, there is no reason why each of the first set would not choose strategy $\{a\}$, yielding the Condorcet choice. But if information were not complete, and these voters for some reason thought that $\{a,b\}$ or $\{a,c\}$ was a "safer" admissible strategy and chose it instead, the resulting outcomes (b or c) would be Nash equilibria and just as stable as a.

Clearly, many outcomes may be Nash equilibria and have little else, besides their stability, to recommend them. Although we shall not give examples here, there are games in which there are no Nash equilibria, or no Nash equilibria that are the product of sincere admissible strategies (in the last example, both sincere and insincere strategies gave rise to Nash equilibria).

The preceding informal analysis can be formalized using tools from game theory. But we think this formalization is premature because general conditions have not yet been found that relate such things as voter preferences and sincere strategies to Condorcet choices, the existence of Nash equilibria, or whether or not these equilibria are Pareto-superior.

Roughly speaking, a game is a situation in which the players (voters) are assumed to have some—though not necessarily complete—information on each others' preferences, from which they can make inferences about others' strategy choices and exploit this information in choosing their own strategies. Unlike the decision-theoretic analysis in earlier chapters, in which voters were assumed not to be informed of each others' preferences or strategy choices—or at best have some information based on polls—game-theoretic calculations are more intricate and subtle. More research is needed to model how information that voters acquire about others' probable voting behavior, from small committees to large electorates, might affect, strategically, their candidate choices in an election.

8.6. The Monotonicity Paradox

We showed in Chapter 7 how poll announcements could influence election results by inducing voters to adjust their plurality and approval voting strategies to distinguish between the two front-runners revealed by the poll. The following example illustrates how preference as well as poll information can be exploited:

1. 6: *abc*
2. 5: *cab*
3. 4: *bca*
4. 2: *bac*.

If the 17 voters choose their sincere strategies under plurality voting, an (accurate) poll would reveal *a* and *b* to be in a dead heat with 6 votes each and *c* to trail with 5 votes. Given this information, it would appear rational for the second set of voters to vote insincerely for *a* to prevent their worst choice, *b*, from winning, thereby ensuring the election of *a* with 11 votes to 6 votes for *b*.

Now assume that all voters have complete information about each others' preferences. Would this additional information cause any further adjustments in voter strategies in the resulting game?

Clearly, the third set of voters, realizing that their sincere votes for *b* will help *a*, their worst choice, to win, could try to strike a deal with the second set of voters in support of *c*. If this deal were consummated, *c* would win with 9 of the 17 votes.

But then a coalition supporting *b* might form in opposition, and in turn a coalition supporting *a* might form in opposition to the *b*-coalition. Suffice it to say that bargaining in this game would be complex, because there is a paradox of voting and hence no Condorcet candidate: a majority of 11 voters prefers *a* to *b*, a different majority of 10 voters prefers *b* to *c*, and a still different majority of 9 voters prefers *c* to *a*.

Would these cyclical majorities continue to create incoherence if the plurality election were followed by a runoff between the top two vote-getters? The answer is "yes," because the contest would then revert to which pair gets into the runoff since the three possible pairs all lead to different winners.

Next suppose, for the sake of argument, that the fourth set of voters changes its preferences and favors *a* over *b* rather than vice versa:

4′. 2: *abc*.

In this case, a poll announcement, based on sincere voting by all four sets of voters under plurality voting, would indicate *a* (8 votes) and *c* (5 votes) to be the top two candidates. Given this information, the third set of voters favoring *b* would be motivated to vote insincerely for *c* to prevent *a* from winning, so the effect of the announcement would be to give the edge to *c* by 9 votes to 8 votes.

In summary, *a* wins after the poll announcement if the voters' preferences are as given at the beginning of this section, but if the fourth set of voters switches from 4 to 4'—favoring a—c wins. This seems extraordinary: a wins when *fewer* voters favor him, loses when more voters favor him.

Obviously the poll has a strange effect, but the paradoxical result it produces may occur without the poll. If the plurality election were followed by a runoff, for example, and all voters voted sincerely, a would make the runoff and then *win* against b in it, given the preference order of the fourth set of voters was bac; but if the preference order of these voters was abc, a would again make the runoff but this time *lose* to c in it.

What the runoff does, if the preferences of the fourth set of voters change in favor of a, is match a different pair. The poll announcement has the same effect as the runoff, as we showed in Section 7.5, by making the contest appear to be one between different pairs, depending on the preferences of the fourth set of voters. Since which pair of candidates is matched determines the winner due to the paradox of voting (which persists if the preferences of the fourth set of voters change from 4 to 4'), the election turns not on voter preferences alone but rather on how these preferences affect which two candidates are matched, either in a runoff or because of a poll announcement.

There is a *monotonicity paradox* if a winner (a in the previous example) is displaced after one or more voters (fourth set in the example) change their preferences in a way favorable to him without changing the order in which they prefer other candidates. Although new information (e.g., from a poll) may give rise to a monotonicity paradox, as we have illustrated, this paradox is usually discussed in the context of voting systems that are vulnerable to it.

Plurality voting, followed by a runoff, is not the only system that is nonmonotonic. So is the Hare system of preferential voting, or "single transferable vote" as it is also known, which extends the idea of a runoff to allow for a series of comparisons. Under this system, voters rank candidates, and if no candidate receives a majority of first-place votes, the candidate with the fewest first-place votes is dropped and his second-place votes are transferred to the other candidates. (In a three-candidate election, this procedure is equivalent to conducting a runoff, under the assumption that supporters of the candidate who does not make the runoff will vote for their second choice in the runoff.)

If there are more than three candidates, candidates continue to be eliminated, with their second-place votes reallocated to the remaining candidates, until one candidate receives a majority of votes. He then is declared the winner, but, as in a single runoff, it is possible for him to win with, say, 10,000 first-place votes but lose if he receives an additional 5,000 votes (from other voters who move him into first place without changing their ordering of other candidates) because of the monotonicity paradox. In a case like this, as Doron and Kronick imagine, many voters would probably be outraged by the election night report: "Mr. O'Grady did not obtain a seat in today's election, but if 5,000 of his supporters had voted for him in second place instead of first place, he would have won!"[18] Some news. Some election.

Unbelievable as this result may sound, the Hare system that can produce it is used today in elections in such places as Australia, Ireland, South Africa, Cambridge, MA, and New York City (in school board elections). Not only is it vulnerable to the monotonicity paradox, but it also does not ensure the election of a Condorcet candidate. (In the Buckley–Goodell–Ottinger race discussed in Section 7.5, the probable Condorcet candidate, Goodell, would have been eliminated at the start under the Hare system or had there been a runoff.) In fairness to the Hare system, however, it has certain strengths in ensuring proportional representation (e.g., of minorities) in multiple-winner elections, such as to a city council; our criticism is mostly directed at its use in single-winner elections.

The monotonicity paradox has been suspected for a long time,[19] but it was not until 1973 that it was conclusively established.[20] Fishburn has shown that a number of ranking and sequential-elimination voting systems are vulnerable to it, but most single-ballot systems, like plurality voting and approval voting, which do not involve the elimination of candidates and the transfer of votes, satisfy monotonicity.[21]

As we showed earlier in the case of plurality voting, however, poll announcements may induce voters to make strategic calculations that engender the monotonicity paradox. What about approval voting? If, in the example at the beginning of this section, the second set of voters switched for strategic reasons from strategy $\{c\}$ to $\{a,c\}$ as a result of the poll announcement, and all other voters approved of just their top candidates, a would still go into the runoff against b and win.

Now consider what would happen if the preferences of the fourth set of voters changed from bac to abc, favoring a as before. If all voters approved of only their top candidates, the poll would indicate a and c to be the top two candidates. Its announcement would induce the third set of voters to switch from $\{b\}$ to $\{b,c\}$, but all this would do is solidify c's place in the runoff against a, and thereby his victory. Thus, poll announcements can render approval voting, as well as plurality voting, nonmonotonic because they induce voters to vote *as if* there were a runoff.

Nonmonotonicity contradicts what seems to us a basic principle of democratic elections: if some voters raise a candidate in their preference orders without changing their ordering of other candidates, and he consequently receives more votes, he will *not* do worse in an election. Unfortunately, as we have shown, being elevated in the preference orders of some voters may torpedo a candidate's victory, depending on the system used for aggregating votes.

In our opinion, this pathology is most serious when it is the product of sincere voting, as it is under the runoff and Hare systems. By contrast, the ascent of a candidate in some voters' preference orders never hurts and sometimes helps him under plurality and approval voting. The rub under these systems comes only when voters react strategically to certain information, such as a poll, indicating the two front-runners.

In elections in which such information is generated, the monotonicity paradox is potentially a problem, though how serious is difficult to say. In an election like the Buckley–Goodell–Ottinger race in 1970, for example, it is not inconceivable that some fraction of Ottinger supporters went from OGB to BGO, favoring Buckley, over the course of the campaign. Then, had they reacted to a poll that said Buckley was out of the running (there was no such poll!) and voted for their second choice (Goodell) instead, Goodell could have won despite the switch in favor of Buckley. (Indeed, the switch is precisely what sets the stage for this reversal.)

Of course, this is only a thought experiment that is at odds with the facts in this election. Nevertheless, it illustrates a heretofore unrecognized (as far as we know) pathology of polls—that they may undermine candidates who are actually favored by changes in voter preferences over the course of a campaign.

8.7. Conclusions

Elections are not conducted in the dark. The most reliable information on the standing of candidates in major races typically comes from public opinion polls, which set up expectations to which voters react. Possible effects of adjustments that voters make to exploit this information, discussed in Chapter 7, were illustrated in a recent United States Senate election and the 1968 presidential election. Significant differences between the effects of plurality and approval voting on the election of Condorcet candidates, and the influence of polls under each type of system, were noted.

Approval voting would appear to be much less sensitive than plurality voting to the number of candidates in a race. Different strategies would be optimal under approval voting—as we illustrated with some spatial calculations—which would probably favor centrist candidates but still give more extremist candidates, like George Wallace in the 1968 presidential election, their proper due. In this election, both Wallace and Richard Nixon would have done relatively better than they actually did—Nixon because he was not only a centrist but also the

Condorcet candidate, Wallace because he would not have suffered from the wasted-vote phenomenon.

Information about voter preferences opens up the possibility of calculating others' best strategies—with a view to determining one's own—in a game. We illustrated such game-theoretic calculations to demonstrate that stable outcomes are not always Pareto-superior, nor do they always result in the election of Condorcet candidates.

Some voting systems, including plurality voting followed by a runoff, are vulnerable to the monotonicity paradox, whereby a candidate's being favored by more voters may cost him an election. This result seems perverse and, in our opinion, inconsistent with democratic choice. Approval and plurality voting are not vulnerable to it if voters are sincere, but it can occur if voters react strategically to poll information.

The lesson we draw from these diverse findings is that the effects of information are not, in general, neutral. Information—even accurate information—may help or hurt a candidate in an election, depending on what strategic calculations it sets in motion. When these calculations produce perverse results, as in the monotonicity paradox, or when they undermine a Condorcet candidate, an evident disservice is done to the voters.

Are there remedies? We think one must begin with an understanding of information pathologies and then ask how their deleterious effects can be minimized. For example, should the publication of polls be banned a week before an election, as is done in presidential elections in France, to discourage insincere voting? Since the French hold a runoff if no candidate receives a majority in the plurality election, sincere voting does not bar the monotonicity paradox in France, but it would be prevented if there were ordinary plurality or approval voting.

This kind of knowledge, we believe, is helpful in designing better voting systems and election procedures. To us, the sensitivity of plurality voting to (often large) numbers of candidates is its most serious failing, especially in primaries. This failing would be greatly attenuated, if not eliminated, by approval voting. Fortunately, the 1980 presidential election did not come to grief because of the multicandidate problem—at least in the general election—but, as we shall show in Chapter 9, the robustness of the system was challenged once again by a significant independent candidate.

Footnotes to Chapter 8

1. Gerald De Maio and Douglas Muzzio, "The 1980 Elections and Approval Voting," *Presidential Studies Quarterly* **9,** 3 (Summer 1981), 341–363.

2. Quoted in Irvin Molotsky, "Javits Says He Would Consider Any Offer of

a Position if Reagan Sought Him," *New York Times*, November 14, 1980, p. B1.

3. Material in this section is based in part on Steven J. Brams and Peter C. Fishburn, "Approval Voting," *American Political Science Review* **72**, 3 (September 1978), 840–842; S. J. Brams, *The Presidential Election Game* (New Haven: Yale University Press, 1978), pp. 221–228; and S. J. Brams, *Comparison Voting*, Innovative Instructional Unit (Washington, DC: American Political Science Association, 1978), pp. 51–66, which will appear in slightly revised form in *Modules in Applied Mathematics: Political and Related Models*, Vol. 2, edited by Steven J. Brams, William F. Lucas, and Philip D. Straffin, Jr. (New York: Springer-Verlag, 1982). However, we also report on studies published since the aforementioned work was done.

4. John Kellett and Kenneth Mott, "Presidential Primaries: Measuring Popular Choice," *Polity* **9**, 4 (Summer 1977), 528–537. Similar results were found for gubernatorial primaries held in New Jersey in June 1981, in which the average voter would have approved of 2.1 candidates. See Steven J. Brams, Arnold Urken, George Sharrard, and Douglas Muzzio, "Results of Exit Poll of New Jersey Voters in Democratic and Republican Gubernatorial Primaries, June 2, 1981" (press release, June 17, 1981).

5. William R. Keech and Donald R. Matthews, *The Party's Choice* (Washington, DC: Brookings Institution, 1976), p. 212.

6. Richard A. Joslyn, "The Impact of Decision Rules in Multi-Candidate Campaigns: The Case of the 1972 Democratic Presidential Nomination," *Public Choice* **25** (Spring 1976), 1–18. The effects of different rules for allocating delegates in the 1972 Democratic presidential primaries (winner-take-all, proportional, and districted) is explored in James I. Lengle and Byron Shafer, "Primary Rules, Political Power, and Social Change," *American Political Science Review* **70**, 1 (March 1976), 25–40; Louis Maisel and Gerald J. Lieberman, "The Impact of Electoral Rules on Primary Elections: The Democratic Presidential Primaries in 1976," in *The Impact of the Electoral Process*, edited by Louis Maisel and Joseph Cooper (Beverly Hills, CA: Sage, 1977), pp. 39–80; and Thomas H. Hammond, "Another Look at the Role of 'The Rules' in the 1972 Democratic Presidential Primaries," *Western Political Quarterly* **33**, 1 (March 1980), 50–72. The effects of allocating delegates in presidential primaries, based on approval votes rather than plurality votes, has not been studied. A potential problem, which Philip D. Straffin, Jr., pointed out to S. J. Brams in conversation in 1980, is that candidates would find it in their interest to set up temporary *Doppelgängers* to run, who would pick up essentially the same approval votes as they would. Then, after the *Doppelgängers* dropped out, a candidate would presumably inherit their delegate votes, gaining an edge over candidates without *Doppelgängers*. This would be a clever strategy but, we think, would soon become so transparent that it would undermine the attractiveness of the *Doppelgängers*, and maybe the candidate himself who set them up. With a high risk of backfiring, we doubt such a strategy would be tried.

7. Samuel Merrill, III, "Strategic Decisions under One-Stage Multi-Candidate Voting Systems," *Public Choice* **36**, 1 (1981), 127, Table 1.

8. See Daniel A. Mazmanian, *Third Parties in Presidential Elections* (Washington, DC: Brookings Institution, 1974).

9. D. Roderik Kiewiet, "Approval Voting: The Case of the 1968 Presidential Election," *Polity* **12**, 1 (Fall 1979), 170–181.

10. Richard M. Scammon and Ben J. Wattenberg, *The Real Majority: An Extraordinary Examination of the American Electorate* (New York: Coward, McCann and Geoghegan, 1970), pp. 171–172.

11. D. R. Kiewiet, "Approval Voting: The Case of the 1968 Election," p. 178.

12. On the debate over the Electoral College and an analysis of its biases, see S. J. Brams, *Presidential Election Game*, Ch. 3. The case for direct popular vote is made in Neal R. Peirce and Lawrence D. Longley, *The People's President: The Electoral College in American History and the Direct Vote Alternative,* Rev. Ed. (New Haven: Yale University Press, 1981).

13. A *median* divides the area under a distribution curve exactly in half, which means in this example that half the voters have attitudes to the left of the point where the median line intersects the horizontal axis and half have attitudes to the right of this point. Moreover, because the distribution is symmetric—the curve to the left of the median is a mirror image of the curve to the right—the same numbers of voters have attitudes equal distances to the left and right of the median. For an elementary analysis of spatial models, and references to the literature, see S. J. Brams, *Presidential Election Game*, Ch. 1.

14. For reasons why voters support third-party candidates under plurality voting, see William H. Riker, "The Number of Political Parties: A Reexamination of Duverger's Law," *Comparative Politics* **9**, 1 (October 1976), 93–106; W. H. Riker, "Duverger's Law: Plurality Voting and Party Systems," *American Political Science Review* **76**, 4 (December 1982), 753–766; and Steven J. Brams and Philip D. Straffin, Jr., "The Entry Problem in a Political Race," in *Political Equilibrium,* edited by Peter C. Ordeshook and Kenneth A. Shepsle (Boston: Kluwer-Nijhoff, 1982), pp. 181–195.

15. Steven J. Brams, *Paradoxes in Politics: An Introduction to the Nonobvious in Political Science* (New York: Free Press, 1976) , pp. 34–37.

16. A more formal development of these ideas is given in Steven J. Brams, *Game Theory and Politics* (New York: Free Press, 1975), Ch. 2. Equilibrium results for approval voting when voters are sincere are given in K. H. Kim and Fred W. Roush, *Introduction to Mathematical Consensus Theory,* Lecture Notes in Pure and Applied Mathematics, Vol. 59 (New York: Marcel Dekker, 1980), pp. 100–102.

17. John Nash, "Non-cooperative Games," *Annals of Mathematics* **54**, 2 (September 1951), 286–295.

18. Gideon Doron and Richard Kronick, "Single Transferrable Vote: An Example of a Perverse Social Choice Function," *American Journal of Political Science* **21**, 2 (May 1977), 303–311.

19. *Report of the Royal Commission Appointed to Enquire into Electoral Systems* (London: HMSO, 1910), Cd. 5163, p. 21; and James Creed Meredith,

Proportional Representation in Ireland (Dublin, 1913), p. 93. We are grateful to Duff Spafford for these references.

20. John H. Smith, "Aggregation of Preferences with Variable Electorate," *Econometrica* **41**, 6 (November 1973), 1027–1041.

21. Peter C. Fishburn, "Monotonicity Paradoxes in the Theory of Elections," *Discrete Applied Mathematics* **4**, 2 (April 1982), 119–134. A related paradox, in which some voters, by truncating their preferences (e.g., indicating only a first choice rather than an ordering over all candidates), can induce a better outcome under the Hare system, is given in Steven J. Brams, "The AMS Nomination Procedure is Vulnerable to 'Truncation of Preferences,'" *Notices of the American Mathematical Society* **29**, 2 (February 1982), 136–138, where an extreme case of nonmonotonicity is also given: a candidate loses when some voters raise him from last to first place in their preference orders. The truncation problem is also shown to affect other preferential voting systems in Hannu Nurmi, "On Taking Preferences Seriously" (mimeographed, 1982). For a catalogue of paradoxes to which preferential voting is vulnerable, see P. C. Fishburn and S. J. Brams, "Paradoxes of Preferential Voting," *Mathematics Magazine* (forthcoming).

Chapter 9

Deducing Preferences and Choices in the 1980 Presidential Election[1]

9.1. Introduction

It is appropriate, we think, to conclude this book by analyzing, as of this writing (June 1982), the most recent presidential election. Fortuitously, included in this election was the most significant independent or third-party candidate since George Wallace in 1968, whose impact on the 1968 race we assessed in Section 8.3. As we shall show, the outcome of the 1980 race would not have changed under approval voting, but the independent candidate, John Anderson, would have done spectacularly better than he did under plurality voting, at least in the popular vote.

This election thus illustrates an advantage of approval voting alluded to earlier—its ability to reflect accurately not only the first-place but also the residual support of the candidates. This overall support for candidates is not picked up by plurality voting and, worse, may be greatly distorted by insincere or strategic voting in plurality elections.

A voting system, in our view, should be a reasonably sensitive barometer of voter feelings toward the candidates. Even when there would have been no displacement of candidates because of approval voting, as was true in 1980, it is desirable to have better information on voter support than is conveyed by plurality voting. This kind of information is politically valuable to both the winners and losers, for from it they can try to fashion future policies and programs with the widest possible voter appeal. We believe a democracy should foster such appeals not just by permitting freedom of association and freedom of press but also by not, more subtly, suppressing information in its election returns. The George Wallaces and John Andersons, despite their lower status, express protest and discontent, and their support should not be stifled or downplayed in a democracy.

In this chapter, we suggest a deductive approach for explaining voting behavior in the 1980 presidential election. We begin by positing a set of assumptions about voting behavior in this election, based on the preferences of voters and their assessments of the strategic environment, and then estimate statistically the numbers of voters who ranked the three major candidates in all possible preference orders. These estimates require both survey and election data, which we assemble from a variety of sources. We next use these data to develop the implications of our assumptions for (1) determining the extent of strategic voting in the 1980 election, (2) approximating the performance of the candidates under approval voting, and (3) measuring the degree to which voter preferences mirrored a single left-right ideological dimension that voters used in the evaluation of their candidates.

Our approach to accounting for voting behavior generally, and understanding its effects in a particular election, is unorthodox. Like the empirical analysis in Chapter 4, we go back to what we consider the roots of voter choices, namely voter preferences. To be sure, since V. O. Key's seminal work,[2] many analysts have argued that voters, generally speaking, make rational choices, but their arguments have been largely based on the prevalence of "issue voting," not on directly linking voter choices to their underlying preference orders.[3]

Probably the most important lesson coming out of our approach is that inferences of the kind we make can be disciplined by a formal model, grounded in explicit assumptions about rational behavior. One important advantage of this approach is that when the results we derive seem suspect, they can be traced back to the assumptions rather than remain hidden in casual statements or a plethora of variables. Indeed, as we shall show later, the robustness of our results can be determined by testing the consequences of alternative assumptions—particularly about the values of certain parameters in the statistical model—through sensitivity analysis.

The statistical model that we develop from the rational-choice assumptions allows us to piece together data in such a way as to derive election results by solving systems of linear equations. These results are speculative, not only because the data are incomplete but also because, in most instances, they describe how voters would behave in hypothetical situations. Nevertheless, we believe they tell us significant things about the 1980 presidential election that are both surprising and not obtainable in the absence of a systematic approach.

This is not to say that intuition has no place in election analysis, or that conventional multivariate statistical analysis cannot be helpful. Rather, we would argue, hunches should be carefully explicated, and statistical analysis should not be burdened with variables that bear no clear logical relationship to the problem at hand. In short, we prefer an austere approach—one which manipulates relevant (if limited) data to maximum advantage.

Some of the assumptions we shall make may seem controversial, and certain "reasonable" parameter values we posit may seem unjustified. We attempt to defend these, but at the same time we are not so wedded to them that we cannot entertain alternative assumptions and values. An important merit of our analysis, we believe, is that these alternatives can be tried out by other researchers, and our inferences revised with simply a reapplication of the rational-choice model and its associated statistical methodology.

This methodology requires little more than an understanding of high school algebra to follow. Essentially, we solve systems of linear equations, but because these systems are usually underdetermined (i.e., there are fewer equations than variables), we must make additional assumptions either to obtain explicit solutions or to show up certain relationships among the variables.

The principal focus of our substantive analysis is on John Anderson's candidacy, which we demonstrate probably had much greater residual, as well as first-place, support than is sometimes thought. In fact, we argue that as many as four-fifths of his supporters, who ranked him ahead of Jimmy Carter or Ronald Reagan, may have deserted him in the election for strategic reasons. Also, we show it is conceivable, though unlikely, that he could have won under approval voting, but that the common perception that he was the candidate in the middle was probably erroneous.

9.2. Preferences and Voter Behavior

The 1980 presidential election was the first presidential election since 1968 in which there was a significant third-party or independent candidate. Although John Anderson's popular-vote total (7 percent) was not sufficient to have swung the popular-vote result from Ronald Reagan (51 percent) to Jimmy Carter (41 percent), throughout the campaign he was thought to pose a serious threat to Carter's candidacy. Although about 1 percent of the vote went to several minor-party candidates—mainly Ed Clark, the Libertarian Party candidate—we shall proceed as if only Reagan (R), Carter (C), and Anderson (A) were running.

To get a total of 100 percent for these three candidates, we increase each of R and C by $\frac{1}{2}$ percent:

R: 51.5
C: 41.5
A: 7.0.

This "correction" is arbitrary but not unreasonable. In any event, any corrections of less than 1 percent—including the actual percentages rounded to the nearest tenth or hundredth of 1 percent—though not without significance, have little impact on our conclusions.

An ABC News exit poll, taken on Election Day as voters left polling booths, showed the following preference percentages in the three hypothetical two-candidate contests:[4]

	R	C	A	Abstain	Total
A vs. R	53	–	41	6	100
A vs. C	–	46	49	5	100
C vs. R	54	43	–	3	100

To begin our rational-choice analysis, we assume a person abstained in a pairwise comparison if and only if he:

    i. did not vote for either candidate in that comparison (in the actual election);

    ii. was indifferent between the two candidates.

When these are tied into later assumptions about voting, they imply that all abstainers, for a given comparison, prefer the candidate left out to the two candidates compared, between whom they are indifferent. For example, the 6 percent who abstained in the A-vs.-R case had preference order $C(AR)$, where the parentheses enclose candidates between whom the voter is indifferent.

We assume that no voter was indifferent among all three candidates. This leaves twelve feasible preference orders, listed in Table 9.1, with symbolic percentages within the voter population denoted by the x_i's. As before, order abc means that a is preferred to b is preferred to c; $a(bc)$ means that a is preferred to b and c, and the voter is indifferent between b and c; and $(ab)c$ means that the voter is indifferent between a and b, and prefers both to c. We categorize the first set of orders as strict, the second as single best, and the third as single worst. Moreover, we require $x_1 + x_2 + \cdots + x_{12} = 100$.

We make the following assumptions with respect to the actual voting:

    iii. a voter with C or R as uniquely best in his preference order voted for C or R, respectively;

    iv. a fraction α of voters with order ACR voted for A; the remaining $1 - \alpha$ fraction voted for C;

    v. a fraction β of voters with order ARC voted for A; the remaining $1 - \beta$ fraction voted for R;

Table 9.1

Feasible Preference Orders*

Category	Preference Order	Percentage of Voters
Strict:	ACR	x_1
	ARC	x_2
	CAR	x_3
	CRA	x_4
	RAC	x_5
	RCA	x_6
Single best:	$A(CR)$	x_7
	$C(AR)$	x_8
	$R(AC)$	x_9
Single worst:	$(CR)A$	x_{10}
	$(AR)C$	x_{11}
	$(AC)R$	x_{12}

*Source: Steven J. Brams and Peter C. Fishburn, "Deducing Preferences and Choices in the 1980 Presidential Election," *Electoral Studies* (forthcoming), Table 1; reprinted with permission.

   vi. all voters with $A(RC)$ voted for A;

   vii. all voters with $(AR)C$ and $(AC)R$ voted for their non-A most preferred [R for $(AR)C$ and C for $(AC)R$]; voters with $(CR)A$ split their votes evenly between R and C.

These assumptions seem quite reasonable. Since A appeared to be out of the running from polls taken before the election, (iii) and (vii) present no problem. Assumptions (iv) and (v) presume only that a voter with A in first place did not vote for his least-preferred candidate. Assumption (vi) applies to voters who liked A best and otherwise did not care, so it seems likely that virtually all these voters would vote for A.

    Assumptions (i)–(iii), and (vi) and (vii), in conjunction with the ABC News exit-poll data, imply that

$$x_7 = 3 \text{ for } A(CR),$$

$$x_8 = 6 \text{ for } C(AR),$$

$$x_9 = 5 \text{ for } R(AC).$$

Put another way, the only way the supporters of a candidate would rank him single best is if they abstained in the pairwise contest between the other two, so the above figures simply match the relevant abstention figures of the ABC News data to the single-best orders.

Assumptions (iii)–(vii), along with the "corrected" election results, yield

vote for R: $51.5 = (x_5 + x_6 + x_9) + (x_{11} + x_{10}/2) + (1 - \beta)x_2$

vote for C: $41.5 = (x_3 + x_4 + x_8) + (x_{12} + x_{10}/2) + (1 - \alpha)x_1$

vote for A: $7 = x_7 + \alpha x_1 + \beta x_2$.

That is, the vote totals of each of the two leading candidates, R and C, include all his strict and single-best supporters, half his supporters who are indifferent between R and C, and some fractions of strict A supporters. By comparison, A picks up only his single-best supporters and certain fractions of his strict supporters.

In view of the values of x_7, x_8, and x_9 noted above, by subtracting out these values from the left sides of the above vote equations and eliminating each of these variables on the right sides, we get

$$R: 46.5 = x_5 + x_6 + x_{11} + x_{10}/2 + (1 - \beta)x_2 \qquad (9.1)$$

$$C: 35.5 = x_3 + x_4 + x_{12} + x_{10}/2 + (1 - \alpha)x_1 \qquad (9.2)$$

$$A: 4 = \alpha x_1 + \beta x_2. \qquad (9.3)$$

These total to 86 since $x_7 + x_8 + x_9 = 14$ is the sum of the values subtracted from the three equations.

Next we turn to assumptions that characterize the basis for choosing between one or two candidates in the ABC News poll pairwise contests. The nonabstaining respondents in the poll, we assume, "vote" for their preferred candidate in each pairwise comparison. Assume also that, in the a-vs.-b comparison, the respondents with $(ab)c$ split evenly between a and b. This coincides with assumption (vii) in the actual election for voters with $(CR)A$ in the hypothetical C-vs.-R contest, but not with (vii) for $(AR)C$ and $(AC)R$. For example, we assume that people with $(AR)C$ voted for R in the general election (since A had no chance); but if only A and R were in the race, it seems reasonable that $(AR)C$ people would split evenly between A and R.[5] Stated formally, the assumption is:

viii. in a comparison between a and b in the ABC News poll, voters who preferred one of a and b to the other voted for their preferred candidate, and those with $(ab)c$ split their votes evenly between a and b.

The foregoing assumptions yield the following, where x_7, x_8, and x_9 have been subtracted out:

$$R \text{ over } A: 48 = x_4 + x_5 + x_6 + x_{10} + x_{11}/2 \qquad (9.4)$$

$$A \text{ over } R: 38 = x_1 + x_2 + x_3 + x_{12} + x_{11}/2 \qquad (9.4')$$

$$A \text{ over } C: 46 = x_1 + x_2 + x_5 + x_{11} + x_{12}/2 \qquad (9.5)$$

$$C \text{ over } A: 40 = x_3 + x_4 + x_6 + x_{10} + x_{12}/2 \qquad (9.5')$$

$$R \text{ over } C: 49 = x_2 + x_5 + x_6 + x_{11} + x_{10}/2 \qquad (9.6)$$

$$C \text{ over } R: 37 = x_1 + x_3 + x_4 + x_{12} + x_{10}/2. \qquad (9.6')$$

For example, the R-over-A comparison of equation (9.4) awards three of six strict preference orders to R (those in which R ranks higher), no single-best order (since the one in which R is preferred is subtracted out), and all of one single-worst order (both R and C preferred over A) and half of another (both R and A preferred over C). The percentages of voters for these "$4\frac{1}{2}$" orders total 53 (for R, as indicated in the ABC News poll) minus 5 (for x_9, or the "diehard" R who would not vote for either C or A), which gives 48.

Note that $(9.4) + (9.4') = (9.5) + (9.5') - (9.6) + (9.6') = 86$, which is the percentage of nonabstaining voters—those who are not diehards for any of the three candidates. This system of six equations yields only three independent equations—one from each pair—along with a fourth independent equation for the total, namely

$$86 = (x_1 + x_2 + x_3 + x_4 + x_5 + x_6) + (x_{10} + x_{11} + x_{12}). \qquad (9.7)$$

Note also that (9.7) is given by $(9.1) + (9.2) + (9.3)$, so that the first three equations provide only two more independent equations.

All told, there are six independent equations but 11 unknowns, namely $x_1 - x_6$; $x_{10} - x_{12}$; and α and β. In Section 9.3 two degrees of freedom will be used up to get estimates of αx_1 and βx_2, i.e., strict-order A supporters. Additional assumptions will then be made to impose greater determinateness on the system of equations, which in turn will allow additional analysis and yield further results.

9.3. Analysis of Anderson Supporters (but Not Voters)

When (9.1) is subtracted from (9.6), and (9.2) is subtracted from (9.6'), the result is

$$2.5 = \beta x_2,$$

$$1.5 = \alpha x_1,$$

the sum of which agrees with (9.3). Given these values of αx_1 and βx_2, (9.1)–(9.3) have no further use since they are subsumed by (9.6) and (9.6').

An independent check on the values of αx_1 and βx_2 is provided by a *New York Times*/CBS News exit poll,[6] which shows that the 7 percent of the electorate who voted for Anderson would have voted as follows if A had not been on the ballot:

R: 49
C: 41
Abstain: 10.

Thus, if A had not been on the ballot and the other 93 percent voted as indicated previously, then the total would have been about 55.3 percent for R and 44.7 percent for C. According to our earlier assumptions, the A voters came from ACR (αx_1), ARC (βx_2), and $A(CR)(x_7)$.

Now suppose that the A voters with ACR indicated they would have voted for C in a C-vs.-R contest; those with ARC would have voted for R in a C-vs.-R contest; and those with $A(CR)$ would either have abstained or split between C and R in a C-vs.-R contest. Then, using the *New York Times*/CBS News data, the 10 percent of the 7 percent of A voters who abstained on the C-vs.-R question gives 0.7 percent of the general electorate who had $A(CR)$ and abstained on the C-vs.-R question in the *New York Times*/CBS News poll, which leaves $x_7 - 0.7 = 3 - 0.7 = 2.3$ of $A(CR)$ that split between C and R on the C-vs.-R question. Therefore,

$$(0.49)7 = 3.43 = \beta x_2 + 2.3/2,$$

$$(0.41)7 = 2.87 = \alpha x_1 + 2.3/2,$$

which, when solved for αx_1 and βx_2, give $\alpha x_1 = 1.72$ and $\beta x_2 = 2.28$. These values are fairly close to those given above ($\alpha x_1 = 1.5$ and $\beta x_2 = 2.5$), lending credibility to our use of the former values.

To obtain at least a rough indication of plausible values of α and β, we shall assume for the moment that $x_{10} = x_{11} = x_{12} = 0$—that is, no voters fall in the single-worst category in Table 9.1. While obviously an oversimplification, this assumption is not as drastic as it at first might seem, though we shall drop it in Section 9.4.

Its rationale is as follows. Because voters with $(CR)A$, $(AR)C$, and $(AC)R$ had no clear first choice, it seems plausible to suppose that they were less numerous than voters with an indifference pair but a clear first choice, i.e., those with $A(CR)$, $C(AR)$, and $R(AC)$, who comprised about 14 percent of the voting population by our earlier assumptions. (Recall these are the abstaining voters, or diehards for one candidate.) Moreover, even if $x_{10} + x_{11} + x_{12}$ comprised, say, 7 percent of the voters, this would not materially affect the present analysis in view of the other uncertainties which surround the data.

Given $x_{10} = x_{11} = x_{12} = 0$, the data from an October 14–16 *Time* poll will be used to estimate α and β. This poll showed that the following percentages of respondents found each of the three major candidates "acceptable":[7]

R: 61
C: 57
A: 49.

Since this poll was taken three weeks before the election, we shall treat it with due caution.

We assume that, in an approval-voting context (this context is dictated by the availability of *Time* "acceptability" data)—whose implications we shall develop later—

    ix. each voter would vote for his most preferred candidate(s), and not vote for his least preferred candidate(s);
    x. voters with strict preference orders who have candidate b as their second choice would vote for b at rate λ_b.

Thus, λ_R of the voters with *ARC* and *CRA* would vote for ("approve of") R as well as their first-place candidate, λ_C of the *ACR* and *RCA* voters would vote for C, and λ_A of the *CAR* and *RAC* voters would vote for A. If we use the admittedly tenuous *Time* data, then

$$R: 61 = \lambda_R(x_2 + x_4) + x_5 + x_6 + x_9$$
$$C: 57 = \lambda_C(x_1 + x_6) + x_3 + x_4 + x_8$$
$$A: 49 = \lambda_A(x_3 + x_5) + x_1 + x_2 + x_7.$$

(If x_{10}, x_{11}, and x_{12} had not been set at zero, x_{10} would be added to the first two lines, and so forth.) With $(x_7, x_8, x_9) = (3, 6, 5)$, we have $x_1 + \cdots + x_6 = 86$ and

$$R: 56 = \lambda_R(x_2 + x_4) + x_5 + x_6$$
$$C: 51 = \lambda_C(x_1 + x_6) + x_3 + x_4$$
$$A: 46 = \lambda_A(x_3 + x_5) + x_1 + x_2.$$

In addition, since $x_{10} = x_{11} = x_{12} = 0$, (9.4′) and (9.5) give

$$x_3 = 38 - x_1 - x_2,$$
$$x_5 = 46 - x_1 - x_2;$$

(9.6′) and (9.6) yield, with the above substitutions for x_3 and x_5,

$$x_4 = 37 - x_1 - x_2 - x_3 = -1 + x_2,$$
$$x_6 = 49 - x_2 - x_5 = 3 + x_1.$$

Making all these substitutions in the three preceding R-C-A equations, we get

$$R: \quad 7 = \lambda_R(2x_2 - 1) - x_2$$

$$C: 14 = \lambda_C(2x_1 + 3) - x_1$$

$$A: 46 = -\lambda_A(2x_1 + 2x_2 - 84) + x_1 + x_2.$$

Finally, when $x_2 = 2.5/\beta$ and $x_1 = 1.5/\alpha$ are substituted into these three equations, we obtain

$$R: \beta = \frac{5\lambda_R - 2.5}{\lambda_R + 7}$$

$$C: \alpha = \frac{3\lambda_C - 1.5}{-3\lambda_C + 14}$$

$$A: \alpha\beta(84\lambda_A - 46) = \alpha(5\lambda_A - 2.5) + \beta(3\lambda_A - 1.5).$$

The first two of these equations, for R and C, are plotted in Figure 9.1 to show how α and β vary as their λ's vary.

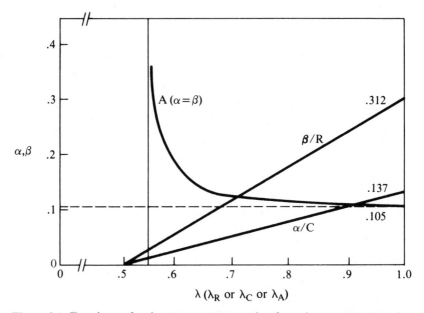

Figure 9.1 Fractions of strict A supporters voting for A but not C (α), and A but not R (β), as a function of those approving of second choices (λ's). (Source: Steven J. Brams and Peter C. Fishburn, "Deducing Preferences and Choices in the 1980 Presidential Election," *Electoral Studies* (forthcoming), Figure 1; reprinted with permission.)

To give feasible values of α and β, note that λ_R and λ_C must be at least $\frac{1}{2}$—that is, at least half of strict-order voters with second choices of R and C would vote for them, as well as their first choices, under approval voting. We also show in Figure 9.1 a horizontal dashed line at 0.105, which indicates that more than 10 percent of strict A supporters will, according to our assumptions, vote only for him because $x_1 + x_2$ cannot exceed 38, according to (9.4'). If, in fact, $x_1 + x_2 = 38$ and $\alpha = \beta$, we then have $\alpha = \beta = \frac{4}{38} = 0.105$. When $\alpha = \beta$, the horizontal dashed line gives a *lower* bound on possible values of α and β.

More generally, (9.4'), with $x_{11} = x_{12} = 0$, requires

$$\frac{1.5}{\alpha} + \frac{2.5}{\beta} = 38 - x_3.$$

Since x_3 is for CAR, which might be in the neighborhood of 15 percent or more, the lowest sensible values for α and β would probably be about 0.16. What Figure 9.1 also shows is that if the *Time* poll figures are even approximately applicable to Election-Day preferences and choices, then α and β are probably not much larger than this. In other words, the large majority of strict A supporters—we estimate 80 percent at the end of this section—almost certainly voted for their second choices (C or R).

The solid curve in Figure 9.1 applies to A supporters under the assumption that $\alpha = \beta$. Its equation, as obtained from the preceding A equation, is

$$\alpha = \beta = \frac{8\lambda_A - 4}{84\lambda_A - 46}.$$

When this is solved for λ_A in terms of α, it shows that values of α in $[0,1]$ are obtained only if λ_A is between 10.5/19, or about 0.55, and 1 (see Figure 9.1).

To obtain realistic values of α and β for the *Time* poll data, it is necessary to take λ_R and λ_C fairly near to 1, while λ_A can be somewhat smaller. Since such λ values seem unlikely, though not impossible, consider the effect of changing the *Time* poll data, which probably would have been different on Election Day. If Reagan's approval percentage is changed from 61 to $61 + r$, then β, as a function of λ_R and r, is given by

$$\beta = \frac{5\lambda_R - 2.5}{\lambda_R + 7 + r}.$$

Positive r values lower the β/R curve in Figure 9.1, and negative r values raise that curve, but one still gets $\beta = 0$ when $\lambda_R = \frac{1}{2}$. For example, to get $\beta = 0.25$, one needs $\lambda_R = 0.89$ when $r = 0$ (61 percent approval for R), $\lambda_R = 1.0$ when $r = 2$ (63 percent approval for R), and

$\lambda_R = 0.68$ when $r = -4$ (57 percent approval for R). When Carter's approval percentage is changed from 51 to $51 + c$, we get

$$\alpha = \frac{3\lambda_C - 1.5}{-3\lambda_C + 14 + c},$$

and to have $\alpha = 0.15$ one needs $\lambda_C = 1.0$ when $c = -1$ (56 percent of approval for C), and $\lambda_C = 0.70$ when $c = -8$ (49 percent approval for C). With these trade-offs between α and λ_C, and β and λ_R, what assumptions are reasonable?

Several polls from mid-October up to Election Day, but particularly after the Carter–Reagan debate on October 28, indicated a slight rise in Reagan's popularity at Carter's (as well as Anderson's) expense.[8] This would argue for lowering the β/R curve perhaps a little (positive r), while raising the α/C curve (negative c).

The modest drift in Reagan's direction, with the polls showing a tight race almost to the end, would suggest that α and β were very close. In fact, one might argue that $\alpha < \beta$ since, on Election Day, ACR voters would have been more likely to vote for C than the ARC voters for R (hence $1 - \alpha > 1 - \beta$) because C was perceived as an underdog to R. However, given C's underdog status, one might suppose a high value of $1 - \beta$ from the ARC group to try to ensure Reagan's election. Either way, it is not at all clear that α and β should differ by much; to simplify the ensuing analysis, assume that $\alpha = \beta$.

More specifically, we shall take

$$\alpha = \beta = \tfrac{1}{5}$$

since $\tfrac{1}{5}$, or 0.2, is consistent with the previous analysis. In particular, the value must be greater than 0.105, with the sensitivity analysis at $\alpha = 0.15$ and $\beta = 0.25$ yielding not unreasonable A's based on the *Time* poll data.

Perhaps more to the point—if there were *not* strategic voting in the race—is that A's total support according to the previous assumptions would be

$$x_1 + x_2 + x_7 + x_{11}/2 + x_{12}/2,$$

or something above 20 percent since $\alpha = \beta = 0.2$ implies

$$x_1 + x_2 = 5(1.5 + 2.5) = 20.$$

If, as assumed previously, $x_{11} = x_{12} = 0$ and $x_3 = 3$, A's sincere support would be 23 percent, a not implausibly high figure since Anderson's "high water" mark was 29 percent when voters were asked by ABC News during the spring primary campaign whom they would vote for in November if Anderson had a real chance of winning.[9] According to this same poll, Anderson would have dropped 6 percentage points to

23 percent—exactly the figure estimated above—if "real chance" were not presumed. To be sure, these data do not reflect the situation that prevailed on Election Day six months later, but it is hard to believe that A was not severely hurt by strategic voting as the campaign wore on.

To sum up the analysis of this section, we believe that on Election Day about 80 percent of voters who had Anderson in first place, and either Carter or Reagan in second place, did *not* vote for Anderson. The actual percentage could have been as low as 75 or as high as 84, but we doubt strongly that it could have been outside this range.

9.4. Inferences from Voter Percentages

At this point we drop the simplifying assumption that $x_{10} = x_{11} = x_{12}$ $= 0$ but retain the other values specified above, namely

$$x_1 = 7.5 \text{ (from } 1.5 = \alpha x_1 \text{ and } \alpha = \tfrac{1}{5}),$$

$$x_2 = 12.5 \text{ (from } 2.5 = \beta x_2 \text{ and } \beta = \tfrac{1}{5}),$$

along with $(x_7, x_8, x_9) = (3,6,5)$. Among other things, these figures indicate that about 23 percent of the voters (x_1, x_2, x_7) favored A uniquely—and would have voted for him in the absence of strategic considerations—though A received only 7 percent of the votes cast. In addition, they allow one to reduce equations (9.4) through (9.6') to

$$48 = x_4 + x_5 + x_6 + x_{10} + x_{11}/2,$$

$$18 = x_3 \qquad\quad + x_{12} + x_{11}/2,$$

$$26 = x_5 \qquad\quad + x_{11} + x_{12}/2,$$

$$40 = x_3 + x_4 + x_6 + x_{10} + x_{12}/2,$$

$$36.5 = x_5 + x_6 \quad + x_{11} + x_{10}/2,$$

$$29.5 = x_3 + x_4 \quad + x_{12} + x_{10}/2.$$

Since only four of these six equations are independent (the sum of each pair gives $66 = x_3 + x_4 + x_5 + x_6 + x_{10} + x_{11} + x_{12}$), and there are seven unknowns, the system is still underdetermined. To give it greater determinacy, assume that the proportion of voters with order $(ab)c$ to those with abc and bac is the same for all arrangements of a, b, and c from $\{A,C,R\}$. That is, we assume that

$$x_{10} = \gamma(x_4 + x_6),$$

$$x_{11} = \gamma(x_2 + x_5),$$

$$x_{12} = \gamma(x_1 + x_3),$$

for some $\gamma \geq 0$. Thus, γ is the ratio of the number of voters who have candidate c in last place, but are indifferent between the other two, to the number of voters who have c in last place and have a definite preference between the other two, assumed to be the same for each c in $\{A,C,R\}$.[10]

This might be called the "nonstrict-to-strict" preference ratio; the higher its value, the less concerned a voter is about which of his preferred candidates wins. In any event, if this ratio is constant whoever is the least-preferred candidate, the preceding system then becomes

$$48 = 6.25\,\gamma \qquad\qquad + (1 + \gamma)x_4 \;\; + (1 + \gamma/2)x_5 \;\; + (1 + \gamma)x_6,$$

$$18 = 13.75\,\gamma + (1 + \gamma)x_3 \qquad\qquad + (\gamma/2)x_5,$$

$$26 = 16.25\,\gamma + (\gamma/2)x_3 \qquad\qquad + (1 + \gamma)x_5,$$

$$40 = 3.75\,\gamma + (1 + \gamma/2)x_3 + (1 + \gamma)x_4 \qquad\qquad + (1 + \gamma)x_6,$$

$$36.5 = 12.50\,\gamma \qquad\qquad + (\gamma/2)x_4 \;\; + (1 + \gamma)x_5 \;\; + (1 + \gamma/2)x_6,$$

$$29.5 = 7.50\,\gamma + (1 + \gamma)x_3 \;\; + (1 + \gamma/2)x_4 \qquad\qquad + (\gamma/2)x_6.$$

The sum of each succeeding pair gives

$$66 = 20\gamma + (1 + \gamma)(x_3 + x_4 + x_5 + x_6),$$

with $x_{10} + x_{11} + x_{12} = 66 - (x_3 + x_4 + x_5 + x_6) = 86\gamma/(1 + \gamma)$.

Once γ is specified, one can obtain a unique solution for (x_3, x_4, x_5, x_6) for the preceding system. Since we would not expect $x_{10} + x_{11} + x_{12}$ to exceed more than about 10 percent of the voters, for reasons given in Section 9.2, values of γ in the range of 0 to 0.1 are of primary interest. Sample values of all x_i for γ's of 0, 0.05, and 0.1 are shown in Table 9.2. Although a firm estimate of γ is lacking, we believe that $\gamma = 0.05$ is a fair guess—that is, one out of twenty voters has a single worst candidate *and* is indifferent between the other two. When $\gamma = 0.05$, $x_{10} + x_{11} + x_{12}$ is about 4.1.

At $\gamma = 0.05$, the six voting groups in Table 9.1 with strict preference orders have the following positional percentages:

	A	C	R	Total
1st place	20.0	27.8	34.1	81.9
2nd place	39.5	18.0	24.4	81.9
3rd place	22.4	36.1	23.4	81.9

These figures indicate that Anderson was a very strong third candidate even though he got only 7 percent of the vote on Election Day.[11] The moral of the story is, of course, that under the extant voting system, a

Table 9.2
Values of x_i for Three γ Values*

Preference Order	Percentage	γ		
		0	0.05	0.1
ACR	x_1	7.5	7.5	7.5
ARC	x_2	12.5	12.5	12.5
CAR	x_3	18.0	15.9	15.2
CRA	x_4	11.5	11.9	10.9
RAC	x_5	26.0	23.6	20.4
RCA	x_6	10.5	10.5	11.6
A(CR)	x_7	3.0	3.0	3.0
C(AR)	x_8	6.0	6.0	6.0
R(AC)	x_9	5.0	5.0	5.0
(CR)A	x_{10}	0	1.1	2.3
(AR)C	x_{11}	0	1.8	3.3
(AC)R	x_{12}	0	1.2	2.3
Total		100.0	100.0	100.0

*Source: Steven J. Brams and Peter C. Fishburn, "Deducing Preferences and Choices in the 1980 Presidential Election," *Electoral Studies* (forthcoming), Table 2; reprinted with permission.

strong third candidate has virtually no chance since many of the voters who favor him will vote strategically for one of the two major-party nominees, which is a result in a presidential election that is probably reinforced by the complicating factor of unit rule in states under the Electoral College.

Of the alternative voting systems that have been considered in previous chapters, the easiest one to analyze with the methodology just developed is approval voting. In analyzing the possible effects of this system, we shall presume that basic voter perceptions would not have changed under approval voting—a rather unlikely presumption, it would appear—and use the x_i values for $\gamma = 0.05$ in Table 9.2. Assumptions (ix) and (x) are invoked, and with these one obtains the following approval voting percentages for the three candidates:

$$R: 42.0 + (24.4)\lambda_R$$

$$C: 36.1 + (18.0)\lambda_C$$

$$A: 26.0 + (39.5)\lambda_A.$$

The first numbers are the sum in Table 9.2 of the sincere (first-place) voting percentages ($x_3 + x_6 + x_9 + x_{10} + x_{11}$ for R), and the coefficients of the λ's are the sums of the second-place voting percent-

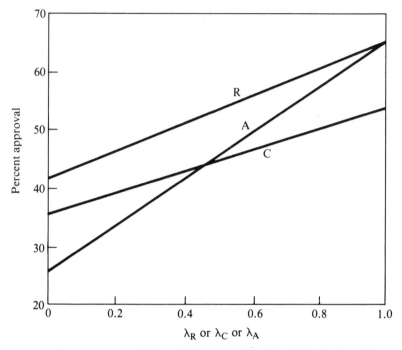

Figure 9.2 Percent approval of candidates as a function of λ's. (Source: Steven J. Brams and Peter C. Fishburn, "Deducing Preferences and Choices in the 1980 Presidential Election," *Electoral Studies* (forthcoming), Figure 2; reprinted with permission.)

ages, provided they are not also worst choices ($x_2 + x_4$ for R). These percentages, as a function of the λ's, are plotted in Figure 9.2.

Although R lies above both A and C for every λ, this does not necessarily mean that R would have won under approval voting, for the values of λ_R, λ_C, and λ_A would differ. Indeed, the preceding equations show that

$$R \text{ beats } A \text{ if } 16 + (24.4)\lambda_R > (39.5)\lambda_A,$$

$$A \text{ beats } R \text{ if } 16 + (24.4)\lambda_R < (39.5)\lambda_A,$$

$$A \text{ beats } C \text{ if } 10.1 + 18\lambda_C < (39.5)\lambda_A,$$

$$C \text{ beats } A \text{ if } 10.1 + 18\lambda_C > (39.5)\lambda_A,$$

$$R \text{ beats } C \text{ if } 6 + (24.4)\lambda_R > 18\lambda_C,$$

$$C \text{ beats } R \text{ if } 6 + (24.4)\lambda_R < 18\lambda_C.$$

For example, R would win when $(\lambda_R,\lambda_C,\lambda_A) = (0.5,0.9,0.7)$, C would win when $(\lambda_R,\lambda_C,\lambda_A) = (0.2,0.7,0.5)$, and A would win when $(\lambda_R,\lambda_C,\lambda_A) = (0.4,0.9,0.7)$.

One final feature of the 1980 presidential election deserves comment. Because it was commonly perceived that C, A, and R were ordered in that way on a liberal-to-conservative ideological scale, one might ask what percentage of voters was "single-peaked" on this dimension (see footnote 10, Chapter 4). Taking only the six strict preference orders as the base, and using the $\lambda = 0.05$ figures again, about 73 percent (i.e., $x_1 + x_2 + x_3 + x_5$, divided by $x_1 + \cdots + x_6$, all times 100) were single-peaked on an underlying CAR order. On the other hand, an underlying ACR order gives about 56 percent single-peaked, and an underlying CRA order gives about 71 percent single-peaked. Since there is a 67 percent expectation of single-peakedness with a random base order, the analysis does not support the idea that most voters adhered to preference orders that were single-peaked, on the basis of the order CAR, from liberal to conservative. This finding is consistent with Anderson supporters' favoring Carter on one set of issues, Reagan on another.[12]

9.5. Conclusions

Probably the most surprising conclusion that emerges from the analysis of this chapter concerns the magnitude of John Anderson's electoral strength, which was hardly registered at all by his 7-percent popular-vote showing in the 1980 presidential election. This strength gave him more second-place support than either Jimmy Carter or Ronald Reagan, according to the foregoing estimates, though the analysis does not establish that he was perceived by an unusually high number of voters as the candidate in the middle on a left-right ideological scale. Moreover, his support was not just residual but also comprised many voters who favored him over the other two candidates but did not vote for him for strategic reasons.

Under approval voting, he would have been a much more significant candidate, though he still probably would not have defeated Reagan. This is consistent with the analysis of De Maio and Muzzio, who show that, in pairwise contests, Anderson was preferred to Carter in all regions except the South but not to Reagan in any region but the Northeast.[13]

The survey data we have analyzed, from four different sources, are both the motivation and limitation of this chapter. In particular, the ABC News exit-poll data on pairwise comparisons of the three major candidates, which gave impetus to our work, are not generally available from standard election surveys, including the SRC/CPS surveys (see Section 8.3). This is unfortunate, because such data are critical in answering certain social-choice questions of the kind we have posed. In the future, we hope that better and richer data can be collected.

But what needs to be stressed in concluding is that the data mean little without a proper model to analyze and relate them. We believe that the model we have postulated, rooted in explicit assumptions about voter behavior, provides a sound methodological basis for estimating voter preferences, and translating these preferences into probable voter choices under different voting systems, that can be very helpful in social-choice and policy-analytic assessments of these different systems. Thereby, we think, a deductive approach can be wedded to empirical data and normative evaluation, which will in turn suggest new data and better models that are useful in extending the analysis and evaluation.

Footnotes to Chapter 9

1. This chapter is based largely on Steven J. Brams and Peter C. Fishburn, "Deducing Preferences and Choices in the 1980 Presidential Election," *Electoral Studies* (forthcoming).

2. V. O. Key, Jr., *The Responsible Electorate: Rationality in Presidential Voting, 1936–1960* (Cambridge: Harvard University Press, 1966).

3. An exception is R. F. Bensel and M. E. Sanders, "Electoral Rules and Rational Voting: The Effects of Candidate Viability Perceptions on Voting Decisions," in *Power, Voting, and Voting Power*, edited by Manfred J. Holler (Würzburg: Physica-Verlag, 1982), pp. 188–200.

4. Jeffrey D. Alderman, "ABC News General Election Exit Poll: GOP Landslide: Realignment or Rejection?" (mimeographed, 1981). We owe special thanks to John C. Blydenburgh for instigating the collection of these data by ABC News.

5. Because the ABC News poll was taken just after the respondents had voted, a "recency effect" (say, for *R*, if a voter's preference order were *ARC* and he had voted for *R*)—induced by a voter's actual vote—could bias the *A*-vs.-*R* comparison. All the survey data reported here and later in this paper are based on national random samples. Details on the sampling and interviews, except for the SRC/CPS data that are available from the Inter-University Consortium for Political and Social Research at the University of Michigan, can be obtained from the following sources: ABC News exit poll—Political Unit, ABC News, 7 West 66th Street, New York, NY 10023; *New York Times*/CBS News exit poll—Election & Survey Unit, CBS News, 524 West 57th Street, New York, NY 10019; *Time* poll—Public Opinion Division, Yankelovich, Skelly and White, Inc., 575 Madison Avenue, New York, NY 10022.

6. Interview with Peter D. Hart, *New York Times*, November 9, 1981, p. E3.

7. John F. Stacks, National Political Correspondent, *Time* (personal communication to S. J. Brams, October 1980).

8. Alvin P. Sanoff, "The Perils of Polling 1980: How the Takers of the Nation's Pulse Missed the Beat," *Washington Journalism Review* 3, 3 (January–February 1981), 32–35; Michael J. Robinson, "The Media in 1980: Was

the Message the Message?" in *The American Elections of 1980*, edited by Austin Ranney (Washington, DC: American Enterprise Institute, 1981), p. 195, Figure 6–3; and Paul R. Abramson, John H. Aldrich, and David W. Rohde, *Change and Continuity in the 1980 Elections* (Washington, DC: Congressional Quarterly, 1982), pp. 44–48, 55–56.

9. Warren Weaver, Jr., "Election in House Studied by Parties," *New York Times*, May 15, 1981, p. B15.

10. When "last place" is replaced here by "first place," the ratios are $x_7/(x_1 + x_2)$, $x_8/(x_3 + x_4)$, and $x_9/(x_5 + x_6)$, which are roughly equal to 0.15, 0.21, and 0.14.

11. One reviewer of an earlier version of the paper on which this chapter is based argued that the post-election SRC/CPS thermometer-scale data (after equal apportionments of respondents to candidates tied on the scale) indicated that Anderson was ranked first by only 16.5 percent of voters, not the 20.0 percent we have estimated. The 16.5 percent is probably an underestimate because of the well-known tendency of survey respondents to downgrade losers after an election. (Carter was first on only 31.5 percent of the respondents' post-election scales, whereas Reagan practically matched his election percentage by being first on 50 percent of the scales.)

12. P. R. Abramson, J. H. Aldrich, and D. W. Rohde, *Change and Continuity in the 1980 Elections*, pp. 180–182.

13. Gerald De Maio and Douglas Muzzio, "The 1980 Elections and Approval Voting," *Presidential Studies Quarterly* **9,** 3 (Summer 1981), 369.

Chapter 10
Epilogue

We have come to the end of what we believe to be a fairly comprehensive and rigorous analysis and appraisal, vintage 1982, of approval voting. Although this system has yet to be used in any public elections, we think that it is a strikingly simple reform that offers compelling advantages over those systems now in widespread use.

As we see it, approval voting is not an attack on vested interests because, as with most things, some interests (and candidates) would benefit and some would not under this system. Rather, we prefer to think of approval voting as a manifestly better way of seeing that public choices—if not the general will, as Rousseau would have liked—get expressed, and candidates with the broadest public appeal get elected.

Under approval voting, we think, the public will not be attracted to candidates who represent only the lowest common denominator. Candidates with ideas who forcefully express them, as approval data from recent elections suggest, will be supported, and those who refuse to take sides on important issues, or simply expound extremist positions, we believe, will not be even minimally acceptable to most voters.

More than intellectual issues are at stake here. As we argued in the Preface, the adoption of approval voting could have far-reaching political consequences. In quantitative terms, there are some 500,000 elected officials serving in approximately 80,000 governments in the United States. And the election rules can make a difference—on who votes, how (sincerely or otherwise), who is elected (Condorcet or minority candidates), whether the winner is viewed as legitimate and the system considered equitable, and what ultimately becomes public policy.

Our hope now is that approval voting will be used in a sufficient number of significant elections to test theoretical claims that have been made of it and to uncover aspects of its empirical operation that might have been overlooked. We do not expect approval voting to take the country or world by storm, but we will be disappointed if it is not tried anywhere. Where and how it gains acceptance could offer some revealing lessons on the role that theoretical and empirical analysis play in the justification of new ideas and in their implementation as political reforms.

Approval voting strikes at the heart of how political debate is resolved. It offers a new approach to the realization of democratic principles by redefining what constitutes a democratic choice. Indeed, the foundation on which representative government is built is periodic elections, and the central problem of elections today is how to translate voter preferences, with as little distortion as possible, into consensus choices in multicandidate races. We believe that approval voting is the best practical way for amalgamating these preferences, fairly and impartially, to produce a winner and thereby ameliorate the multicandidate problem.

Appendix: Bill to Enact Approval Voting in New York State

Voting; system of approval voting. 1. In any election in which more than two candidates' names appear for nomination or election to the same public office on the official ballot; or in which more than two candidates' names appear on the official ballot for election to the same party position which position is to be filled by the election of only one candidate; or in which more candidates' names appear on the official ballot than are to be elected to the same party position which position is to be filled by the election of a group of candidates; the voter shall be permitted to vote for (and thereby to approve of) as many or as few of the candidates for such same public office or party position as the voter chooses to vote for, without limitation, except that the voter may not vote more than once for the same candidate in such election for nomination or election to such office or position. The candidate who receives the greater total number of votes cast in the election for nomination or election to such same public office or party position shall be nominated or elected thereto. Any provisions of this chapter or the education law which appear to limit or restrict a voter's right to vote in accordance with this section or which are inconsistent with these provisions shall be deemed to be modified or superseded by the provisions of this section.

Glossary

Admissible Strategy. A strategy is admissible if and only if it is feasible and there is no other feasible strategy that dominates it.

Approval Voting System. *See* Nonranked Voting Systems.

Borda Voting System. The Borda voting system is a preferential voting system in which the candidate ranked highest by a voter receives the most points, the candidate ranked next-highest the next-most points, and so on; the outcome is the subset of candidates with the largest point total. When there are m candidates, the usual Borda points are $m - 1$, $m - 2$, . . ., 0 for first choice, second choice, . . ., last choice.

Concerned Voter. A concerned voter is a voter who is not indifferent among all candidates.

Condorcet Candidate. A Condorcet candidate is a candidate who in every pairwise contest against another candidate is preferred to the other candidate by at least as many voters as prefer the other candidate to him.

Connected Preferences. A voter's preferences are connected if, for every pair of candidates, either he strictly prefers one to the other or is indifferent between the two.

Consistent Preferences. A voter's preferences are consistent with a strategy and an assumption about voting behavior if the assumed behavior could give rise to the choice of the strategy.

Contingency. A contingency specifies the numbers of votes each candidate receives from all voters other than the focal voter.

Cyclical Majorities. Majorities cycle when majorities of voters prefer candidate a to b, b to c, and c to a, indicating the lack of a social choice or consensus.

Dichotomous Preferences. A voter's preferences are dichotomous if and only if he can divide the set of candidates into exactly two subsets—

preferred and nonpreferred—such that he is indifferent among all candidates in each subset but strictly prefers each member of the preferred subset to each member of the nonpreferred subset.

Dominance. A strategy for a focal voter is dominant if and only if it leads to outcomes at least as good as any other strategy for all possible contingencies, and a better outcome for at least one contingency.

Efficacy. Efficacy is measure of a voter's ability, on the average, to change the outcome from what it would have been if he had abstained. The efficacy of a particular strategy defines the power of the voter who possesses it.

Equity. Equity is a measure of the fairness of a voting system, based on the ratio of the largest to the smallest expected-utility gain for voters when they choose their optimal strategies. The larger this ratio for a given number of candidates, the more inequitable the voting system is.

Feasible Strategy. A strategy is feasible for a particular voting system if and only if it is permitted by that system.

Focal Voter. A focal voter is the voter singled out in the definition of dominance.

Game Theory. Game theory is a mathematical theory of strategy to explicate optimal choices in interdependent decision situations, wherein the outcome depends on the choices of two or more actors, or players.

Hare System. *See* Majority Preferential Voting.

Indifference. A voter is indifferent among a subset of candidates when he does not strictly prefer one to any other; the subset is referred to as an indifference subset for that voter.

Integer Programming. Integer programming provides techniques for assigning integers to things, such as voters to the possible preference scales they might have, that satisfy assumptions relating what is assigned to the things to which they are assigned.

Majority Preferential Voting. Under majority preferential voting, which is also known as the Hare system or single transferable vote, if no candidate receives a majority of first-place votes, the candidate with the fewest first-place votes is dropped and his second-place votes are given to the remaining candidates. This elimination process continues, with lower-place votes of the voters whose preferred candidates are eliminated being transferred to the candidates that survive, until one candidate receives a simple majority.

Median. A median divides the area under a voter distribution curve exactly in half.

Monotonicity. A preferential voting system is monotonic if a candidate cannot be hurt by being raised in the preference rankings of some voters while remaining the same in the rankings of all others. A nonranked voting system is monotonic if a candidate cannot be hurt when he receives additional votes from some voters. To be "hurt" means to rank lower in the social choice ordering under preferential voting systems, and to receive fewer total votes under nonranked voting systems; when this happens, a monotonicity paradox is said to exist.

Multichotomous Preferences. A voter's preferences are multichotomous if and only if he can divide the set of candidates into four or more subsets—say, A_1, A_2, A_3, A_4, . . .—such that he is indifferent among all candidates in each subset but strictly prefers each member of A_1 to each member of A_2, each member of A_2 to each member of A_3, and so on.

Nash Equilibrium. A Nash equilibrium is an outcome from which no player would have an incentive to depart unilaterally because he would do worse, or at least not better, if he did.

Negative Voting System. A negative voting system is a system in which each voter is allowed one vote, either for or against a candidate but not both, and the outcome is the subset of candidates with the largest net vote total (*for* minus *against* votes).

Nonranked Voting Systems. A nonranked voting system is a system in which a voter can vote for, but not rank, the candidates according to his preferences. Such systems range from vote for exactly one candidate (plurality voting) to vote for from one to all the candidates (approval voting); they also include multiballot nonranked voting systems such as runoff systems. In each of these systems, the outcome is the subset of candidates with the largest vote total on the final ballot.

Ordinary Voting System. An ordinary voting system is a single-ballot voting system.

Outcome. An outcome is the subset of candidates who have the largest vote total.

Paradox of Voting. The paradox of voting occurs when there is no Condorcet candidate: every candidate can be beaten by at least one other candidate in a pairwise contest.

Plurality Voting System. *See* Nonranked Voting Systems.

Power. *See* Efficacy.

Preferential Voting Systems. Preferential voting systems are systems that allow voters to rank candidates from best to worst.

Runoff Voting System. A runoff voting system is a two-ballot system in which the top two candidates in the first election face each other in a second election. In practice, the second (runoff) election is not held unless the winner in the first election fails to receive a certain minimum number of votes, such as a simple majority.

Sincerity. A voting strategy is sincere for a voter if and only if it includes voting for all candidates ranked above the lowest-ranked candidate included in the voter's admissible strategy. (It is strongly sincere if, whenever a strategy contains at least one member of an indifference subset, it contains all members of that subset.) A voting system is sincere if and only if all admissible strategies for voters, whatever their preferences, are sincere.

Single-Peakedness. Single-peakedness refers to the shape of voter preferences and occurs when there exists a single dimension underlying the preferences of voters (e.g., a liberalism-conservatism scale) along which alternatives (e.g., candidates) can be ordered; it precludes the existence of a paradox of voting.

Single Transferable Vote. *See* Majority Preferential Voting.

Strategic Voting. Strategic voting is voting that is not sincere.

Strategy. A strategy under a nonranked voting system is a subset of candidates.

Strategy-proofness. A voting system is strategy-proof if and only if exactly one strategy is admissible for each voter, whatever his preferences (in which case this strategy must also be sincere).

Strict Preferences. For every pair of candidates, a voter's preferences are strict if he definitely prefers one to the other: he is not indifferent between any two candidates.

Symmetric Voter Distribution. A symmetric voter distribution has the same shape to the left and right of its median.

Transitivity. If a voter strictly prefers a to b, and b to c, he will strictly prefer a to c, and similarly for nonstrict preference/indifference relations. This concept is also applicable to social-choice orderings of candidates; when these orderings are not transitive, majorities are said to be cyclical.

Trichotomous Preferences. A voter's preferences are trichotomous if and only if he can divide the set of candidates into exactly three subsets—say, A_1, A_2, and A_3—such that he is indifferent among all candidates in each subset but strictly prefers each member of A_1 to each member of A_2, each member of A_2 to each member of A_3, and (by transitivity) each member of A_1 to each member of A_3.

Unimodal Voter Distribution. A unimodal voter distribution has one peak, or mode.

Voting System. *See* Nonranked Voting Systems; Preferential Voting Systems.

Bibliography

Abramson, Paul R., John H. Aldrich, and David W. Rohde. *Change and Continuity in the 1980 Elections*. Washington, DC: Congressional Quarterly, 1982.

Alderman, Jeffrey D. "ABC News General Election Exit Poll: GOP Landslide: Realignment or Rejection?" Mimeographed, 1981.

Aranson, Peter H. *American Government: Strategy and Choice*. Cambridge, MA: Winthrop, 1980.

Banzhaf, John F. "Weighted Voting Doesn't Work: A Mathematical Analysis." *Rutgers Law Review* 19, no. 2 (Winter 1965): 317–343.

Bensel, R. F., and M. E. Sanders. "Electoral Rules and Rational Voting: The Effects of Candidate Viability Perceptions on Voting Decisions." In *Power, Voting, and Voting Power*, ed. Manfred J. Holler. Würzburg: Physica-Verlag, 1982, pp. 188–200.

Bishop, Cortlandt F. *History of Elections in the American Colonies*. New York: Burt Franklin, 1968 (originally published in 1893).

Black, Duncan. *The Theory of Committees and Elections*. Cambridge: Cambridge University Press, 1958.

Boehm, George A. W. "One Fervent Vote against Wintergreen." Mimeographed, 1976.

Borda, Jean-Charles de. "Mémoire sur les élections au scrutin." *Histoire de l'Académie Royale des Sciences*. Paris, 1781.

Bordley, Robert F. "A Pragmatic Scheme for Evaluating Voting Schemes." *American Political Science Review* (forthcoming).

Brams, Steven J. "The AMS Nomination Procedure Is Vulnerable to 'Truncation of Preferences.'" *Notices of the American Mathematical Society* 29, no. 2 (February 1982): 136–138.

Brams, Steven J. "Approval Voting: A Better Way to Elect a President?" *Annal of the Science and Public Policy Section*, New York Academy of Sciences (forthcoming).

Brams, Steven J. "Approval Voting in Multicandidate Elections." *Policy Studies Journal* 9, no. 1 (Autumn 1980): 102–108.

Brams, Steven J. "Approval Voting: One Candidate, One Vote." In *Representation and Redistricting Issues in the 1980s,* ed. Bernie Grofman, Arend Lijphart, Robert McKay, and Howard Scarrow. Lexington, MA: Lexington, 1982, pp. 137–142.

Brams, Steven J. "Approval Voting: A Practical Reform for Multicandidate Elections." *National Civic Review* 68, no. 10 (November 1979): 549–553, 560.

Brams, Steven J. *Comparison Voting.* Innovative Instructional Unit. Washington, D.C.: American Political Science Association, 1978. Published in slightly revised form in *Modules in Applied Mathematics: Political and Related Models,* vol. 2, ed. Steven J. Brams, William F. Lucas, and Philip D. Straffin, Jr. New York: Springer-Verlag, 1982, pp. 32–65.

Brams, Steven J. "Deception in 2 × 2 Games." *Journal of Peace Science* 2, no. 2 (Spring 1977): 171–203.

Brams, Steven J. *Game Theory and Politics.* New York: Free Press, 1975.

Brams, Steven J. "Is This Any Way to Elect a President?" In *Selection/Election: A Forum on the American Presidency,* ed. Robert S. Hirschfield. Hawthorne, NY: Aldine, 1982, pp. 173–177.

Brams, Steven J. "One Candidate, One Vote." *Archway: The Magazine of Arts & Science at New York University* 2 (Winter 1981): 10–14.

Brams, Steven J. "One Man, n Votes." Module in Applied Mathematics, Mathematical Association of American. Ithaca, NY: Cornell University, 1976.

Brams, Steven J. *Paradoxes in Politics: An Introduction to the Nonobvious in Political Science.* New York: Free Press, 1976.

Brams, Steven J. "Strategic Information and Voting Behavior." *Society* 19, no. 6 (September/October 1982): 4–11.

Brams, Steven J. *The Presidential Election Game.* New Haven: Yale University Press, 1978.

Brams, Steven J. "When Is It Advantageous to Cast a Negative Vote?" In *Mathematical Economics and Game Theory: Essays in Honor of Oskar Morgenstern,* ed. R. Henn and O. Moeschlin. Lecture Notes in Economics and Mathematical Systems, vol. 141. Berlin: Springer-Verlag, 1977, pp. 564–572.

Brams, Steven J., and Peter C. Fishburn. "Approval Voting." *American Political Science Review* 72, no. 3 (September 1978): 831–847.

Brams, Steven J., and Peter C. Fishburn. "Deducing Preferences and Choices in the 1980 Presidential Election." *Electoral Studies* 1 (1982): 333–346.

Brams, Steven J., and Peter C. Fishburn. "Reconstructing Voting Processes: The 1976 House Majority Leader Election." *Political Methodology* 7, nos. 3 & 4 (1981): 95–108.

Brams, Steven J., and George Sharrard. "Analysis of Pilot Study Questions on Preference Rankings and Approval Voting." Mimeographed, 1979.

Brams, Steven J., and Philip D. Straffin, Jr. "The Entry Problem in a Political Race." In *Political Equilibrium,* ed. Peter C. Ordeshook and Kenneth A. Shepsle. Boston: Kluwer-Nijhoff, 1982, pp. 181–195.

Brams, Steven J., Arnold Urken, George Sharrard, and Douglas Muzzio. "Results of Exit Poll of New Jersey Voters in Democratic and Republican Gubernatorial Primaries, June 2, 1981." Press release, June 17, 1981.

Brams, Steven J., and Frank C. Zagare. "Deception in Simple Voting Games." *Social Science Research* 6, no. 3 (September 1977): 257–272.

Brams, Steven J., and Frank C. Zagare. "Double Deception: Two against One in Three-Person Games." *Theory and Decision* 13, no. 1 (March 1981): 81–90.

Browne, Malcolm W. "Can Voting Become Safer for Democracy?" *New York Times,* June 1, 1980, p. E7.

Chamberlin, John, and Michael D. Cohen. "Toward Applicable Social Choice Theory: A Comparison of Social Choice Functions under Spatial Model Assumptions." *American Political Science Review* 72, no. 4 (December 1978): 1341–1356.

Clem, Alan L. *American Electoral Politics: Strategies for Renewal.* New York: D. Van Nostrand, 1981.

Condorcet, Marquis de. *Essai sur l'application de l'analyse à la probabilité dés decisions rendues à la pluralité des voix.* Paris, 1785.

Cronin, Thomas E. *The State of the Presidency,* 2d ed. Boston: Little, Brown, 1980.

de Grazia, Alfred. "Mathematical Derivation of an Election System." *ISIS* 44, nos. 135–136 (June 1953): 42–51.

De Maio, Gerald, and Douglas Muzzio. "The 1980 Election and Approval Voting." *Presidential Studies Quarterly* 9, no. 3 (Summer 1981): 341–363.

De Maio, Gerald, Douglas Muzzio, and George Sharrard. "Approval Voting: The Empirical Evidence." *American Politics Quarterly* (forthcoming).

Doron, Gideon, and Richard Kronick. "Single Transferable Vote: An Example of a Perverse Social Choice Function." *American Journal of Political Science* 21, no. 2 (May 1977): 303–311.

Dutta, Bhaskar, and Prasanta K. Pattanaik. "On Nicely Consistent Voting Systems." *Econometrica* 46, no. 1 (January 1978): 163–170.

Epstein, Laurily K., and Gerald Strom. "Election Night Projections and West Coast Turnout." *American Politics Quarterly* 9, no. 4 (October 1981): 479–491.

Faith, Roger L., and James M. Buchanan. "Towards a Theory of Yes-No Voting." *Public Choice* 37, no. 2 (1981): 231–245.

Fishburn, Peter C. "An Analysis of Simple Voting Systems for Electing Committees." *SIAM Journal on Applied Mathematics* 41, no. 3 (December 1981): 499–502.

Fishburn, Peter C. "Axioms for Approval Voting: Direct Proof." *Journal of Economic Theory* 19, no. 1 (October 1978): 180–185.

Fishburn, Peter C. "Condorcet Social Choice Functions." *SIAM Journal on Applied Mathematics* 33, no. 3 (November 1977): 469–489.

Fishburn, Peter C. "Deducing Majority Candidates from Election Data." *Social Science Research* 9, no. 3 (September 1980): 216–224.

Fishburn, Peter C. "Dimensions of Election Procedures: Analyses and Comparisons." *Theory and Decision* (forthcoming).

Fishburn, Peter C. "Dominant Strategies and Restricted Ballots with Variable Electorate." *Mathematical Social Sciences* 2, no. 4 (June 1982): 383–395.

Fishburn, Peter C. "Monotonicity Paradoxes in the Theory of Elections." *Discrete Applied Mathematics* 4, no. 2 (April 1982): 119–134.

Fishburn, Peter C. "Paradoxes of Voting." *American Political Science Review* 68, no. 2 (June 1974): 537–546.

Fishburn, Peter C. "Simple Voting Systems and Majority Rule." *Behavioral Science* 19, no. 3 (May 1974): 166–176.

Fishburn, Peter C. "A Strategic Analysis of Nonranked Voting Systems." *SIAM Journal on Applied Mathematics* 35, no. 3 (November 1978): 488–495.

Fishburn, Peter C. "Symmetric and Consistent Aggregation with Dichotomous Voting." In *Aggregation and Revelation of Preferences,* ed. Jean-Jacques Laffont. Amsterdam: North-Holland, 1979, pp. 201–208.

Fishburn, Peter C. *The Theory of Social Choice.* Princeton: Princeton University Press, 1973.

Fishburn, Peter C. *Utility Theory for Decision Making.* New York: John Wiley and Sons, 1970.

Fishburn, Peter C., and Steven J. Brams. "Approval Voting, Condorcet's Principle, and Runoff Elections." *Public Choice* 36, no. 1 (1981): 89–114.

Fishburn, Peter C., and Steven J. Brams. "Deducing Simple Majorities from Approval Voting Ballot Data." *Social Science Research* 10, no. 3 (September 1981): 256–266.

Fishburn, Peter C., and Steven J. Brams. "Efficacy, Power, and

Equity under Approval Voting." *Public Choice* 37, no. 3 (1981): 425–434.

Fishburn, Peter C., and Steven J. Brams. "Expected Utility and Approval Voting." *Behavioral Science* 26, no. 2 (April 1981): 136–142.

Fishburn, Peter C., and Steven J. Brams. "Paradoxes of Preferential Voting." *Mathematics Magazine* (forthcoming).

Fishburn, Peter C., and William V. Gehrlein. "An Analysis of Simple Two-stage Voting Systems." *Behavioral Science* 21, no. 1 (January 1976): 1–23.

Fishburn, Peter C., and William V. Gehrlein. "An Analysis of Voting Procedures with Nonranked Voting." *Behavioral Science* 22, no. 3 (May 1977): 178–185.

Fishburn, Peter C., and William V. Gehrlein. "Collective Rationality versus Distribution of Power for Binary Social Choice Functions." *Journal of Economic Theory* 15, no. 1 (June 1977): 72–91.

Fishburn, Peter C., and William V. Gehrlein. "Majority Efficiencies for Simple Voting Procedures: Summary and Interpretation." *Theory and Decision* 14, no. 2 (June 1982): 141–153.

Franklin, Ben A. "31 on Ballot Tomorrow for House Seat in Maryland." *New York Times,* April 6, 1981, p. B15.

Galton, Francis. "One Vote, One Value." *Nature* 75 (February 28, 1907): 414.

Gardner, Martin (written by Lynn Arthur Steen). "Mathematical Games (From Counting Votes to Making Votes Count: The Mathematics of Elections)." *Scientific American,* October 1980, pp. 16ff.

Gehrlein, William V. "Condorcet Efficiency and Constant Scoring Rules." *Mathematical Social Sciences* 2, no. 2 (March 1982): 123–130.

Gehrlein, William V., and Peter C. Fishburn. "Coincidence Probabilities for Simple Majority and Positional Voting Rules." *Social Science Research* 7, no. 3 (September 1978): 272–283.

Gehrlein, William V., and Peter C. Fishburn. "Constant Scoring Rules for Choosing One among Many Alternatives." *Quality and Quantity* 15, no. 2 (April 1981): 203–210.

Gehrlein, William V., and Peter C. Fishburn. "The Effects of Abstentions on Election Outcomes." *Public Choice* 33, no. 2 (1978): 69–82.

Gehrlein, William V., and Peter C. Fishburn. "Effects of Abstentions on Voting Procedures in Three-Candidate Elections." *Behavioral Science* 24, no. 5 (September 1979): 346–354.

Gibbard, Allan. "Manipulation of Voting Schemes: A General Result." *Econometrica* 41, no. 3 (May 1973): 587–601.

Gillett, Raphael. "The Asymptotic Likelihood of Agreement between Plurality and Condorcet Outcomes." *Behavioral Science* 25, no. 1 (January 1980): 23–32.

Gordon, Julie P. "Report of the Secretary." *Econometrica* 48, no. 1 (January 1981): 229–233.

Hammond, Thomas H. "Another Look at the Role of 'The Rules' in the 1972 Democratic Presidential Primaries." *Western Political Quarterly* 33, no. 1 (March 1980): 50–72.

Heil, Barbara J., and Steven J. Brams. "How to Improve DC's Crazy Elections." *DC Gazette* 13, no. 220 (May 1982): 2–4.

Hess, Stephen. "Approval Voting." *Baltimore Sun*, May 8, 1981, p. A23.

Hoffman, Dale T. "A Model for Strategic Voting." *SIAM Journal on Applied Mathematics* 42, no. 4 (August 1982): 751–761.

Hoffman, Dale T. "Relative Efficiency of Voting Systems: The Cost of Sincere Behavior." Mimeographed, 1979.

Inada, Ken-ichi. "A Note on the Simple Majority Decision Rule." *Econometrica* 32, no. 4 (October 1964): 525–531.

Interview with Peter D. Hart, *New York Times,* November 9, 1981, p. E3.

Jackson, John E., and William H. McGee III. "Election Reporting and Voter Turnout." Mimeographed, 1981.

Joslyn, Richard A. "The Impact of Decision Rules in Multicandidate Campaigns: The Case of the 1972 Democratic Presidential Nomination." *Public Choice* 25 (Spring 1976): 1–18.

Keech, William R., and Donald Matthews. *The Party's Choice.* Washington, DC: Brookings Institution, 1976.

Kellett, John, and Kenneth Mott. "Presidential Primaries: Measuring Popular Choice." *Polity* 11, no. 4 (Summer 1977): 528–537.

Kelly, Jerry S. *Arrow Impossibility Theorems.* New York: Academic Press, 1978.

Key, V. O., Jr. *The Responsible Electorate: Rationality in Presidential Voting, 1936–1960.* Cambridge: Harvard University Press, 1966.

Kiewiet, D. Roderick. "Approval Voting: The Case of the 1968 Presidential Election." *Polity* 12, no. 1 (Fall 1979): 170–181.

Kim, K. H., and Fred W. Roush. *Introduction to Mathematical Consensus Theory.* Lecture Notes in Pure and Applied Mathematics, vol. 59. New York: Marcel Dekker, 1980.

Lakeman, Enid, and James D. Lambert. *Voting in Democracies: A Study of Majority and Proportional Electoral Systems.* London: Faber and Faber, 1955.

Lembke, Bud. "A Proposal for Legal Ballot-Box 'Stuffing.'" *Los Angeles Times* (Orange County section, part 2), May 12, 1979, p. 13.

Lengle, James I., and Byron Shafer. "Primary Rules, Political Power, and Social Change." *American Political Science Review* 70, no. 1 (March 1976): 25–40.

Levin, Murray B. *The Alienated Voter: Politics in Boston.* New York: Holt, Rinehart, and Winston, 1960.

Maisel, Louis, and Gerald J. Lieberman. "The Impact of Electoral Rules on Primary Elections: The Democratic Presidential Primaries in 1976." In *The Impact of the Electoral Process,* ed. Louis Maisel and Joseph Cooper. Beverly Hills, CA: Sage, 1977, pp. 39–80.

Mazmanian, Daniel A. *Third Parties in Presidential Elections.* Washington, DC: Brookings Institution, 1974.

Mendelsohn, Harold. "Election-Day Broadcasts and Terminal Voting Decisions." *Public Opinion Quarterly* 30, no. 2 (Summer 1966): 212–225.

Meredith, James Creed. *Proportional Representation in Ireland.* Dublin, 1913.

Merrill, Samuel. "For Approval Voting." *New York Times,* July 20, 1979, p. A25.

Merrill, Samuel, III. "Approval Voting: A 'Best Buy' Method for Multicandidate Elections?" *Mathematics Magazine* 52, no. 2 (March 1979): 98–102.

Merrill, Samuel, III. "A Comparison of Multicandidate Electoral Systems in Terms of Optimal Voting Strategies." *American Journal of Political Science* (forthcoming).

Merrill, Samuel, III. "Decision Analysis of Multicandidate Voting Systems." UMAP Module 384. Newton, MA: Education Development Center, n.d.

Merrill, Samuel, III. "Strategic Decisions under One-Stage Multicandidate Voting Systems." *Public Choice* 36, no. 1 (1981): 115–134.

Merrill, Samuel, III. "Strategic Voting in Multicandidate Elections under Uncertainty and under Risk." In *Power, Voting, and Voting Power,* ed. Manfred J. Holler. Würzburg: Physica-Verlag, 1982, pp. 179–187.

Molotsky, Irwin. "Javits Says He Would Consider Any Offer of a Position if Reagan Sought Him." *New York Times,* November 14, 1980, p. B1.

Morin, Richard A. *Structural Reform: Ballots.* New York: Vantage Press, 1980.

Mueller, Dennis C. *Public Choice.* Cambridge: Cambridge University Press, 1979.

Nagel, Jack H. *The Descriptive Analysis of Power.* New Haven: Yale University Press, 1975.

Nash, John. "Non-cooperative Games." *Annals of Mathematics* 54, no. 2 (September 1951): 286–295.

National Academy of Sciences: Constitution and Bylaws (April 28, 1981).

Niemi, Richard G., and William H. Riker. "The Choice of Voting Systems." *Scientific American,* June 1976, pp. 21ff.

Nossiter, Bernard D. "China Continues to Bar Waldheim Nomination." *New York Times,* October 29, 1981, p. A8.

Nossiter, Bernard D. "Security Council Elects a Peruvian Secretary General." *New York Times,* December 12, 1981, pp. 1, 6.

Nossiter, Bernard D. "Someone Is Trying to Fire Waldheim." *New York Times,* November 1, 1981, p. E5.

Nossiter, Bernard D. "U.N. Security Council Fails to Agree on Waldheim." *New York Times,* October 28, 1981, p. A14.

Nurmi, Hannu. "Majority Rule: Second Thoughts and Refutations." *Quality and Quantity* 14, no. 6 (1981): 19–32.

Nurmi, Hannu. "On the Properties of Voting Systems." *Scandinavian Political Studies* 4 (1981): 19–32.

Nurmi, Hannu. "Review Article: Voting Procedures." *British Journal of Political Science* (forthcoming).

Nurmi, Hannu. "On Taking Preferences Seriously." Mimeographed, 1982.

"One Voter, Two Votes . . . or Three, or Four . . ." *Research for Managers at Penn State.* University Park, PA: College of Business Administration, Pennsylvania State University, 1978, pp. 22–23.

Oppenheimer, Bruce I., and Robert L. Peabody. "The House Majority Leader Contest, 1976." Mimeographed, 1977.

Oppenheimer, Bruce I., and Robert L. Peabody. "How the Race for Majority Leader Was Won—by One Vote." *Washington Monthly* 9 (November 1977): 46–56.

Ottewell, Guy. "The Arithmetic of Voting." *In Defense of Variety* 4 (July-August 1977): 42–44.

Peirce, Neal R., and Lawrence D. Longley. *The People's President: The Electoral College in American History and the Direct Vote Alternative,* rev. ed. New Haven: Yale University Press, 1981.

Peleg, Bezalel. "Consistent Voting Systems." *Econometrica* 46, no. 1 (January 1978): 153–162.

Report of the Royal Commission Appointed to Enquire into Electoral Systems. London: HMSO, 1910, Cd. 5163.

Richelson, Jeffrey T. "A Comparative Analysis of Social Choice Functions." *Behavioral Science* 20, no. 5 (September 1975): 331–337.

Richelson, Jeffrey T. "A Comparative Analysis of Social Choice Functions, II." *Behavioral Science* 23, no. 1 (January 1978): 38–44.

Richelson, Jeffrey T. "A Comparative Analysis of Social Choice Functions, III." *Behavioral Science* 23, no. 3 (May 1978): 169–178.

Richelson, Jeffrey T. "A Comparative Analysis of Social Choice Functions, I, II, III: A Summary." *Behavioral Science* 24, no. 5 (September 1979): 355.

Richelson, Jeffrey T. "A Comparative Analysis of Social Choice Functions, IV." *Behavioral Science* 26, no. 4 (October 1981): 346–353.

Richelson, Jeffrey T. "Running off Empty: Run-off Point Systems." *Public Choice* 35, no. 4 (1980): 457–468.

Riker, William H. "Duverger's Law: Plurality Voting and Party Systems." *American Political Science Review* 76, no. 4 (December 1982): 753–766.

Riker, William H. "The Number of Political Parties: A Reexamination of Duverger's Law." *Comparative Politics* 9, no. 1 (October 1976): 93–106.

Riker, William H. *Liberalism against Populism: A Confrontation between the Theory of Democracy and the Theory of Social Choice.* San Francisco: W. H. Freeman, 1982.

Riker, William H. "Some Ambiguities in the Notion of Power." *American Political Science Review* 48, no. 3 (September 1964): 787–792.

Robinson, Michael J. "The Media in 1980: Was the Message the Message?" In *The American Elections of 1980,* ed. Austin Ranney. Washington, DC: American Enterprise Institute, 1981, pp. 177–211.

Russell, Mary. "Representative Wright Is Elected House Majority Leader." *Washington Post,* December 7, 1976, pp. A1, A6.

Sanford, Terry. *A Danger of Democracy: The Presidential Nominating Process.* Boulder, CO: Westview, 1981.

Sanoff, Alvin P. "The Perils of Polling 1980: How the Takers of the Nation's Pulse Missed the Beat." *Washington Journalism Review* 3, no. 3 (January-February 1981): 32–35.

Satterthwaite, Mark Allen. "Strategy-Proofness and Arrow's Conditions: Existence and Correspondence Theorems for Voting Procedures and Social Welfare Functions." *Journal of Economic Theory* 10, no. 2 (April 1975): 187–217.

Scammon, Richard M., and Ben J. Wattenberg. *The Real Majority: An Extraordinary Examination of the American Electorate.* New York: Coward, McCann and Geoghegan, 1970.

"Scott and Hoyer Nominated in Maryland 5th District." *Congressional Quarterly Weekly Report* 39, no. 5 (April 11, 1981): 645.

Sidney, Jeffrey B. "Single Ballot Non-Ranked Voting Systems for Committee Selection." Mimeographed, 1981.

Smith, John H. "Aggregation of Preferences with Variable Electorate." *Econometrica* 41, no. 6 (November 1973): 1027–1041.

Straffin, Philip D., Jr. *Topics in the Theory of Voting.* UMAP Expository Monograph. Boston: Birkhäuser Boston, 1980.

Stratmann, William C. "The Calculus of Rational Choice." *Public Choice* 18 (Summer 1974): 93–105.

Teune, Henry, Morton Lustig, Jack Nagel, and Oliver P. Williams. *A New Government for Atlantic City: A Strong Mayor-Strong Council*

Plan. Philadelphia: Government Study Group, Department of Political Science, University of Pennsylvania, 1979.

Urken, Arnold. "Two from Column A . . ." *New Jersey Reporter,* June 1981, pp. 9–12.

von Neumann, John, and Oskar Morgenstern. *Theory of Games and Economic Behavior,* 3d ed. Princeton: Princeton University Press, 1953.

Weaver, Warren Jr. "Elections in House Studied by Parties." *New York Times,* May 15, 1981, p. B15.

Weaver, Warren Jr. "New System Urged in Presidential Primary Voting." *New York Times,* April 13, 1979, p. A15.

Weber, Robert J. "Comparison of Voting Systems." Mimeographed, 1977.

Weber, Robert J. "Multiply-Weighted Voting Systems." Mimeographed, 1977.

Weber, Robert J. "Reproducing Voting Systems." Mimeographed, 1977.

Index

About the authors—

Steven J. Brams is Professor of Politics at New York University, and author of *Game Theory and Politics* (1975), *Paradoxes in Politics: An Introduction to the Nonobvious in Political Science* (1976), *The Presidential Election Game* (1978), and *Biblical Games: A Strategic Analysis of Stories in the Old Testament* (1980).

Peter C. Fishburn is a member of the technical staff at Bell Laboratories, Murray Hill, New Jersey, and is the author of *Decision and Value Theory* (1964), *Utility Theory for Decision Making* (1970), *Mathematics of Decision Theory* (1972), *The Theory of Social Choice* (1973), and *The Foundations of Expected Utility* (1982).